The Earliest Christian Artifacts

The Earliest Christian Artifacts

MANUSCRIPTS AND CHRISTIAN ORIGINS

Larry W. Hurtado

WILLIAM B. EERDMANS PUBLISHING COMPANY

GRAND RAPIDS, MICHIGAN / CAMBRIDGE, U.K.

Published 2006 by
Wm. B. Eerdmans Publishing Co.
2140 Oak Industrial Drive N.E., Grand Rapids, Michigan 49505 /
P.O. Box 163, Cambridge CB3 9PU U.K.

Printed in the United States of America

11 10 09 08 07 06   7 6 5 4 3 2 1

Library of Congress Cataloging-in-Publication Data

Hurtado, Larry W., 1943-
    The earliest Christian artifacts: manuscripts and Christian origins /
    Larry W. Hurtado.
        p.   cm.
    Includes bibliographical references.
    ISBN-10: 0-8028-2895-7 / ISBN-13: 978-0-8028-2895-8 (pbk.: alk. paper)
    1. Christian literature, Early — Manuscripts. 2. Christianity — Origin.
    I. Title.

BR62.H87   2006
270.1 — dc22

                                              2006022843

www.eerdmans.com

To

Professor Edwin Judge and other colleagues and friends
in the Ancient History Documentary Research Centre,
Macquarie University,

with gratitude for kindness and generosity during my time as
Visiting Fellow of the University, April–May 2005

CONTENTS

PREFACE   viii

ABBREVIATIONS   xii

Introduction   1

1. The Texts   15

2. The Early Christian Preference for the Codex   43

3. The *Nomina Sacra*   95

4. The Staurogram   135

5. Other Scribal Features   155

Concluding Remarks   191

SELECT BIBLIOGRAPHY   193

APPENDIX 1: Christian Literary Texts in Manuscripts
of the Second and Third Centuries   209

APPENDIX 2: Photographic Plates of Selected Manuscripts   231

INDEX OF AUTHORS   243

INDEX OF MANUSCRIPTS   245

Whenever I had hesitation about the value of writing this book, I found myself repeatedly energized over the last year through occasional conversations with a number of scholars in New Testament and Christian origins (including some senior ones). When I was asked about what I was working on during my year-long research leave, and I responded that I was writing a book on the wider historical importance of early Christian manuscripts, the result was usually a blank stare, and a request to illustrate specifically what things I had in mind. They then characteristically were surprised to learn that our earliest manuscripts already attest efforts at punctuation, larger sense-unit demarcation, and a curiously strong preference for the codex, especially for biblical writings. And they were often intrigued that these matters might have interesting implications for familiar historical questions about early Christianity. I have the strong impression that the material discussed in this book is not as well known as it deserves to be among scholars in the field. Thus one of my key aims here is to draw attention to an important body of data that is often overlooked.

But I have attempted to do more than introduce and review what others have said. My aim here is also to advance the discussion of a number of particular matters, which I hope will be of further benefit to those who may already be reasonably well informed about these topics. I offer this discussion in grateful response to those whose scholarly work on early manuscripts has been of such stimulation and benefit to me in doing the research embodied in this book.

Thanks to a semester of research leave granted by the University of Edinburgh, and a further period of research leave funded by the Arts and Humanities Research Council (AHRC), I was able to have the full year of 2005 free from teaching and administrative duties to complete the research for this book and to write it. I am, indeed, very grateful for this period of research leave, and I hope that what I offer here will help to demonstrate the usefulness to scholarship of affording such extended times for research/ writing projects.

In the spring of 2005, I was able to spend several weeks in Macquarie University as a Visiting Fellow, which substantially advanced the research for this book. This visit enabled extended collaboration with colleagues there in the Ancient History Documentary Research Centre (AHDRC), particularly those involved in the project on Papyri from the Rise of Christianity in Egypt (PRCE). I was also permitted free and full access to their copious files on early Christian manuscripts. Professor Alanna Nobbs nominated me for this appointment, and I want to register here my gratitude to her and to Macquarie University for that splendid opportunity to advance my knowledge of things papyrological. In addition to Alanna, I also want to single out Dr. Don Barker and Dr. Malcolm Choat, who gave me generously their time and expertise. Professor Samuel Lieu (co-director of the AHDRC) also took a friendly interest in my research.

Moreover, they kindly provided me with a computing station in the Centre, and comfortable lodging for me and my wife during our stay. Don Barker and his wife took us on a delightful day trip out to the Blue Mountains, and Alanna thoughtfully arranged several lunchtime occasions to meet additional colleagues in Macquarie. Sam Lieu took my wife and me along with graduate students for a very enjoyable dinner in a Chinese restaurant, where he expertly ordered superb delicacies for the party. All these colleagues also showed up for a lovely farewell dinner toward the end of our stay. In our whole time "down under," we felt warmly welcomed and kindly treated.

A further personal pleasure for me in my time in Sydney was the opportunity to confer with Professor Edwin Judge, the founding father of the Centre and the PRCE project. Among his publications, several have been of special direct benefit to students of Christian origins, since his groundbreaking volume, *The Social Pattern of Christian Groups in the First Century* (1960). He and the other PRCE staff kindly included me in several sessions in which we discussed the shape, aims, and format of their impressive project, which is to produce a descriptive catalogue of all papyri relating to Christianity in Egypt in the pre-Constantinian period. As a small token of appreciation for his many contributions to scholarship, for the splendid boon to my research afforded by my appointment as a Visiting Fellow of the University, and for all the kindnesses extended to me during my stay, I am pleased to dedicate this book to him and all the Macquarie colleagues, who also have become friends.

It was an additional benefit of the visit to Australia to be invited to Melbourne, to give a public lecture in the Australian Catholic University. Dr. Ann Hunter arranged this, and graciously entertained us over an enjoyable and informative ANZAC Day holiday. We were also able to make a short side trip to Dunedin (particularly appropriate for visitors from Edinburgh!), thanks to the invitation of Professor Paul Trebilco (University of Otago) to give public lectures and a seminar presentation. He kindly arranged for our lodgings in St. Margaret's College, where staff and students made us feel entirely welcome.

During our time away, our son, Jess, both fended for himself capably and took diligent care of Cupar, our feline flatmate (perhaps the most talkative cat in Edinburgh), who allows us to provide him with food and attention, in exchange for his mischief of various types. Both cat and flat were fully in operational order upon our return, thanks to Jess.

I also want to mention gratefully a grant from the Association of Commonwealth Universities and the British Academy in support of the collaboration with scholars from Macquarie. In particular, this grant made it possible to bring Professor Nobbs, Dr. Barker, and Dr. Choat to Edinburgh for a day conference in June 2005, in which they presented their papyri project and gave some interesting case studies of particular manuscripts. Colleagues and graduate students from several British universities were on hand and shared in the benefits of this grant.

Further thanks are due to the Bodleian Library (Oxford), the British Library (London), the Chester Beatty Library (Dublin), the Martin Bodmer Library (Geneva), and the Houghton Library of Harvard University for photos of papyri and permissions to include these photos in this book. I also thank the Bodleian Library for the opportunity to examine a number of their many important manuscripts in July 2005. During that same visit to Oxford, Dr. Nick Gonis kindly allowed me to examine a number of Oxyrhynchus papyri now held in the impressive Sackler building adjacent to the Ashmolean Museum. Professor Willy Clarysse, who established the Leuven Database of Ancient Books (LDAB), responded to various queries about using this valuable online resource, and generously allowed adaptation of charts and graphs from the LDAB.

One of the valuable resources of the School of Divinity in the last few years has been our two experts in computing support, Dr. Jessie Paterson and Bronwyn Currie. Bronwyn kindly took my data from the LDAB and prepared the graphs and charts included in this book. Jessie fashioned the "Christograms" included in chapter four. In addition, both of these kind souls responded to my other pleas and cries of frustration about various computing matters with serenity and efficiency.

Robert Kraft gave me comments on an earlier draft of chapter two. Bob is well informed in the subjects of this book, and not inclined always to agree with my own views, so it was all the more valuable to have his input. I doubt that I have persuaded him on some key issues of disagreement, but his vigorous comments certainly helped me to sharpen my argument. One of my current graduate students, Michael Leary, read chapters two and five, catching a number of typos and raising some helpful queries. Scott Charlesworth gave me a number of corrections and suggestions from his reading of an early draft of chapters one through five.

New College, Edinburgh
13 February 2006

Arts & Humanities
Research Council

The AHRC funds postgraduate training and research in the arts and humanities, from archaeology and English literature to design and dance. The quality and range of research supported not only provides social and cultural benefits but also contributes to the economic success of the UK. For further information on the AHRC, please see our website: www.ahrc.ac.uk.

Abbreviations of ancient texts follow those given in *The SBL Handbook of Style for Ancient Near Eastern, Biblical, and Early Christian Studies,* ed. Patrick H. Alexander et al. Peabody, MA: Hendrickson, 1999.

ABD	*Anchor Bible Dictionary,* ed. D. N. Freedman, 6 vols. New York: Doubleday, 1992
AHDRC	Ancient History Documents Research Centre
Aland	Kurt Aland, *Kurzgefasste Liste der griechischen Handschriften des Neuen Testaments.* 2nd ed. Berlin: de Gruyter, 1994
ANF	Ante-Nicene Fathers
ANTF	Arbeiten zur neutestamentlichen Textforschung
APIS	Advanced Papyrological Information System. http://www.columbia.edu/cu/lweb/projects/digital/apis
BA	*Biblical Archaeologist*
BAGD	W. Bauer, W. F. Arndt, F. W. Gingrich, and F. W. Danker, *Greek-English Lexicon of the New Testament and Other Early Christian Literature,* 2nd ed. Chicago: University of Chicago Press, 1979
BETL	Bibliotheca ephemeridum theologicarum lovaniensium
BibSem	Biblical Seminar
BICSSup	Bulletin of the Institute of Classical Studies, Supplements
BIOSCS	*Bulletin of the International Organization for Septuagint and Cognate Studies*
BJRL	*Bulletin of the John Rylands Library* (Manchester)
BWANT	Beiträge zur Wissenschaft vom Alten und Neuen Testament

DJD	Discoveries in the Judaean Desert
EEC	*Encyclopedia of Early Christianity,* ed. E. Ferguson. 2nd ed. 2 vols. New York: Garland, 1997
EncJud	*Encyclopedia Judaica,* ed. G. Wigoder, 16 vols. Jerusalem: Keter, 1971-72
GCS	Die griechische christliche Schriftsteller der ersten [drei] Jahrhunderte
HTR	*Harvard Theological Review*
JAC	*Jahrbuch für Antike und Christentum*
JBL	*Journal of Biblical Literature*
JQR	*Jewish Quarterly Review*
JRASup	Journal of Roman Archaeology Supplement Series
JSNTSup	Journal for the Study of the New Testament Supplement Series
JSOTSup	Journal for the Study of the Old Testament Supplement Series
JTS	*Journal of Theological Studies*
LDAB	Leuven Database of Ancient Books. http://ldab.arts.kuleuven.ac.be/
NHS	Nag Hammadi Studies
NIGTC	New International Greek Testament Commentary
NovT	*Novum Testamentum*
NovTSup	Novum Testamentum Supplements
NTOA	Novum Testamentum und Orbis Antiquus
NTS	*New Testament Studies*
PG	Patrologia Graeca, ed. J.-P. Migne, 167 vols. Paris, 1857-66
PRCE	Papyri from the Rise of Christianity in Egypt
Rahlfs	Alfred Rahlfs and Detlef Fraenkel, *Verzeichnis der griechischen Handschriften des Alten Testaments.* Göttingen: Vandenhoeck & Ruprecht, 2004
SBLMS	Society of Biblical Literature Monograph Series
SBLTT	Society of Biblical Literature Texts and Translations
SD	Studies and Documents
SJLA	Studies in Judaism in Late Antiquity
SPap	*Studia Papyrologica*
STDJ	Studies on the Texts of the Desert of Judah
Sup	Supplement(s)
TDNT	*Theological Dictionary of the New Testament,* ed. G. Kittel and G. Friedrich, trans. G. W. Bromiley. 10 vols. Grand Rapids: Eerdmans, 1964-76

TU	Texte und Untersuchungen
TynBul	*Tyndale Bulletin*
VC	*Vigiliae christianae*
VH	Joseph van Haelst, *Catalogue des papyrus littéraires juifs et chrétiens*. Paris: Publications de la Sorbonne, 1976
WMANT	Wissenschaftliche Monographien zum Alten und Neuen Testament
WUNT	Wissenschaftliche Untersuchungen zum Neuen Testament
ZNW	*Zeitschrift für die neutestamentliche Wissenschaft*
ZPE	*Zeitschrift für Papyrologie und Epigraphik*

Introduction

P rominent among the earliest physical evidence of Christianity is a body
of manuscripts of canonical and extracanonical texts that continues to
grow in number. Indeed, the very earliest of these manuscripts are the most
ancient of identifiably Christian artifacts extant. In this book I want to draw
attention to this evidence, and emphasize the particular import of these
valuable (and too frequently overlooked) items for the study of the New Testament and the origins of Christianity. Although ours is a period of intense
scholarly focus on *historical* analysis of earliest Christianity, with an impressively proliferating assortment of issues and approaches deployed by scholars today, it is striking that the manuscripts that constitute our earliest artifacts of Christianity are so widely ignored.[1] In his wide-ranging study of
early Christian books and reading, Harry Gamble noted that we now possess
manuscripts of very early date, and lamented that "the close study of these
manuscripts has remained almost exclusively the preserve of paleographers
and textual critics, historians of early Christian literature having taken little
interest in exploiting them for the history of Christianity and its literature."[2]

---

1. This basic point was made earlier by Erich Dinkler, "Älteste christliche Denkmäler:
Bestand und Chronologie," *Signum Crucis* (Tübingen: Mohr [Siebeck], 1967), 134-78, repr. in
Paul Corby Finney, ed., *Art, Archaeology, and Architecture of Early Christianity* (New York: Garland, 1993), 22-66. The point still bears repeating, as illustrated by a recent conversation with
another senior scholar in Christian origins. After telling him about the subject of this book, he
replied, "Ah, but I'm not so interested in manuscripts, and more interested in artifacts." It is
precisely the failure to realize that manuscripts *are* artifacts that I seek to correct in this book.

2. Harry Y. Gamble, *Books and Readers in the Early Church: A History of Early Christian
Texts* (New Haven: Yale University Press, 1995), 43.

My main purpose here, however, is not to complain about this but to encourage greater recognition of what these manuscripts have to offer to all of us who are interested in historical questions about early Christianity, whether we are scholars, students, or wider public. Let us begin by considering further their chronological significance.

Manuscripts and Other Early Artifacts

It is instructive to consider early Christian manuscripts in the context of other early physical evidence of Christianity. The earliest example of a Christian church building remains the third-century structure at Dura Europos (dated ca. 241-256 CE).[3] As for early epigraphical data, virtually all inscriptions that can be dated with any confidence are from the third century and later.[4] There is, for example, a frequently studied body of Christian inscriptions from Phrygia from this period.[5] If it is dated correctly to about 200, the Aberkios inscription (found at Hierapolis) perhaps remains our earliest identifiably Christian inscription.[6] Although one finds confi-

3. The Dura Europos structure appears to have been a house that was renovated for use as a church building, and destroyed with the rest of the city in 256 CE during incursions by the Sassanians. It was identified during the excavations of Dura-Europos in 1922-39. For basic information and further bibliographical references, see L. Michael White, "Dura-Europos," *EEC*, 1:352-53; idem, "Architecture," *EEC*, 1:104-6; Graydon F. Snyder, *Ante Pacem: Archaeological Evidence of Church Life Before Constantine* (Macon, GA: Mercer University Press, 1985), 67-117. Robert Kraft pointed me to the more recent find of a fourth-century basilica at Aqaba: http://www.chass.ncsu.edu/history/rapweb/1996.htm.

4. For a concise recent survey on Christian epigraphical material, see Michael P. McHugh, "Inscriptions," *EEC*, 1:574-76 (with references). Snyder (*Ante Pacem*, 119-48) gives a more detailed analysis of pre-Constantinian inscriptions and graffiti. Older but still worth consulting is H. V. P. Nunn, *Christian Inscriptions* (Eton: Saville, 1951).

5. W. Tabbernee, "Christian Inscriptions from Phrygia," in *New Documents Illustrating Early Christianity*, 3, ed. G. H. R. Horsley (North Ryde, NSW: AHDRC, Macquarie University, 1983), 128-39; Gary J. Johnson, *Early Christian Epitaphs from Anatolia*, SBLTT 35 (Atlanta: Scholars Press, 1995).

6. R. A. Kearsley, "The Epitaph of Aberkios: The Earliest Christian Inscription?" in *New Documents Illustrating Early Christianity*, 6, ed. S. R. Llewelyn (North Ryde, NSW: AHDRC, Macquarie University, 1992), 177-81; W. K. Wischmeyer, "Die Aberkiosinschrift als Grabepigramm," in *Studia Patristica*, ed. E. A. Livingstone (Oxford: Pergamon, 1982), 777-81. Margherita Guarducci (*The Tomb of St. Peter*, trans. J. McLellan [London: Harrap, 1960], esp. 131-36) argued that one or two graffiti found under the Vatican may be dated to the mid/late

dent references to second-century catacombs and catacomb art in some older publications, it is now generally recognized among specialists that these as well should probably be dated to sometime in the third century.[7] It is, in fact, difficult to identify any art as unambiguously Christian from before about 200.

Therefore, it is important to recognize that a significant body of Christian manuscripts is as early as any of these other types of artifacts, and a small number may be somewhat earlier still. Some 400 papyri from prior to the official recognition of Christianity by the emperor Constantine have been logged as either from Christian hands or at least directly referring to Christians.[8] About half of these are copies of biblical texts (both Christian OT and what became NT writings), about a quarter are classified as other literary or "subliterary" texts (e.g., treatises, other extracanonical writings, liturgical and magical texts), and the rest include a number of letters and other types of documents.[9] Among these pre-Constantinian manuscripts, a small but growing number are dated as early as the second century, and these second-century manuscripts now constitute the earliest extant artifacts of Christianity. Consequently, early Christian manuscripts, especially those from the second and third centuries, should be given close attention in all historical analysis of the Christian movement in the pre-Constantinian period.

Granted, in the case of nearly every one of the earliest manuscripts, at least those containing literary texts, what we have represents only a portion of the original manuscript, sometimes just a single leaf or even as little as a few fragments. But I aim to show that even such small portions of ancient manuscripts can provide us with a surprising amount of valuable information. In addition to giving us our earliest witnesses to the texts that

---

second century, including one that she read as "Peter is within" (ΠΕΤΡ[ΟΣ] ΕΝΙ), which may have been intended to mark the traditional site of Peter's tomb. Cf. D. M. O'Connor, "Peter in Rome: A Review and Position," in *Christianity, Judaism and Other Greco-Roman Cults: Studies for Morton Smith at Sixty,* ed. Jacob Neusner, 4 vols., SJLA 12 (Leiden: Brill, 1975), 2:146-60.

7. Paul Corby Finney, "Art," *EEC*, 1:120-26; idem, *The Invisible God: The Earliest Christians on Art* (Oxford: Oxford University Press, 1994); Robin Margaret Jensen, *Understanding Early Christian Art* (London: Routledge, 2000).

8. I draw here upon findings from the research project on "Papyri from the Rise of Christianity in Egypt" (PRCE), based in the AHDRC, Macquarie University (Australia). See http://www.anchist.mq.edu.au/doccentre/PCEhomepage.html.

9. For a concise overview see Edwin A. Judge, "Papyri," *EEC*, 2:867-72.

they convey, we have a number of other matters to consider. The physical and visual features of these manuscripts (which I will specify later in this introduction) also constitute a body of data that, when analyzed carefully, can yield potentially significant evidence that is relevant for various questions about early Christianity.

Simply to take a slightly more specific account of the texts attested in second- and third-century manuscripts yields an impressive inventory.[10] In addition to copies of the writings that became part of the New Testament and the writings of the Christian Old Testament (the earliest Christian scriptures), we have copies of apocryphal Christian texts such as the *Gospel of Thomas, Gospel of Mary, Acts of Paul;* correspondence between Paul and the church at Corinth; the *Protevangelium (Infancy Gospel) of James;* several unidentified Gospel-like writings (e.g., the so-called *Egerton Gospel*); and other important early Christian texts such as Irenaeus's *Against Heresies* and the *Shepherd of Hermas.* There are also fragments of Christian liturgical texts, hymns, prayers, amulets, and letters. In short, Christian manuscripts from the second and third centuries witness strongly to the rich and diverse fund of texts produced, read, copied, and circulated among Christians. That is, these early manuscripts not only give us extremely early witnesses that are very valuable for our grasp of the textual history of early Christian writings but also allow us to construct more broadly a picture of the history and "culture" of Christianity in the second and third centuries.

---

10. Joseph van Haelst, *Catalogue des papyrus littéraires juifs et chrétiens* (Paris: Publications de la Sorbonne, 1976), remains the most essential reference tool. It is ordered according to the types of texts contained in manuscripts, but there is an index arranged according to their likely dating (409-14). The other principal printed catalogues of Christian papyri are the two volumes by Kurt Aland, *Repertorium der griechischen christlichen Papyri, I: Biblische Papyri, Altes Testament, Neues Testament, Varia, Apokryphen,* Patristische Texte und Studien 18 (Berlin: de Gruyter, 1976); and *Repertorium der griechischen christlichen Papyri, II: Kirchenväter-Papyri, Teil 1: Beschreibungen* (Berlin: de Gruyter, 1995). Cornelia Römer (University College London) has an online bibliographical update of van Haelst's catalogue: http://www.ucl.ac.uk/GrandLat/research/christianpapyri.htm, and since 1997 she has produced an annual review of publications on "Christian Papyri" in *Archiv für Papyrusforschung,* taking up the mantle of the late Kurt Treu, who produced such annual surveys in the journal from 1969 through 1991.

Early Christian Manuscripts as Artifacts

In this book I urge that we take earliest Christian manuscripts seriously as historical artifacts, paying attention to their physical and visual characteristics as well as the texts that they contain.[11] As a preview of matters elaborated in the following chapters of this book, here are the sorts of phenomena that should be noted. At this point, I will simply mention features of early Christian manuscripts and briefly pose some questions about their possible significance, leaving for subsequent chapters a fuller exploration of these matters.

To commence with an elementary observation, the overwhelming number of the earliest Christian manuscripts are papyrus, whereas parchment became increasingly favored from the fourth century onward. Moreover, it is interesting to note by comparison that the fund of early Jewish manuscripts from various sites in Roman Judea appears to exhibit a preference for leather, especially for literary texts.[12] Is there any significance to the predominance of papyrus as writing material for earliest Christian manuscripts, or is it simply indicative of what material was most readily to hand at that time and place (second- and third-century Egypt)? Either way, it is a matter worth considering.

A somewhat better-known set of questions concerns what to make of the clear Christian preference for the codex over the roll/scroll, evident from our earliest evidence onward, especially (but by no means exclusively) for texts that Christians regarded most highly, such as their copies of Old Testament writings and the Christian writings that were coming to be regarded as scripture. This contrasts with a preference for the roll in the wider contemporary culture, especially for literary texts. How did the codex so quickly and so early come to be preferred by Christians? Does this preference basically reflect a Christian judgment about some superior

11. I develop here proposals made in an essay a few years ago: Larry W. Hurtado, "The Earliest Evidence of an Emerging Christian Material and Visual Culture: The Codex, the *Nomina Sacra* and the Staurogram," in *Text and Artifact in the Religions of Mediterranean Antiquity: Essays in Honour of Peter Richardson,* ed. Stephen G. Wilson and Michel Desjardins (Waterloo, Ont.: Wilfrid Laurier University Press, 2000), 271-88; and in "The 'Metadata' of Earliest Christian Manuscript," an invited presentation given at the annual meeting of the Society of Biblical Literature, San Antonio, Texas, November 2004.

12. See now Emanuel Tov, *Scribal Practices and Approaches Reflected in the Texts Found in the Judean Desert,* STDJ 54 (Leiden: Brill, 2004), esp. 31-55.

practicality and usefulness of the codex, or did it have some semiotic significance, representing an expression of emergent Christian identity, especially in the second and third centuries? There are, however, also instances of Christian texts written on rolls, though they form a small minority of the total number of early Christian manuscripts. So, we may ask, in light of the clear Christian preference for the codex, what does the choice to copy a given Christian writing on a roll signal? It seems that the choice to use a codex or a roll was not made indifferently, but what precisely are we to make of particular choices?

Another curious feature of early Christian manuscripts is the special scribal treatment accorded certain words, written in an abbreviated form, and normally with a horizontal stroke over the abbreviation. Scholars refer to these distinctive abbreviations as the *nomina sacra* (literally, "sacred names"), and several issues remain under lively debate. Does this scribal practice represent an early Christian convention that reflects Christian piety, or was it merely a kind of labor-saving standardized way of writing certain familiar key words in the early Christian religious vocabulary? Also, did Christians invent this scribal practice, or did they share it with, or derive it from, Jewish scribal tradition?

What about the interesting monogram-like combination of the two Greek letters *tau* and *rho* that appears in certain early manuscripts of New Testament writings? Is it significant that the earliest Christian use of this *tau-rho* device is as part of abbreviated forms of the Greek words for "cross" and "crucify"? Is it, as some scholars have proposed, perhaps even an early pictogram of a crucified Jesus from about 200 (which would be considerably earlier than is conventionally thought to be the date of the earliest visual references to Jesus on the cross)?

Do their earliest manuscripts tell us anything significant about the social and economic status and cultural aspirations of Christians in the second and third centuries? For example, might the scribal "hands" of various manuscripts (the nature and quality of the copyists' writing) indicate something relevant? What about the size and shape of manuscripts, and whether the text is written in columns? Perhaps even the size of the margins and the number of lines of writing per page signal something. Is it significant that these manuscripts often feature spacing apparently used to mark sense units (such as sentences), and does the presence of punctuation and some other scribal devices represent a particular effort to facilitate reading, perhaps public/liturgical reading?

Do corrections in early manuscripts tell us anything more than that copyists made mistakes? Might corrections indicate a concern for careful copying of a text, or do they signal instead a certain fluidity in textual transmission? And does it matter whether corrections were made by the copyist or by someone else? Might corrections in another contemporary hand suggest a setting something like a scriptorium, in which the work of a scribe was proofread by someone else, perhaps a scribal supervisor of some sort?

All of these questions point to features of early Christian manuscripts that are well known among specialists in Greek paleography and papyrology. I want to show, however, that these phenomena may also comprise evidence relevant for wider questions about early Christianity, and I want to urge that a larger circle of scholars and students concerned with the origins of Christianity should become more acquainted with these matters.

Scholarly Neglect

Part of the rationale for this book is to overcome an unwitting neglect of early Christian manuscripts. This lamentable neglect of manuscripts is most pointedly illustrated with reference to what New Testament scholars usually regard as the most important ones of all, the early manuscripts of New Testament writings. Even these are insufficiently considered, especially beyond those scholars who focus on New Testament textual criticism. Of course, a wider circle of scholars know of key early manuscripts of the writings of the New Testament, and will have at least a general appreciation of their significance for the task of tracing the textual history of these writings and for constructing modern critical editions of them. Textual variants supported in early manuscripts appear in the apparatus of critical editions commonly used by New Testament scholars, such as the Nestle-Aland Greek New Testament.[13] But neither manuscripts of New Testament writings nor the many others that contain other early Christian texts have been given their due broadly in the field of New Testament and Christian origins.

I emphasize how striking it is that this wide neglect extends even to early manuscripts of New Testament writings, and I want to explore this

---

13. *Novum Testamentum Graece*, ed. Barbara Aland et al., 27th ed. (Stuttgart: Deutsche Bibelgesellschaft, 1993), often referred to as "Nestle-Aland."

more fully. Sadly, most contemporary New Testament scholars have scant direct acquaintance with these manuscripts, and often only a limited sense of what they have to offer. This is partly a reflection of the way most scholars in the field are prepared today. Few doctoral programs in New Testament and Christian origins involve training in reading ancient manuscripts, or even any serious exhortation or opportunities to consult them. Moreover, most New Testament scholars today probably have little direct familiarity with the materials, procedures, and issues involved in textual criticism of the New Testament, and basically rely on the judgments and products of specialists in the subject.[14] Granted, this is simply one manifestation of the consequences of a proliferation of subspecialties that characterizes virtually all academic disciplines nowadays. The field of New Testament studies in particular now reflects the continuing emergence of new and additional approaches and foci, which can have the effect of making more traditional lines of inquiry seem a bit out of current fashion.

With all due appreciation for the richness and diversity of the current state of New Testament studies, however, in one respect we are in what I regard as quite a regrettable situation for a field that is traditionally characterized by textual scholarship. Though texts are central to our work in the field, we too often engage them at considerable remove from their historical and physical manifestation as *manuscripts*. Indeed, even the variant readings of early manuscripts of the New Testament presented in the apparatus of critical editions of the Greek New Testament are often inadequately considered. Instead, scholars, including those who avowedly pursue historical questions about early Christianity, often treat the text of a printed edition of the Greek New Testament as all they need to consider. Further, if the truth be admitted, many New Testament specialists today and, still more worrying for the future of the field, many or most of those of recent vintage, can barely navigate the critical apparatus of a modern printed edition of the Greek New Testament, such as Nestle-Aland. So scholars sometimes do not adequately engage questions of textual variation in doing their exegesis of the New Testament.

14. These are not exaggerations, but judgments formed through some thirty years in the field of NT and Christian origins, based on numerous conversations with fellow scholars. A number of NT scholars even find the apparatus of the Nestle-Aland edition too daunting, and prefer the United Bible Societies' *Greek New Testament* (ed. Barbara Aland et al.; 4th ed.; repr. Stuttgart: Deutsche Bibelgesellschaft, 2004) because it has a simpler apparatus (but less adequate for scholarly exegesis of the NT).

In part, this also reflects the decline in the fortunes of New Testament textual criticism in the latter half of the twentieth century, particularly in English-speaking countries.[15] Indeed, in the late 1970s a leading scholar in the discipline, Eldon Epp, went so far as to warn starkly that New Testament textual criticism was perhaps at the point of its demise in English-speaking settings, especially in North America, styling his essay as a putative "requiem" for the discipline.[16]

Since Epp's somber jeremiad appeared in 1979, however, in some respects things have started looking a bit better.[17] For example, nowadays sessions of the program unit devoted to New Testament textual criticism in annual meetings of the Society of Biblical Literature regularly draw an attendance of fifty or so, and often significantly more. It is also encouraging that a number of those attending these sessions with serious interest in the subject are younger scholars and even some students in or aiming for Ph.D. work. The flourishing of the Internet has facilitated the production of various World Wide Web sites devoted to New Testament textual criticism, including a number aimed at the general public, and indicating a certain popular interest.[18] Moreover, there are now several university settings in English-speaking countries in which Ph.D. students can pursue research in New Testament textual criticism, a significant improvement over the situation when Epp wrote his "requiem" article.[19] Nevertheless, be-

15. When I completed a Ph.D. in 1973 with a thesis in NT textual criticism, I was quite aware that I was one of very few scholars of my generation who chose to do doctoral work in this subject, and I often had the sense that many contemporaries found my choice a bit of a curiosity. The thesis, revised and the data augmented, was published later: Larry W. Hurtado, *Text-Critical Methodology and the Pre-Caesarean Text: Codex W in the Gospel of Mark*, SD 43 (Grand Rapids: Eerdmans, 1981).

16. Eldon J. Epp, "New Testament Textual Criticism in America: Requiem for a Discipline," *JBL* 98 (1979): 94-98. In the German scene, however, the Institute for New Testament Textual Research in the University of Münster has continued to be a major center for important text-critical work.

17. L. W. Hurtado, "Beyond the Interlude? Developments and Directions in New Testament Textual Criticism," in *Studies in the Early Text of the Gospels and Acts*, ed. D. G. K. Taylor (Birmingham: University of Birmingham Press; Atlanta: Society of Biblical Literature, 1999), 26-48.

18. Note, e.g., the various links on Mark Goodacre's "New Testament Gateway" Web site: http://www.ntgateway.com/resource/textcrit.htm.

19. Among other current English-speaking scholars who particularly focus on NT textual criticism in university settings are Bart Ehrman (University of North Carolina, USA), David Parker (University of Birmingham, UK), and J. Keith Elliott (University of Leeds,

yond the circle of those who focus on New Testament textual criticism (albeit, a circle a bit larger in recent years), for many other New Testament scholars the subject remains somewhat esoteric, technical, and, frankly, not particularly obligatory.

Even those who commendably do develop an acquaintance with textual criticism of the New Testament and are accustomed to take account of variant readings and weigh the witnesses that support them often have little direct familiarity with actual manuscripts. Granted, if all one seeks to know is what readings of a given New Testament passage are supported by various ancient textual witnesses, the apparatus of a good critical edition, and perhaps the printed editions of key manuscripts, or even collations of manuscripts, are adequate and readily available in good research libraries.[20] Also, undeniably, all of us today, accustomed as we are to modern printed texts, find it much easier to read printed transcriptions, rather than to deal with the very different (and sometimes demanding) features of ancient handwritten manuscripts.[21]

But if even the early manuscripts of New Testament writings are rarely accessed by New Testament scholars, beyond those with some specific interest and training in textual criticism, it is not surprising that other early Christian manuscripts are hardly consulted at all outside the small circles of certain specialists. To be sure, as the case with New Testament writings, scholars are often interested in the *texts* conveyed in these early manuscripts, and appreciate the importance of these manuscript witnesses for estimating how early these texts may have been written, and are interested in tracing their textual history. But scholars all too often leave to papyrologists and paleographers the consideration of the actual manuscripts as historical/physical artifacts.

Certainly, it requires impressive expertise to identify, date, and edit an-

UK). If we widen the circle to include specialists in cognate material (e.g., LXX, apostolic fathers, Nag Hammadi), opportunities and resources are somewhat greater still.

20. As confession is good for the soul, I acknowledge that my focus in my own Ph.D. thesis was on comparing textual variants, with little attention then to what else could be learned from the manuscripts in question.

21. The problem extends to other text-oriented disciplines too. John Dagenais has similarly complained about modern textual critics of medieval texts often overlooking what all actual manuscripts have to offer: *The Ethics of Reading in Manuscript Culture* (Princeton: Princeton University Press, 1994), xviii (noted in H. Gregory Snyder, *Teachers and Texts in the Ancient World* [London: Routledge, 2000], 4).

cient manuscripts, and it is perfectly appropriate for other scholars to rely gratefully upon those with expertise in these sorts of matters. In this book, however, I want to urge that the kinds of phenomena that papyrologists and paleographers note and discuss among themselves, especially the physical features of ancient Christian manuscripts, have potentially wider significance. I want to show some of the reasons why it will prove rewarding for the study of the New Testament and early Christianity if a wider circle of scholars take the trouble to acquaint themselves with these important Christian artifacts. We cannot, and need not, all be specialists in papyrology and paleography; but we can learn to take account of what such specialists make available, and we can harvest important data for the study of Christian origins.[22] In his valuable study of early Christian use of books, Harry Gamble recognized that the proliferation of specialties in the study of the New Testament and early Christianity has led to impressive expertise in particular approaches, issues, and bodies of evidence, but has also resulted in an unfortunate insulation of scholars in this or that specialty from findings in other specialties that may well have relevance for their own concerns. Lamenting the neglect of the questions and evidence that his book so helpfully highlighted, Gamble urged, "Unless the knowledge gained through disciplinary specialization is deployed across the boundaries of narrower subjects and applied to larger issues, it cannot bear its full fruit."[23] I concur with him, and this book, like his, is also intended to contribute to a cross-specialty enrichment of the historical analysis of early Christianity.

Encouraging Developments

Notwithstanding the widespread neglect of early Christian manuscripts, there are also some more encouraging developments in recent decades. In recent years annual meetings of the Society of Biblical Literature have included a program unit on "Papyrology and Early Christian Backgrounds," and its sessions have attracted interest of a respectable number of scholars in biblical studies. Likewise, recent international meetings of the SBL have

---

22. It is not too much, however, to expect scholars in Christian origins to acquire a basic acquaintance with the study of manuscripts. Eric G. Turner provides an excellent, even intriguing, entrée in *Greek Papyri: An Introduction* (Oxford: Clarendon, 1980).

23. Gamble, *Books and Readers*, xi.

featured a program unit on manuscripts. Since the mid-1990s several publications further reflect and contribute to an interest in early Christian manuscripts. I have already mentioned Harry Gamble's valuable study of how texts featured in early Christianity, and his book probably deserves pride of place. A few years later, Kim Haines-Eitzen focused on the copyists/scribes who produced early Christian manuscripts, posing intriguing questions about who they were and how they operated.[24] Also, Alan Millard produced a broad-ranging discussion of writing and reading practices, with special attention to the Roman period.[25] More recently still, there is Philip Comfort's volume, which includes discussion of physical features of New Testament manuscripts.[26] The Macquarie University project on "Papyri from the Rise of Christianity in Egypt" represents an ambitious and valuable undertaking, from which I have benefited in researching for this book.[27]

Of the publications of respected papyrologists, Colin Roberts's volume from his 1977 Schweich Lectures probably represents the most influential and best-known effort to illustrate the importance of manuscript evidence for wider questions about early Christianity.[28] Though some of his proposals remain controversial, the book is essential reading on the subject. In essays published at about the same time as Roberts's important little volume, Edwin Judge and Stuart Pickering were making a congruent emphasis on the wider historical importance of early papyri.[29] There are

24. Kim Haines-Eitzen, *Guardians of Letters: Literacy, Power, and the Transmitters of Early Christian Literature* (New York: Oxford University Press, 2000).

25. Alan Millard, *Reading and Writing in the Time of Jesus*, BibSem 69 (Sheffield: Sheffield Academic Press, 2000).

26. Philip Comfort, *Encountering the Manuscripts: An Introduction to New Testament Paleography of Textual Criticism* (Nashville: Broadman & Holman Publishers, 2005). I note also the recent multiauthor volume edited by Thomas J. Kraus and Tobias Nicklas, *New Testament Manuscripts: Their Texts and Their World* (Leiden: Brill, 2006).

27. Professor Alanna Nobbs is current leader of the project, originally inspired and led by Professor Edwin Judge. Their aim is to publish a detailed catalogue of all pre-Constantinian papyri of Christian provenance (literary and documentary texts) through Cambridge University Press. Further information is available from their Web site: http://www.anchist.mq.edu.au/doccentre/PCEhomepage.html.

28. Colin H. Roberts, *Manuscript, Society and Belief in Early Christian Egypt*, Schweich Lectures 1977 (London: Oxford University Press, for the British Academy, 1979).

29. Edwin A. Judge and S. R. Pickering, "Papyrus Documentation of Church and Community in Egypt to the Mid-Fourth Century," *JAC* 20 (1977): 47-71; idem, "Biblical Papyri Prior to Constantine: Some Cultural Implications of Their Physical Form," *Prudentia* 10 (1978): 1-13.

still other scholars whose work I gratefully acknowledge and draw upon in the following chapters. I do not posture myself in this book as a lone voice crying in the wilderness. Instead, I want to draw much wider attention to the historical significance of material that is too often overlooked.

Although not particularly focused on Christian manuscripts, a small book by Roger Bagnall intended mainly for scholars and students in ancient history may serve as an analogy for what I aim to provide here. Bagnall illustrated more broadly the usefulness of papyri for historical study of the early centuries, addressing himself also to a wider circle, in his case primarily scholars and students in classics and ancient history.[30] In the following chapters, I focus more specifically on how useful early Christian papyri are in understanding Christianity in its first influential centuries.

30. Roger Bagnall, *Reading Papyri, Writing Ancient History* (London: Routledge, 1995).

CHAPTER ONE

The Texts

U ndeniably, the foremost value of manuscripts is that they convey texts. In subsequent chapters, I discuss the historical relevance of other physical and visual properties of early Christian manuscripts, but before turning to these matters I focus on the evidence that manuscripts supply concerning the texts used among early Christians. Of course, in tracing the history of the transmission of a text, and also in reconstructing an edition of a text as close as possible to its "original" form, we particularly prize early manuscripts.[1] For these aims, in general, the earlier the manuscript, the better. But we can also pursue other questions concerning what early manuscripts tell us about ancient Christian texts, as I will illustrate in this chapter.[2]

---

1. The traditional text-critical aim of establishing an "original" text of a given writing has come under a great deal of criticism recently. I do not take time here to engage the matter. See, e.g., Eldon Jay Epp, "The Multivalence of the Term 'Original Text' in New Testament Textual Criticism," *HTR* 92 (1999): 245-81.

2. In several valuable essays, Eldon Jay Epp has offered analyses of the manuscript evidence from Oxyrhynchus in particular, exploring the texts read, possible implications on early Christian literacy, and other matters: "The New Testament Papyri at Oxyrhynchus in Their Social and Intellectual Context," in *The Sayings of Jesus: Canonical and Non-Canonical: Essays in Honour of Tjitze Baarda,* ed. William L. Petersen, Johan S. Vos, and Henk J. de Jonge, NovTSup 89 (Leiden: Brill, 1997), 47-68; "The Codex and Literacy in Early Christianity and at Oxyrhynchus: Issues Raised by Harry Y. Gamble's *Books and Readers in the Early Church," Critical Review of Books in Religion 1997,* ed. Charles Prebish (Atlanta: American Academy of Religion and Society of Biblical Literature, 1998), 15-37; "The Oxyrhynchus New Testament Papyri: 'Not Without Honor Except in Their Hometown'?" *JBL* 123 (2004): 5-55.

Texts Witnessed in Earliest Christian Manuscripts

We may begin with a very basic question about what texts appear in the earliest Christian manuscripts.[3] As indicated briefly in the introduction, simply to note the texts witnessed in these manuscripts yields interesting and potentially instructive results. Even if we limit our definition of "earliest" Christian manuscripts to those that can be dated with some confidence to the second and third centuries, the inventory of texts is ample enough to make it helpful to organize them in several major categories. Because the aim at this point is simply to take stock of what texts are attested, we can restrict ourselves to basic information about the manuscripts in question. This will involve the sort of manuscript identifiers used by paleographers and papyrologists concerning contents of the manuscript, probable date, and other notable features.[4]

Before we look at the data, however, I want to say a brief word about dates. Nearly all the manuscripts that we will survey are dated paleographically, that is, by the nature of the scribal "hand," essentially the way the letters of the text are formed. To make this judgment with competence requires an admirably wide and detailed knowledge of the scribal characteristics of ancient Greek manuscripts; the more thorough this knowledge, the better. But paleographical dating is still a judgment call, and even those scholars with this sort of expertise often disagree in their dating of a manuscript, a surprising number of times by a century or more. Let me be clear on my own limitations. I can follow the paleographical analysis of experts, but I cannot claim sufficient expertise in Greek paleography to offer a deciding judgment, and so I shall simply give the dates of manuscripts supplied in the standard catalogues, noting any significant disagreements.[5]

---

3. Appendix 1 gives a list, with information on each text in manuscripts that can be dated ca. 300 CE or earlier.

4. In addition to the formal manuscript identifier (e.g., P.Yale 1), I also note the reference numbers in important catalogues. See the list of abbreviations for full titles of these.

5. The Leuven Database of Ancient Books (LDAB) is a valuable (but not inerrant) Internet-accessible catalogue intended to list all "literary" texts from the Roman era: http://ldab.arts.kuleuven.ac.be/. For early Jewish and Christian manuscripts, note also the van Haelst *Catalogue* (though it is now a bit dated in light of the most recent publications of Oxyrhynchus papyri and some Jewish texts from Judean sites). Another important Internet site is the Advanced Papyrological Information System (APIS), which links various sources

Old Testament Texts

We start with those texts that are known in Christian tradition as the "Old Testament." Of course, this term is a bit anachronistic for this early period, especially for the second century. To cite one reason, the expression connotes an association and comparison with the collection of writings that we know as the "New Testament." But, although a number of texts that came to form part of the New Testament were already circulating and receiving a growing regard in Christian circles, along with scriptures inherited from Jewish tradition, the boundaries of the Christian canon were still not firmly defined, and the question of which writings should be included was still not resolved. That is, neither the "Old Testament" nor the "New Testament" was then an agreed and closed list of texts.[6] So both terms are somewhat anachronistic with reference to the very early period that concerns us here. Nevertheless, in spite of the slight anachronism involved, it is convenient to review first the early Christian manuscript evidence for those writings that came to be part of the "Old Testament" (in the wider sense of the term reflected in Roman Catholic and Orthodox traditions), and in a later section the evidence for "New Testament" texts.

To take note of another preliminary matter that calls for brief comment, in a few cases, especially some Greek manuscripts of Old Testament texts, it is difficult to be sure whether the provenance of the artifact is Christian or Jewish. Devout Jews and also (most) Christians of the time regarded these texts as scriptures.[7] For obvious reasons, Greek biblical manuscripts that can be dated with confidence prior to the emergence of Christianity, such as those from Judean sites, and manuscripts written in

---

of information on literary texts written on papyrus, but at present only papyri from a number of North American centers: http://www.columbia.edu/cu/lweb/projects/digital/apis/.

6. For a concise overview of the early steps in the development of the Christian canon, see Lee M. McDonald, "Canon (of Scripture)," *EEC*, 1:205-10. For more extensive treatment, see the multiauthor volume edited by Lee M. McDonald and James A. Sanders, *The Canon Debate* (Peabody, MA: Hendrickson, 2002).

7. Of course, Marcionite Christians and probably most of those usually referred to by scholars as "gnostic" Christians rejected the OT texts as scripture. I have argued that one of the key features of the circles that make up "proto-orthodox" Christianity was their regard for the scriptures of Jewish tradition as their scriptures also: L. W. Hurtado, *Lord Jesus Christ: Devotion to Jesus in Earliest Christianity* (Grand Rapids: Eerdmans, 2003), esp. 494-96, 563-78.

Hebrew or Aramaic are readily posited as Jewish.[8] Likewise, we presume that manuscripts containing Christian texts, such as those that came to form part of the New Testament, derive from a Christian setting. But manuscripts of Old Testament texts from the early centuries CE can be more difficult to place as to religious provenance.

Scholars often use some key earmarks of manuscripts, however, to try to make this judgment, and in most cases there is wide agreement.[9] For instance, the specially abbreviated forms of words known as *nomina sacra* (discussed in chapter three) are widely taken by specialists in ancient Greek manuscripts as indicating a probable Christian provenance. Likewise, in light of the early Christian preference for the codex, scholars often view codex manuscripts of Old Testament texts as probably Christian. In contrast, the use of Hebrew characters to write the divine name (יהוה) suggests a manuscript probably prepared for Jewish usage. But the problem is that a few manuscripts exhibit a mixture of these earmarks, making it difficult to decide between a Jewish and a Christian provenance.[10] I will note these dif-

---

8. See now Tov, *Scribal Practices*, esp. 299-316; idem, "The Greek Biblical Texts from the Judean Desert," in *The Bible as Book: The Transmission of the Greek Text*, ed. Scot McKendrick and Orlaith A. O'Sullivan (London: British Library, 2003), 97-122.

9. Note, e.g., Tov's summary of these in *Scribal Practices*, 303. See also Robert Kraft's discussion: http://ccat.sas.upenn.edu/rs/rak/jewishpap.html#jewishmss. Kraft gives a current list of Greek biblical manuscripts (with photographs) dated first century CE and earlier (and so commonly taken as Jewish): 4QLXXDeut (4Q122, fragment of parchment, Deuteronomy, roll, second century BCE), P.Ryl. 458 (fragment of Deuteronomy, papyrus roll, second century BCE), 7QpapLXXEx (7Q1, fragment of Exodus, papyrus roll, ca. 100 BCE), 4QLXXLeva (4Q119, fragment of Leviticus parchment roll, ca. 100 BCE), 4QpapLXXLevb (4Q120, papyrus roll of Leviticus, first century BCE), 7QLXXEpJer (7Q2, papyrus roll of *Epistle of Jeremiah* = *Bar.* 6, ca. 100 BCE), P.Fouad 266a (papyrus roll of Genesis, first century BCE), P.Fouad 266b (papyrus roll of Deuteronomy, first century BCE), P.Fouad 266c (papyrus roll of Deuteronomy, first century BCE), 4Q127 ("Paraphrase of Exodus," papyrus roll, first century BCE), 4QLXXNum (4Q121, fragment of parchment roll, end of first century BCE), 8HevXIIgr (Hab. 2–3, fragment of parchment roll of Minor Prophets, end of first century BCE), P.Oxy. 3522 (fragment of papyrus roll of Job, first century BCE), P.Oxy. 4443 (fragment of papyrus roll of Esther, late first/early second century CE). Kraft also includes the following manuscripts: 4Q126 (fragment of parchment roll, unidentified Greek text, late first century BCE), 4Q127 (4QParaphrase of Exodus, fragment of papyrus roll, late first century BCE), and P.Fouad 203 (fragment of papyrus roll, unidentified Greek text, first/second century CE). Cf. the list in Tov, *Scribal Practices*, 304-10, which includes all Greek papyrus manuscripts of biblical texts down through the fourth century CE. Kraft also gives a list of early Greek manuscripts (and a few other items) that he proposes may be either Jewish or Christian.

10. To anticipate here a discussion of these matters later in this book, these problematic

ficult cases as we proceed. Fortunately, however, they are comparatively few, and for the far greater number of manuscripts of Old Testament texts scholars agree widely on which to take as early Christian copies.

Because my aim at this point is simply to show the range and number of texts for which our earliest Christian manuscripts bear witness, in what follows I merely list texts, with the number of second- and third-century manuscript witnesses for each in parentheses. After we take note of these data, we will then consider some questions and inferences. I have attempted to take account of all Christian Greek manuscripts dated to the second or third century, including some dated as third/fourth century (i.e., ca. 275-325 CE). In footnotes I have added comments on some particular cases. For more information on relevant manuscripts, consult appendix 1.[11]

Here are the results: Genesis (8),[12] Exodus (8),[13] Leviticus (3), Numbers (1), Deuteronomy (2), Joshua (1), Judges (1), 2 Chronicles (2),[14] Esther (2),[15] Job (1), Psalms (18),[16] Proverbs (2), Ecclesiastes (2),[17] Wisdom of Solomon

---

manuscripts may be evidence that in these early centuries contact and interchange between those whom we would identify as Jews and Christians remained more lively than we might sometimes assume.

11. Cf. Epp's survey of copies of OT texts at Oxyrhynchus: "Oxyrhynchus New Testament Papyri," 18-20.

12. Three of these are manuscripts somewhat more difficult to identify confidently as Jewish or Christian: P.Oxy. 1007 (a parchment codex, but with the Tetragrammaton written as ZZ with a horizontal stroke through this device), P.Oxy. 656 (a papyrus codex, but with Κυριος not abbreviated), and P.Oxy. 1166 (a papyrus roll). The earliest extant Greek manuscript of Genesis is P.Fouad 266 (a papyrus roll of Genesis and Deuteronomy), which because of the date (first century BCE) is clearly a Jewish manuscript and is not included in the total given here.

13. This includes P.Harris 2.166, a third-century CE papyrus roll, which some scholars have identified as Jewish. It is possible that this was an excerpt text, rather than a continuous text of Exodus, and so of Jewish or Christian provenance. Also included in the total is P.Oxy. 1075 (third-century CE papyrus roll).

14. These two (P.Lond.Christ. 3 and P.Barc.inv. 3) may be portions of the same manuscript. See VH 51 (##75-76).

15. In addition there is an early papyrus roll (P.Oxy. 4443), which may well be Jewish.

16. Includes *PSI* 8.921v, an opisthograph, P.Harris 31 (papyrus roll, third/fourth century), and also P.Vindob.G. 39777 (parchment roll, third/fourth century CE), and P.Barc.inv. 2 (parchment roll, early second century CE), either or both of which might well be Jewish. Excludes some others that appear to be an amulet (P.Ryl.Gk Add.Box 3.1, N), a school exercise (P.Lit.Lond. 207), or a single sheet (P.Monts. II Inv. 10).

17. P.Med. 1.13 (Rahlfs 989, VH #264) and P.Mich. 3.135 (VH #265), both single leafs of papyrus codices, are probably part of the same manuscript. The other one, Hamb. Staats/

(1), Sirach (2), Isaiah (6),[18] Jeremiah (2), Ezekiel (2),[19] Daniel (2),[20] Bel and Susanna (1), Minor Prophets (2),[21] Tobit (2), and 2 Maccabees (1).[22]

New Testament Texts

Again, I simply list writings that came to form the New Testament that are witnessed in manuscripts dated to the second and third centuries CE, giving in parentheses the number of manuscripts for each writing:[23] Matthew (12),[24] Mark (1),[25] Luke (7),[26] John (16),[27] Acts (7), Romans

---

Univ. Bibliothek pap. bil. 1, contains (in this order) a Greek text of *Acts of Paul*, Song of Songs and Lamentations in Old Fayumic, and a complete Greek text of Ecclesiastes.

18. Includes P.Alex. inv. 203 (VH #300; Rahlfs 850, third/fourth century CE), a papyrus roll, with one instance of κυριος written in the contracted form κς. It is judged "probably Jewish" by van Haelst. But this judgment may rest (too?) heavily on the assumption that by this point all Christians used only the codex for their scripture texts.

19. P.Chester Beatty IX-X (published separately and later united) contained (in this order) Ezekiel, Daniel (with Greek additions), and Esther.

20. Does not include P.Lit.Lond. 211 (fourth-century parchment roll).

21. Of these, MPER 18.257 contains only Hosea and Amos. In addition, the Crosby-Schøyen Codex 193 (third century CE papyrus) includes the earliest complete text of Jonah, but in Sahidic Coptic. For studies of this composite codex, see James E. Goehring, ed., *The Crosby-Schøyen Codex: MS 193 in the Schøyen Collection* (Leuven: Peeters, 1990).

22. The sole witness is again the Crosby-Schøyen Codex 193, and it gives 2 Maccabees in Sahidic.

23. Cf. Epp, "Oxyrhynchus New Testament Papyri," 14-18, who surveys manuscripts down through the fourth century CE. Unfortunately he incorrectly dates seven copies of *Shepherd of Hermas* "up to around 200 C.E." (p. 18). By my count, there may be eight copies of *Hermas* from before 300 CE, but at most only three that can be dated earlier than 200 CE. Cf. Epp's more accurate statement (p. 17) that the surviving copies of *Hermas* "are spread evenly from the late second through the fourth centuries."

24. A few of these manuscripts include two or more Gospels: 𝔓45 (Chester Beatty I, four Gospels + Acts); 𝔓4 (Paris Bib. Nat. 1120) + 𝔓64 (Mag. 18) + 𝔓67 (P.Barc. 1), now widely accepted as one manuscript containing at least Matthew and Luke; 𝔓53 (P.Mich. 6652, only portions of Matthew and Acts survive), and Gregory-Aland 0171 (P.Berl. 11863, Matthew and Luke, but quite possibly fourth century CE).

25. The only manuscript witness to the Gospel of Mark from the second-third centuries is 𝔓45 (P.Chester Beatty I).

26. Several manuscripts have Luke and one or more other Gospels: 𝔓45 (Chester Beatty I, all four Gospels + Acts), 𝔓75 (P.Bod. XIV-XV, Luke and John), 𝔓4 + 𝔓64 + 𝔓67 (Matthew and Luke), Gregory-Aland 0171 (Matthew and Luke).

27. Four of these are dated fourth century CE and later by some scholars: 𝔓39, 𝔓80,

(4),[28] 1 Corinthians (2), 2 Corinthians (1), Galatians (1), Ephesians (3), Philippians (2), Colossians (1), 1 Thessalonians (3), 2 Thessalonians (2), Philemon (1), Titus (1), Hebrews (4),[29] James (3),[30] 1 Peter (1),[31] 2 Peter (1), 1 John (1?),[32] 2 John (1),[33] Jude (2), and Revelation (5).[34]

Other Early Christian Writings

In addition to the writings that became familiar Scriptures, a number of other Christian texts are attested in early manuscripts. These include writings usually referred to today as early Christian "apocrypha," that is, writings "similar in form and content" to the writings that came to make up the New Testament and often claiming some sort of apostolic authorship or authority, but not included as part of the Christian canon (though perhaps at least some of these writings may have been read as scripture in some Christian groups).[35]

Christian "apocrypha" attested in early manuscripts include the fol-

---

Gregory-Aland 0162, and 𝔓95. Still, John and Matthew are rather more frequently attested among early manuscript witnesses than the other canonical Gospels.

28. Excluding 𝔓40 (P.Heidelberg 45), dated to the fifth/sixth century CE by the editor who published the manuscript, but to the third century CE by Kurt Aland, *Studien zur Überlieferung des Neuen Testaments und seines Textes,* ANTF 2 (Berlin: de Gruyter, 1967), 105.

29. Includes, however, 𝔓12 (P.Amherst 1.3, third/fourth century CE, papyrus amulet or writing exercise?) and 𝔓13 (P.Oxy. 657 + *PSI* 12.1292, third/fourth century CE, papyrus opisthograph, Hebrews written on verso of a roll originally used for a copy of the Epitome of Titus Livy).

30. Two of these, however, 𝔓23 and 𝔓100, are dated third/fourth century CE, toward the end of, or perhaps beyond, the period of our concern here.

31. In addition, Crosby-Schøyen Codex 193 includes a Sahidic Coptic text of 1 Peter, which may be the earliest complete text of this writing.

32. The one manuscript witness is 𝔓9 (P.Oxy. 402), which is generally dated fourth/fifth century CE, though Aland dates it third century.

33. A single leaf of a codex with a pagination number suggesting that the complete manuscript, P.Ant. 1.12 (Gregory-Aland 0232), may have comprised a collection of Johannine writings, including the Gospel of John, Revelation, and Johannine Epistles. See, e.g., VH #555; and my further discussion of this item later in this chapter.

34. This includes 𝔓18 (P.Oxy. 1079, third/fourth century CE, papyrus roll/opisthograph, Revelation on the verso, Exodus on the recto). This may be another part of the same roll as P.IFAO 2.31, which also has a portion of Revelation on the verso of a roll. See Epp's intriguing thoughts on this manuscript, "Oxyrhynchus New Testament Papyri," 18-19.

35. I paraphrase the definition of Christian "apocrypha" from D. M. Scholer, "Apocrypha, New Testament," *EEC,* 1:74-77.

lowing:[36] *Gospel of Thomas* (3), *Protevangelium of James* (1),[37] *Gospel of Mary* (2),[38] *"Egerton" Gospel* (1),[39] *Gospel of Peter* (2?),[40] *"Fayum" Gospel* (1),[41] *Acts of Paul* (3),[42] *Correspondence of Paul and Corinth* (1),[43] *Apocalypse*

36. I have not included here the text previously thought to be a "Naasene Psalm" (P.Fay. 2), accepting the analysis by Roberts that it is instead some unknown "pagan" account of an underworld visit (*Manuscript*, 81-82).

37. The text (also referred to as *Nativité de Marie*) is part of a composite codex also containing the apocryphal correspondence of Paul and Corinth, *Odes of Solomon*, Epistle of Jude, Melito's *Pascal Homily*, 1-2 Peter, Psalms 33–34, and the *Apology of Phileas*. The last two texts are dated to the fourth century, and the construction of the composite codex is dated to the same period. See Michel Testuz, *Papyrus Bodmer VII-IX* (Cologny-Genève: Bibliotheca Bodmeriana, 1959); supplemented and corrected by Eric G. Turner, *The Typology of the Early Codex* (Philadelphia: University of Pennsylvania Press, 1977), 79-82 (discussing this and other examples of composite codices); and now Tommy Wasserman, "Papyrus 72 and the Bodmer Miscellaneous Codex," NTS 51 (2005): 137-54.

38. See now the discussion of the manuscripts of the *Gospel of Mary* by Dieter Lührmann, *Die apokryph gewordenen Evangelien: Studien zu neuen Texten und zu neuen Fragen*, NovTSup 112 (Leiden: Brill, 2004), 105-24.

39. P.Egerton 2 was previously dated to ca. 150 CE, but more recently ca. 200 CE in light of a further fragment of the manuscript (P.Köln 255) identified: Michael Gronewald, "Unbekanntes Evangelium oder Evangelienharmonie (Fragment aus dem 'Evangelium Egerton')," in *Kölner Papyri (P.Köln)*, VI (Cologne: Rheinisch-Westfälischen Akademischer Wissenschaften unter Universität Köln, 1987), 136-45; Lührmann, *Apokryph gewordenen Evangelien*, 125-43. P.Egerton 2 comprises two leaves and fragments of a third leaf of a papyrus codex, and it is not clear whether the text was some unknown Gospel or a harmonizing rendition of Synoptic material. See, e.g., J. K. Elliott, *The Apocryphal New Testament* (Oxford: Clarendon, 1993), 37-40 (but Elliott takes no note of the revised dating). Unfortunately, Jon Daniels's Ph.D. thesis on the text has not been published: "The Egerton Gospel: Its Place in Early Christianity" (Ph.D. diss., Claremont Graduate School, 1989). Wieland Wilker has produced a very helpful Web site on the manuscript: http://www-user.uni-bremen.de/~wie/Egerton/Egerton_home.html.

40. Fragments of two different manuscripts, P.Oxy. 2949 and P.Oxy. 4009, have been proposed as parts of the *Gospel of Peter* by Dieter Lührmann, "POx 2949: EvPt 3-5 in einer Handschrift des 2./3. Jahrhunderts," ZNW 72 (1981): 216-26; idem, "POx 4009: Ein neues Fragment des Petrusevangeliums?" *NovT* 35 (1993): 390-410. As indicated later in this chapter, however, this suggestion is now contested.

41. It is not entirely clear whether this seven-line fragment (P.Vind. G2325) is part of some unknown Gospel or some sort of rendition of material from the Synoptic Gospels. For brief introduction and translation see Elliott, *Apocryphal New Testament*, 43-45.

42. *Acts of Paul* is a composite of three component texts: *Acts of Paul and Thecla*, *Correspondence of Paul and the Corinthians*, and *Martyrdom of Paul*. See, e.g., VH #609; Elliott, *Apocryphal New Testament*, 350-89.

43. These apocryphal letters form part of the collection of material that came to be the *Acts of Paul*.

of Peter (1),[44] *Apocryphon of Jannes and Jambres* (1),[45] and *Apocryphon of Moses* (1).[46]

There are as well other early Christian texts of several types. Some are also known from later copies. In the case of some others, the identification is an inference based on resemblances of the contents to references to particular texts by ancient Christian writers. In a few remaining cases, we simply have to acknowledge that we are not able to identify the texts. Again, I simply list the texts, with comments in footnotes: *Shepherd of Hermas* (11);[47] Irenaeus, *Against Heresies* (2); Melito, *Paschal Homily* (1); Melito, *On Prophecy?* (1);[48] Melito, *Paschal Hymn?* (1);[49] Tatian, *Diatessaron?* (1);[50] *Odes of Solomon* (1); Julius Africanus, *Cesti* (1); Origen, *Gospel Commentary* (1); Origen, *Homily* (1); Origen, *De Principiis* (1);[51] *Sibylline Oracles* (1);[52] Theonas, *Against Manichaeans?* (1);[53] other unidentified theological

44. What were previously two separately catalogued manuscripts (Bodl. MS Gr.th.f4 and P.Vindob.G. 39756) are now widely thought to be portions of the same one. The Bodleian manuscript was previously dated to the fifth century, and the other one to the third/fourth century. The earlier dating now appears favored, which puts the manuscript toward the later end of the period we focus on here.

45. This Christian text appears on the verso of a roll, on the recto an unidentified Hermetic or "gnostic" text, probably pre/non-Christian.

46. P.Ludg.Bat. II W comprises twenty-fives pages of a papyrus codex containing two creation accounts and magical formulas, perhaps a portion of some esoteric/"gnostic" circle or orientation. See, e.g., VH 333 (#1071).

47. One of these, P.Oxy. 404, is dated third/fourth century, toward the end of, or just beyond, our period. Another, P.Oxy. 1828, a parchment codex dated third century, may be part of the same manuscript as P.Oxy. 1783, which is dated fourth century! This illustrates the approximate nature of paleographical dating, and how specialists can differ.

48. P.Oxy. 5 (VH #682). The identification is not certain, but is widely accepted as the best suggestion available.

49. The identification is widely accepted but not absolutely certain.

50. The widely repeated identification of this fragment has been stoutly challenged: D. C. Parker, D. G. K. Taylor, and M. S. Goodacre, "The Dura-Europos Gospel Harmony," in *Studies in the Early Text of the Gospels and Acts,* ed. D. G. K. Taylor (Birmingham: University of Birmingham Press; Atlanta: Society of Biblical Literature, 1999), 192-228; but cf. Jan Joosten, "The Dura Parchment and the Diatessaron," *VC* 57 (2003): 159-75.

51. This manuscript is dated to the third century by some and to the fourth century by others.

52. *Sibylline Oracles* (esp. books 1, 2, and 5) is widely thought to have originated as a Jewish text, thereafter expanded in Christian hands. This could well be a Jewish manuscript.

53. Theonas was bishop of Alexandria, 282-300; this is the oldest anti-Manichaean text known, but comes toward the end of the period of our concern.

texts (3); an unidentified eschatological discourse (1); other unidentified homilies/letters (2); a Jewish/Christian dialogue text (1);[54] prayer texts (3);[55] Hymn to the Trinity (1);[56] and exorcistic/apotropaic texts.[57]

I have restricted myself here to texts that can be regarded as "literary," but even so I have been a bit generous. For example, it is debatable whether the exorcistic texts qualify. In any case, there are a number of other items, which appear to be separate sheets containing short prayers, hymns, and such.[58] But the items that I have listed will suffice for the purpose of illustrating the diversity of texts in use by Christians in these early centuries. With this concise inventory of texts before us, let us now consider some questions, observations, and inferences.

Questions, Observations, and Inferences

The first and most immediate observation is that, indeed, we have an impressive number of texts attested in these very early manuscripts. Though nearly all are only portions, and in many cases mere fragments, of the full manuscripts, enough survives to tell us that collectively early Christians produced, copied, and read a noteworthy range of writings. With all due allowance for the limitations in the likely extent of literacy in this period, the impression given is that early Christianity represented a religious movement in which texts played a large role.[59] But we may be able to probe

54. P.Oxy. 2070 is two damaged columns of some anti-Jewish dialogue on the recto, and some other text in a later cursive hand on the verso.

55. One (BKT 6.6.1; VH #722) appears to be a compilation of prayers. Another (P.Würzb. 3; VH #1036) may be a eucharistic prayer, and the remaining one (P.Oxy. 407; VH #952) is likely a single sheet used as an amulet, so not strictly a Christian "literary" text.

56. P.Oxy. 1786 has a hymn on the verso of a single papyrus sheet (a financial account document on the recto), with the earliest extant Christian musical notation.

57. One of these (P.Fouad 203; VH #911) is judged more likely to be a Jewish adjuration against unclean spirits (so, e.g., van Haelst), and the other (VH #850) is a single golden leaf rolled up inside a golden box, so not strictly a Christian "literary" text, but instead an amulet.

58. The conspectus of the project on "Papyri from the Rise of Christianity in Egypt" (PRCE) aims to give a complete list of items that can be taken as of Christian provenance: http://www.anchist.mq.edu.au/doccentre/Conspectus.pdf.

59. This is one of the main emphases in Gamble's excellent study, *Books and Readers*. See also John Sawyer, *Sacred Languages and Sacred Texts* (London: Routledge, 1999). I can-

a bit farther. Even if we must be somewhat cautious in drawing our inferences, these data invite intriguing questions. It is a further reason for caution that only about 1% of the estimated 500,000 manuscripts from this
period have been published.

Perhaps the most basic question is whether the extant manuscripts reflect broadly the pattern of usage of texts in Christian circles in the lo-
cale(s) where the manuscripts were found. A great number of early Christian manuscripts come from the ancient Egyptian city of Oxyrhynchus,
and it appears that in the main these were found in the city refuse site,
where they had lain for centuries in the dry climate of that area.[60] Thou-
sands of manuscripts (mostly fragmentary, and mostly non-Christian
texts) were found there, deposited over six centuries or more. But what
were the circumstances for the disposal of manuscripts in the city refuse
site? Were manuscripts discarded when they wore out? If so, did Christians
simply throw out copies of their own prized texts, including those that
they treated as Scripture? Why are so many of the manuscripts, particularly the Christian texts, only pieces of their originals (e.g., individual
leaves of codices or pieces of rolls)? Is this simply the result of centuries of
incomplete decay, or does it reflect some policy or effort to destroy the
texts before throwing them on the refuse mounds?

To my knowledge, we simply do not have sufficient information to answer these questions about why and how Christian texts wound up where
they were excavated by Grenfell and Hunt and others. But, with due recognition of the danger in doing so, we will assume here that, however the
texts came to be discarded, the Christian manuscripts found in the
Oxyrhynchus rubbish mounds and other places in Egypt may broadly reflect Christian use of these texts, at least in these parts of Egypt. More spe-

---

not here attempt to engage the thorny and controverted issue of the extent of Roman-era
literacy. Cf., e.g., William V. Harris, *Ancient Literacy* (Cambridge: Harvard University Press,
1989); Mary Beard et al., *Literacy in the Roman World,* JRASup 3 (Ann Arbor: Journal of Roman Archaeology, 1991). Suffice it to say that the extent of literacy does not determine the
extent of the appreciation for and influence of texts. Even illiterates can admire and appreciate texts and be influenced by them through hearing them read. Turner (*Greek Papyri,* 82-
83) gives an interesting discussion of the matter, showing, e.g., that "illiterate" can in some
cases mean someone unable to read *Greek* but able to read and write Egyptian (i.e., de-
motic).

60. The Oxyrhynchus Web site has accessible information on the excavation and the
finds. http://www.papyrology.ox.ac.uk/index.html

cifically (and, again, recognizing that it is a bit of a risk to do so), we shall assume that extant material reflects both something of the range of texts used by Christians and perhaps also the broadly comparative popularity of individual texts in the second and third centuries. In any case, there is no reason to suspect that we are dealing with aberrant Christians behind the fragments from Oxyrhynchus and other Egyptian sites.

We must consider nevertheless whether the earliest Christian manuscripts, which all come from Egypt, are at least somewhat representative of the pattern of Christian preferences and usage of texts more generally, both more widely in Egypt and in other locales. Of course, it is always dangerous to generalize on the basis of such limited evidence. Moreover, in these early centuries Christianity was by no means monochrome; there was diversity, sometimes radical, among Christians.[61] There are likely to have been Christian circles with very different textual preferences from those of other Christian groups. So let it be clear that I am not naively proposing to treat monolithically the textual preferences of all Christians in the second and third centuries. But I contend that we should make use of the evidence that we do have, and that it likely indicates the textual preferences of those from whom the manuscript remains derive. Moreover, I believe that we have sufficient reasons for assuming (until we may have better evidence to the contrary) that we can take the papyri evidence from Egypt as broadly indicative of relevant attitudes and practices among many Christian circles more widely in the second and third centuries.

As one reason for taking this view, all indications are that early Christians were very much given to what we today would call "networking" with one another, and that includes translocal efforts. Indeed, the Roman period generally was a time of impressive travel and translocal contacts, for trading, pilgrimages, and other purposes.[62] Eldon Epp has marshaled evidence that the early Christian papyri, mainly from Egypt, reflect "extensive and lively interactions between Alexandria and the outlying areas, and also between the outlying areas [of Egypt] and other parts of the Roman world . . . and . . . the wide circulation of documents in this early pe-

---

61. I have discussed some examples of "radical diversity" in second-century Christianity in *Lord Jesus Christ*, esp. 519-61.

62. See Lionel Casson, *Travel in the Ancient World* (London: Allen & Unwin, 1974); and Richard Bauckham's discussion in his essay, "For Whom Were the Gospels Written?" in *The Gospels for All Christians: Rethinking the Gospel Audiences*, ed. Richard Bauckham (Grand Rapids: Eerdmans, 1998), 32 (9-48).

riod."[63] In another essay Epp also demonstrated how readily people expected to send and receive letters all across the Roman Empire, reflecting more broadly a "brisk 'intellectual commerce' and dynamic interchanges of people, literature, books, and letters between Egypt and the vast Mediterranean region."[64]

In illustration of this, note that we have at least three copies of the *Shepherd of Hermas* that are dated to the late second/early third century, at most only a few decades later than the composition of this text. Thus this Roman-provenance writing made its way to Egypt very quickly, and was apparently received positively. Even more striking is the appearance of a copy of Irenaeus's *Against Heresies* that has been dated to the late second or early third century. Again, within a very short time, we have a writing composed elsewhere (Gaul) finding its way to Christians in Oxyrhynchus (about 120 miles south of Cairo). We could also note the several early copies of writings of Melito of Sardis (Roman Asia Minor). In short, the extant manuscript evidence fully supports the conclusion that the Oxyrhynchus material reflects a wide, translocal outlook.

Thus in what follows I shall explore the implications of the papyrus evidence, on the working assumption that, though largely of Egyptian provenance, these early Christian papyri reflect attitudes, preferences, and usages of many Christians more broadly in the second and third centuries. I turn now to consider what we might infer from the list of textual witnesses provided to us in these papyri.

To start with writings that came to make up the Christian Old Testament, the Psalms are far and away the most attested text. Even if we set aside the two Psalms parchment rolls from our totals (which could be Jewish copies), there remain sixteen copies that are almost certainly of Christian

---

63. Eldon Jay Epp, "The Significance of the Papyri for Determining the Nature of the New Testament Text in the Second Century: A Dynamic View of Textual Transmission," in *Gospel Traditions in the Second Century: Origins, Recensions, Text, and Transmission*, ed. William L. Petersen (Notre Dame: University of Notre Dame Press, 1989), 81 (71-103).

64. Eldon Jay Epp, "New Testament Papyrus Manuscripts and Letter Carrying in Greco-Roman Times," in *The Future of Early Christianity: Essays in Honor of Helmut Koester*, ed. Birger A. Pearson (Minneapolis: Fortress Press, 1991), 55 (35-56). As another particular piece of evidence of Christian networking across imperial distances, Malcolm Choat pointed me to a third-century letter sent from an unknown individual Christian in Rome to fellow Christians in Egypt (P.Amherst 1.3), requesting certain financial transactions. For discussion see Charles Wessely, "Les plus ancients monuments du Christianisme écrits sur papyrus," *Patrologia Orientalis, Tomus Quartus* (Paris: Librairie de Paris, 1908), 135-38.

provenance, far outnumbering the tally for any other Old Testament writing. Indeed, the only other writings identifiably used by Christians that approach the number of copies of Psalms are the Gospel of Matthew (twelve copies), the Gospel of John (at least eleven copies and likely as many as fifteen, depending on the dating of four of them), and *Hermas* (eleven).[65]

The popularity of the Psalms surely occasions no surprise. Other evidence indicates that the Psalms were cherished and pondered by Christians from the earliest days. Importantly, the Psalms are the most frequently cited portion of the Old Testament in the New Testament. To cite one measure of this, in the current (27th) edition of the Nestle-Aland Greek New Testament, there are nine columns of citations and identified allusions to the Psalms, more than for any other Old Testament writing (Isaiah coming next, with about eight columns). Moreover, scholars have long noted that from the outset the Psalms were perhaps the most frequently mined portions of the Old Testament as earliest Christians sought particularly both to understand and to articulate for others the significance of Jesus. Psalm 110 is the single most frequently cited and alluded to Old Testament passage in the New Testament.[66] Moreover, from earliest years Psalms appear to have featured in Christian worship.[67]

It is a bit more curious, however, that among Old Testament writings the next best attested are Genesis and Exodus (eight copies each), suggesting a greater interest in these writings than we might have supposed. Interestingly, for Isaiah, which comes closest to Psalms in frequency of citation and allusion in the New Testament, we have only six early manuscript witnesses. Given the considerable importance that early Christians attached to Isaiah, especially as predictive of Jesus' works and in defense of their claims about his glorious significance, we might well expect the writing to be more frequently represented.[68]

It is also worthwhile to consider the Old Testament writings that are at-

65. In appendix 1 the four copies of John referred to here are numbered 118, 119, 121, 122, each of which is dated sometime between the late third and early fourth century.

66. See esp. David M. Hay, *Glory at the Right Hand: Psalm 110 in Early Christianity*, SBLMS 18 (Nashville: Abingdon, 1973). More generally, see now Steve Moyise and J. J. Maarten, eds., *The Psalms in the New Testament* (London: T&T Clark International, 2004).

67. Hughes Oliphant Old, "The Psalms of Praise in the Worship of the New Testament Church," *Interpretation* 39 (1985): 20-33.

68. John F. A. Sawyer, *The Fifth Gospel: Isaiah in the History of Christianity* (Cambridge: Cambridge University Press, 1996).

tested and those that are not.[69] We have Christian copies of each of the five books of the Pentateuch. Curiously, these include three copies of Leviticus, compared with two copies of Deuteronomy. Among what Christians consider Old Testament "historical" books, there are a copy of Joshua, and one manuscript witness each for 2 Chronicles and Esther. Of the prophets, in addition to the several copies of Isaiah, we also have witnesses to Jeremiah, Ezekiel, Daniel, and the Minor Prophets. Of the "wisdom" writings, there are copies of Proverbs, Ecclesiastes, Job, Wisdom of Solomon, and Sirach. We also have copies of Tobit, one copy of 2 Maccabees in Sahidic Coptic, and one witness to the two additional stories attached to Daniel in the LXX and known as Bel and the Dragon, and Susanna.

I propose that all this indicates Christian interest in, and appreciation for, texts received from Jewish tradition as scriptures and edifying writings. In one sense, of course, this is hardly remarkable, for it appears that most Christians identified themselves, and linked their faith, with their Old Testament. To be sure, there were Christians (especially Marcionites, but also other Christian "demiurgical traditions") who in varying ways regarded the deity emphasized in the Old Testament as inferior to the true or high deity, with whom they linked Christ and themselves.[70] But one of the characteristics of the forms of early Christianity that came to be regarded as "orthodox" and "catholic" was their usage of the Old Testament writings as sacred scripture.[71] To judge from the remnants of writings of the Old Testament in the papyri from early Egyptian Christianity, we seem to have in them artifacts of Christians of recognizably mainstream, "orthodox" stance.

When we consider the evidence of usage of writings that were composed by Christians, there are further interesting results. To judge by the

69. Gamble (*Books and Readers*, 233-34) cites *Apostolic Constitutions* 2.4-6, which gives advice to Christians about (private) reading choices, which include books of the Pentateuch, Kings, Prophets, and Psalms as well as "the Gospel." We have to take account of both public (liturgical) and private reading of texts among Christians.

70. I borrow the expression "demiurgical traditions" from Michael A. Williams, *Rethinking "Gnosticism": An Argument for Dismantling a Dubious Category* (Princeton: Princeton University Press, 1996), who offers an incisive analysis of various "gnostic" expressions of early Christianity.

71. See my discussion of earmarks of "proto-orthodox" Christianity in *Lord Jesus Christ*, 494-95, and on proto-orthodox expressions of devotion to Jesus in the second century, 563-648.

number of extant copies, the Gospel of Matthew (12) and the Gospel of John (15) seem to have been the most popular Christian texts in the second and third centuries. The next most frequently attested Christian texts are *Shepherd of Hermas,* and then the Gospel of Luke and the Acts of the Apostles. It occasions no real surprise, however, that witnesses to Matthew and John outnumber those for any other Christian writing, and that in particular they even have such strong support among the very earliest Christian manuscripts, those dated to the second and early third century. These two seem always to have been the favorite Gospels in Christian usage, both liturgically and in private devotion. Stephen Llewelyn's tables of the number of copies of New Testament writings on papyrus and parchment, and on the comparative frequency of citation of New Testament writings in patristic authors, all show a heavy preference for these two Gospels, well above any other New Testament writing.[72]

It has been frequently echoed that the Gospel of John was especially used in "gnostic" Christian circles. But a recent and rather thorough study by Charles Hill seems to demand a major revision of opinion. Hill shows that heterodox Christians were not especially given to John, and made use of a number of New Testament writings. Moreover, early "orthodox" Christian texts indicate a familiarity with and positive view of John.[73] The manuscript evidence seems to be consistent with Hill's judgment. The numerous copies of John in the papyri from Egypt suggest a notable popularity of this text, and the copies of other texts from the same site and approximate time period as the manuscripts of John suggest that those among whom John was so popular also enjoyed a panoply of texts that reflect mainstream Christian tastes and preferences.

Some may find it a bit puzzling, however, that the Gospel of Mark has only one manuscript witness, and that from the third century, $\mathfrak{P}$45 (ca. 250). But it is rather clear that, although Mark was probably the first narrative Gospel to be written, it was not nearly so widely copied and used as any of the other canonical Gospels in the earliest centuries from which our manuscript evidence survives. Sifting evidence of second-century use of and comments on Mark, Clifton Black argued that Mark seems to have

---

72. Stephen R. Llewelyn, *New Documents Illustrating Early Christianity, 7* (North Ryde, NSW: AHDRC, Macquarie University, 1994), 257-62.

73. Charles E. Hill, *The Johannine Corpus in the Early Church* (Oxford: Oxford University Press, 2004).

been regarded as inferior to Matthew or Luke, probably because it contained fewer of Jesus' sayings and appeared overall to be a less elegant narrative.[74] There is no reason to think that Mark was regarded with disapproval, but the manuscript evidence suggests that Mark was considerably less frequently and less widely used.

Turning now to evidence concerning the other New Testament writings, we also have early (third-century) copies of every epistle ascribed to Paul, except 1 and 2 Timothy. The most frequently attested Pauline writings are Romans (4 copies), Ephesians (3 copies), and 1 Corinthians and 1-2 Thessalonians (2 copies each). In addition, we have single copies of Philemon and Titus.

It is also interesting that there are four early copies of Hebrews, which suggests that this writing was rather more frequently used than we might have expected. We also know that Hebrews was regarded by some Christians in the second and third centuries as a Pauline writing. This is illustrated in material form most famously in the earliest codex collection of Pauline epistles, Chester Beatty codex 𝔓46, where Hebrews is included right after Romans (all the "Pauline" writings are placed in an order of decreasing length).[75]

Among the remaining New Testament writings represented, there are single copies of 1 Peter (plus a third-century Sahidic copy), 2 Peter, 1 John, 2 John, two copies of Jude, and, interestingly, three copies of James. Do these several copies of James reflect something of the interest in Jesus' brother in early Christianity?[76] Or was it simply the contents of the epistle that led to it being one of the New Testament writings that featured early Christian usage?

Still more interesting, perhaps, is the comparative popularity of the book of Revelation, with several copies from our period, including one dated to late second or early third century. This copy of Revelation (P.IFAO 2.31) and another as well (P.Oxy. 1079) are examples of what paleographers

---

74. C. Clifton Black, *Mark: Images of an Apostolic Interpreter* (Columbia, SC: University of South Carolina Press, 1994), 77-113.

75. Frederic G. Kenyon, *The Chester Beatty Biblical Papyri, Fasciculus III Supplement: Pauline Epistles* (London: Walker, 1936).

76. John Painter, *Just James: The Brother of Jesus in History and Tradition* (Columbia, SC: University of South Carolina Press, 1997). But in his discussion of the early reception history of the Epistle of James (234-48), Painter makes no reference to these early papyri copies.

call an "opisthograph," a roll that was originally used to accommodate one text (on the inner, "recto" side), and then subsequently reused to accommodate another text copied on the outer (verso) side. In chapter two we shall look more closely at the possible significance of various physical forms of books (the roll, the codex, and opisthographs). In the case of P.Oxy. 1079, we can identify the text on the inner surface of the roll as Exodus. Scholars have not been able to identify the Greek text on the inner side of P.IFAO 2.31 because the writing is so heavily eroded, but it is possible that this manuscript and P.Oxy. 1079 are actually portions of the same reused roll.[77] In any case we have at least four early copies of Revelation, which puts it in a three-way tie with Romans and Hebrews as the fifth-most-attested New Testament writing (behind John, Matthew, Luke, and Acts). So, in spite of the lengthy time that it took for Revelation to be accepted as part of the emerging New Testament canon, particularly in the East, it appears to have enjoyed a reasonable popularity, at least among Christian circles reflected in the earliest extant papyri. If, as Hill argues, already in the second century many Christians linked Revelation with the Gospel of John and one or more of the Johannine Epistles as forming what we could regard as a "Johannine corpus" of writings, this early tradition of apostolic authorship may partially account for why Revelation appears to have been copied so frequently.

It is also clear, however, that early Christians read and circulated many other texts beyond those that became part of the Christian canon. Among these, the fascinating text known as the *Shepherd of Hermas* is by far the most frequently attested, with eleven manuscripts that have been dated to the second or third century.[78] In fact, this total exceeds the number of witnesses for any other text in Christian manuscripts of the period, except for

---

77. If they are parts of the same opisthograph, then the differing dates assigned to them (P.Oxy. 1079 dated mid-to-late third century, and P.IFAO 237 dated to the late second or early third century) would have to be reconsidered. I leave this, however, to the paleographical experts. See Dieter Hagedorn, "P.IFAO II 31: Johannesapokalypse 1,13-20," *ZPE* 92 (1992): 243-47.

78. In his introduction to the three most recently published copies, Nick Gonis refers to twenty-three papyri manuscripts of *Hermas*, of which twelve are dated fourth century and later. Nick Gonis et al., eds., *The Oxyrhynchus Papyri, Volume LXIX* (London: Egypt Exploration Society, 2005), 1. It is worth noting that the earliest copies of *Hermas* (P.Mich. 130 and P.Oxy. 4706) are rolls. In chapter two I discuss the likely significance of the use of a codex or a roll for a Christian text.

the Psalms and the Gospels of Matthew and John. On the basis of manuscript witnesses and citations in early Christian writers, Carolyn Osiek judged, "No other noncanonical writing was as popular before the fourth century."[79] Although *Hermas* originated in Rome sometime in the first half of the second century, it quickly acquired a wide reception, being cited by Tertullian (Carthage) and Irenaeus (Gaul) by the end of the century, and by Origen (Egypt) early in the third century.[80] Indeed, as the papyri show, in the early centuries *Hermas* enjoyed "immense popularity" in Egypt.[81] The appearance of *Hermas* in the great fourth-century Codex Sinaiticus at the end of the New Testament, and Athanasius's endorsement of *Hermas* and the *Didache* with some "deutero-canonical" writings of the Old Testament as suitable for reading by catechumens (though not to be included in the canon) further reflect a high estimate of *Hermas* that is consistent with the goodly number of early copies among extant papyri.

On the other hand, for some other Christian texts that might have been intended to function as scripture, or might have been so considered by some Christians, the manuscript support is not nearly so strong. If we consider the several extracanonical Gospel texts, we have only single copies (the "Egerton Gospel" fragment, the "Fayum Gospel" fragment, and the *Protevangelium of James*), except for the *Gospel of Thomas* (3 copies), the *Gospel of Mary* (2 copies), and possibly the *Gospel of Peter* (depending on whether one accepts Lührmann's proposal that both P.Oxy. 2949 and P.Oxy. 4009 are fragments of this text, and opinion is divided on this question).[82]

So, if the single copy of Mark in 𝔓45 from the early third century suggests that in these early centuries Mark was not very frequently copied and used, then the same must be said for these other Gospel texts as well. In-

---

79. Carolyn Osiek, *The Shepherd of Hermas*, Hermeneia (Minneapolis: Fortress Press, 1999), 1.

80. See Osiek's discussion of the reception of *Hermas*, ibid., 4-8. Osiek considers various theories of multiple authorship, but sides with what she considers now the dominant view, that one author wrote the book but probably in several stages (10).

81. Ibid., 5. Osiek notes that Clement of Alexandria was "the most enthusiastic early user of *Hermas*," and gathers other indications of how highly the text was valued early in Egypt (ibid., 5-6).

82. Lührmann, "POx 2949"; idem, "POx 4009." But Lührmann's proposal is not assured. See now Thomas J. Kraus and Tobias Nicklas, eds., *Das Petrusevangelium und die Petrusapokalypse: Die griechischen Fragmente mit deutscher und englischer Übersetzung*, GCS 11 (Berlin: de Gruyter, 2004); and Paul Foster, "Are There Any Early Fragments of the So-called *Gospel of Peter*?" *NTS* 52 (2006): 1-28.

deed, for putative *second-century* copies of extracanonical Gospel(-like) texts, we have only the Oxyrhynchus fragments 2949 and 4009, which may be early witnesses to the *Gospel of Peter,* or perhaps fragments of one or even two otherwise unknown writings, and possibly the "Egerton Gospel" fragment (now dated ca. 200). For the remaining extracanonical Gospels, our earliest copies are dated to sometime in the third century.

But, to be sure, it is very interesting that we have fragments of three distinguishable third-century manuscripts of what we call the *Gospel of Thomas* (hereafter *GThomas*). This clearly suggests that a collection of Jesus' sayings that was also likely somehow connected with the figure of Thomas enjoyed some notable popularity in at least some Christian circles of the time. Although we cannot go into the matter here, it is important to note, however, that the Greek fragments indicate that *GThomas* was transmitted with a noticeable fluidity in contents and arrangement. Furthermore, what survives in the Oxyrhynchus Greek fragments are only a few of the 114 sayings that make up the fourth-century Coptic text of *GThomas* from Nag Hammadi. So it would be dubious to use the Nag Hammadi text as directly indicative of what may have constituted the Greek *GThomas* in the second century. Indeed, in considering the origins of this writing, proper scholarly method requires us to give primary place to the early-third-century Greek manuscripts, something that, unfortunately, is not always done.[83]

Nevertheless, it is clear that *GThomas* was among the writings that enjoyed a certain level of popularity among the Christians reflected in the Oxyrhynchus papyri. But was *GThomas* used there by some particular circle(s) of "Thomistic" Christians, or were those who copied and read the extant Greek manuscripts of *GThomas* basically the same sort of Christians who also read and prized the other texts found in the site (which otherwise seem to reflect recognizably mainstream Christian textual preferences)? The latter seems to me more likely, given that the copies of *GThomas* come from the same site in which the other writings of Christian provenance were found. That is, the Oxyrhynchus copies of *GThomas* do not particularly seem to be instances of "gnostic scriptures." These copies do not seem to be artifacts of Christians who gave preference to *GThomas* over against the better-known

---

83. I refer readers to my more extended discussion of *GThomas* in *Lord Jesus Christ,* 425-79, which includes a much fuller citation of, and interaction with, other scholarship. The popular interest in the text is reflected in the following helpful Web sites: http://www.earlychristianwritings.com/thomas.html; http://www.misericordia.edu/users/davies/thomas/Thomas.html.

Gospels that became canonical. Indeed, it is not even evident that these particular copies of *GThomas* reflect a regard for this text as "scripture" to be read in worship and treated as somehow authoritative for faith.[84]

I say this in part because of the physical form of the Oxyrhynchus copies of *GThomas*. Of the three copies, one was a codex, one a roll (i.e., *GThomas* on the recto/inner side), and the remaining copy a reused roll (an opisthograph, the roll originally used for a secular documentary text). In the next chapter, I discuss the significance of the strong early Christian preference for the codex, and in the light of this preference probe further the inferences that we might make on the basis of the book form in which Christian texts appear. For now, I simply want to anticipate that discussion by noting that the physical forms of the three *GThomas* manuscripts from Oxyrhynchus should not be ignored and may well signal something of how the text was regarded and used.

In addition to considering which texts are attested, and how many copies of each we have, we can also note another interesting feature of early Christian manuscripts that has not received sufficient attention: the practice of combining more than one text in the same manuscript. For any inquiry into how a particular text was regarded and used in early Christian circles, it may well be worth noting whether it was associated directly with one or more other texts. It must have been a deliberate choice to place particular texts together, and that means that it probably reflects some view of the texts in question. I suggest specifically that the physical linkage of texts in one manuscript probably reflects a view of them as sharing some common or related subject matter or significance for readers. In any case, that certain texts got physically linked by placement in the same manuscript is another artifactual feature that we should not overlook.[85]

---

84. I allude here to (and express caution about) the title of the very useful collection of texts by Bentley Layton, *The Gnostic Scriptures: A New Translation with Annotations and Introductions* (New York: Doubleday, 1987). I respectfully suggest that the title of Layton's book is a bit misleading. We do not actually know that all the texts in question were treated as "scripture," and it is not particularly clear what would have made this or that group "gnostic" either. As Michael Williams *(Rethinking "Gnosticism")* has shown, scholars use "gnostic" and "gnosticism" with such diversity of reference and meaning that one cannot tell what is being designated.

85. Note that I restrict the focus here to manuscripts of the second and third centuries, and I also omit composite codices such as P.Bod. VII-IX, which involved the *secondary* binding together of originally discrete codices.

The comparatively better known examples of this are among the Bodmer and Chester Beatty papyri. Dated to about 175-225 CE, Bodmer XIV-XV (𝔓75) comprises major remnants of a codex that surely included both the Gospel of Luke and the Gospel of John. However, T. C. Skeat suggested that 𝔓75 may have been a four-Gospel codex, with Luke and John forming one of two quires, and perhaps Matthew and Mark forming the other quire.[86] Skeat also presented an elaborate case that the three other manuscript remnants known as 𝔓64 (fragments of Matthew housed at Magdalen College, Oxford), 𝔓67 (further fragments of Matthew now in Barcelona), and 𝔓4 (fragments of Luke held in the Bibliothèque nationale, Paris), are all portions of the same codex, and that this manuscript, too, originally contained all four canonical Gospels, making it the earliest known four-Gospel codex (late second century).[87] Peter Head has recently contended rather cogently, however, that Skeat's argument that 𝔓64, 𝔓67, and 𝔓4 are remnants of a four-Gospel codex is flawed and not convincing.[88]

Whatever the force of either of Skeat's proposals about these other manuscripts, however, in the Chester Beatty codex known as 𝔓45 (P.Chester Beatty I, now usually dated ca. 250) we undeniably have all four canonical Gospels (in the order Matthew, John, Luke, Mark), plus Acts in one codex, originally comprising 224 pages.[89] So it is clear that by the late second

86. T. C. Skeat, "The Origin of the Christian Codex," *ZPE* 102 (1994): 263-68, now repr. in *The Collected Biblical Writings of T. C. Skeat*, ed. J. K. Elliott, NovTSup 113 (Leiden: Brill, 2004), 79-87; strongly endorsed by Graham N. Stanton, *Jesus and Gospel* (Cambridge: Cambridge University Press, 2004), esp. 71-75.

87. T. C. Skeat, "The Oldest Manuscript of the Four Gospels?" *NTS* 43 (1997): 1-34; repr. in *Collected Biblical Writings*, ed. Elliott, 158-92. Roberts (*Manuscript*, 12-13) had come to this view earlier. Two years prior to Skeat's article, Philip W. Comfort ("Exploring the Common Identification of Three New Testament Manuscripts: 𝔓4, 𝔓64 and 𝔓67," *TynBul* 46 [1995]: 43-54) had argued similarly, but this article is not noted by Skeat. It remains for me an inadequately addressed question as to why and how such a fine-quality manuscript as 𝔓4 was used for binding a copy of Philo. Did it wear out, and did the owner feel no compunction about using the copy of Luke as packing material? Cf. Comfort's brief discussion ("Exploring," 52). But, contra Comfort, 𝔓46 is not a good analogy, and actually illustrates the question. It was apparently used for as much as a century and then buried with a Coptic monk, not torn up and used for binding material!

88. Peter M. Head, "Is 𝔓4, 𝔓64 and 𝔓67 the Oldest Manuscript of the Four Gospels? A Response to T. C. Skeat," *NTS* 51 (2005): 450-57.

89. The original description of 𝔓45 (P.Chester Beatty I) by Frederic G. Kenyon (*The Chester Beatty Biblical Papyri, Fasciculus II: The Gospels and Acts: Text* [London: Walker, 1933]) has been updated with some corrections by T. C. Skeat, "A Codicological Analysis of

century some Christians were beginning to put two or more Gospels together in one manuscript.

This makes it worth noting which Gospel texts were linked and copied together. To my knowledge, the only Gospels so treated in the extant evidence are those that became part of the New Testament canon. None of the other (apocryphal) Gospel texts is linked with any other Gospel. This is the case even in manuscripts dated after the practice of combining Gospels developed (i.e., third century and later). I propose that, at least for those Christians whose views are represented in the extant manuscripts, those Gospel texts that were copied together were regarded as in some way complementary and sufficiently compatible with one another to be so linked. Along the same lines of reasoning, those Gospel writings that did not get linked with other texts were probably regarded as in some way sufficiently different in significance and/or usefulness that they did not belong in the same manuscript.

As we have noticed, these other (ultimately extracanonical) Gospel writings were read, and apparently in the very Christian circles that seem also to have also read and revered the familiar canonical Gospels. But the manuscript data suggest that, though these Christians regarded texts such as the "Egerton Gospel" and the sayings collection we know as the *Gospel of Thomas* as suitable for Christian reading, they did not consider these texts as appropriate for inclusion in the early Gospel collections that reflect steps toward a New Testament canon.

In addition to the four Gospels, the inclusion of Acts in $\mathfrak{P}$45 also merits further brief comment. It is unusual among early codices of the Gospels to have Acts as well.[90] Most scholars today believe that the author of Luke

---

the Chester Beatty Papyrus Codex of the Gospels and Acts ($\mathfrak{P}$45)," *Hermathena* 155 (1993): 27-43 (= *Collected Biblical Writings*, ed. Elliott, 141-57).

90. The extant portions of $\mathfrak{P}$53 (mid-third century) comprise bits of Matthew and Acts, so it might have been another codex of Gospels and Acts. See Henry A. Sanders, "A Third Century Papyrus of Matthew and Acts," in *Quantulacumque: Studies Presented to Kirsopp Lake*, ed. Robert P. Casey, Silva Lake, and Agnes K. Lake (London: Christophers, 1937), 151-61. Sanders calculated, however, that some 325 leaves would have been required, certainly a very large manuscript for its time; and he judged it more likely that the codex contained only Matthew and Acts (153). The pages of $\mathfrak{P}$53 contained about 25 lines, each line about 25-27 letters. In $\mathfrak{P}$74 (seventh century), Acts is followed by a collection of the Catholic Epistles. The other papyri copies of Acts ($\mathfrak{P}$29, $\mathfrak{P}$38, $\mathfrak{P}$48, $\mathfrak{P}$50, $\mathfrak{P}$91) are so fragmentary that we cannot confidently determine whether in the original codices Acts stood on its own or with other texts.

intended Acts as a closely linked sequel to his account of Jesus' ministry, the early Christians thus portrayed as continuing the story begun in Jesus. Yet it is also clear that at a very early point the Gospel of Luke was copied and circulated separately from Acts, and was linked with the other accounts that made up the fourfold Gospels. So perhaps the inclusion of Acts in $\mathfrak{P}$45 reflects a view of some Christians that this narrative of the earliest church should be linked with the four Gospels and read as a sequel to their accounts of Jesus. That is, $\mathfrak{P}$45 may well reflect both regard for, and interpretation of, the five texts that it contains, giving us a valuable artifact of at least one early Christian appropriation and construal of these texts.

In addition to combinations of Gospel texts, we have other somewhat similar developments evidenced in early manuscripts. Another important Chester Beatty codex, $\mathfrak{P}$46 (P.Chester Beatty II, ca. 200), is our earliest unambiguous instance of a collection of Pauline epistles. I noted earlier in this discussion that this codex includes Hebrews among the Pauline Epistles, artifactual evidence of an early Christian view of the authorship of this fascinating text. But here my focus is on the phenomenon of a Pauline epistles collection itself, and what it may signify about how Christians who assembled the collection regarded the texts in question. Before we explore this, however, I want to note briefly suggestions that we have remnants of other codices that were originally Pauline letter collections.[91]

It has been proposed that $\mathfrak{P}$15 (P.Oxy. 1008), a portion of 1 Corinthians, and $\mathfrak{P}$16 (P.Oxy. 1009), a portion of Philippians, may be remnants of the same codex (dated variously to the third or early fourth century). If so, the original codex may have constituted a Pauline collection, as it seems more difficult otherwise to account for 1 Corinthians and Philippians being in the same manuscript. Similarly, $\mathfrak{P}$49 (P.Yale 2), containing portions of Ephesians, and $\mathfrak{P}$65 (PSI 14.1373), portions of 1 Thessalonians, are possibly remnants of one codex. Once again, a codex containing Ephesians and 1 Thessalonians likely also contained a fuller collection of Pauline epistles.

$\mathfrak{P}$30 (P.Oxy. 1598) is four fragments of two consecutive codex leaves containing portions of 1 Thessalonians and 2 Thessalonians. But pagination survives on a couple of the fragments, indicating that these are portions of pages 207 and 208 of the original codex. It is a reasonable supposition that this too was a codex of Pauline epistles. Finally, $\mathfrak{P}$92 (P.Medinet

91. See Philip W. Comfort, "New Reconstructions and Identifications of New Testament Papyri," *NovT* 41 (1999): 214-30.

Madi 69.39a + 69.229a), portions of Ephesians and 2 Thessalonians, may be remnants of yet another example of an early codex containing a Pauline epistles collection.

In his magisterial study of the text of Paul's epistles in 𝔓46, Günther Zuntz contended that an "archetypal *Corpus*" of Paul's letters was assembled sometime around 100, perhaps in Alexandria, and that this edition of Pauline epistles was prepared with a concern for textual accuracy.[92] We cannot engage here Zuntz's main concern, which was focused more on text-critical questions about the Pauline Epistles. His proposal about an early Pauline "corpus" did not require that the letter collection was transmitted from the outset in single-codex format, only that by 100 CE a list of Pauline epistles had become associated in the minds of some influential Christians as forming a letter collection. To use modern parlance, this could be thought of as a "virtual" collection. But as indisputably shown in 𝔓46, and very possibly also in some or all of the other proposed remnants of Pauline codices that we have noted briefly, at a very early point (certainly by sometime in the second century and perhaps even in the late first century) Pauline letters were physically treated as a collection by copying them in a single codex. In this development we have a material indication that the Christians behind it clearly regarded the Pauline Epistles very highly. Indeed, the copying of multiple Pauline epistles in one codex would have had the effect of marking off all of them as enjoying a high regard, the smaller and less weighty epistles as well as the larger ones.

Also, Colin Roberts suggested that P.Ant. 12 (Gregory-Aland 0232, a late-third-/early-fourth-century parchment codex, #170 in appendix 1) may have originally contained a collection of writings ascribed to the apostle John, a "Johannine Corpus."[93] The extant single codex leaf contains 2 John 1-9, but page numbers at the top of the two pages, 164 and 165 (by a hand other than the copyist), indicate a codex of good size that obviously contained much more than 2 John. Roberts calculated that the preceding 163 pages would have been too much space for all the other Catholic epistles, but could well have accommodated the Gospel of John, Revelation, and 1 John.

---

92. Günther Zuntz, *The Text of the Epistles: A Disquisition upon the Corpus Paulinum*, Schweich Lectures 1946 (London: Oxford University Press for the British Academy, 1953), 279.

93. As noted by Hill, *Johannine Corpus*, 455-56. See also VH #555. First noted in C. H. Roberts et al., *The Antinoopolis Papyri* (London: Egypt Exploration Society, 1950-67), 1:24-25.

Obviously, this cannot be proven, for the codex could have contained a more diverse body of texts. The quality of the scribal hand and the parchment writing material suggest a copy commissioned for a well-to-do individual, and its miniature size (9 x 10 cm.) also suggests a personal copy. This means that the codex was probably not merely an eclectic collection of texts, but had some coherence. A collection of writings linked to the apostle John would fit both the space and the probable purpose quite nicely.

Summary

I hope that this deliberately limited and somewhat preliminary analysis of the texts that are attested in Christian manuscripts of the second and third centuries will at least have demonstrated that it is worthwhile to give attention to these matters. My aim has been to show that the pattern of texts attested in earliest Christian manuscripts is an important subject for analysis and reflection, insufficiently noted in current discussion and debates about Christianity in the second and third centuries. If we take account of which texts are attested in the extant manuscripts, and the comparative numbers of copies of each text, we likely have some direct indication of what texts were read and their comparative popularity. More broadly, the evidence also confirms other indications that texts were an important feature of Christian circles in these early centuries.

The inventory of texts witnessed reflects some further interesting early Christian practices, including a usage of Old Testament writings and most of the writings that came to form the New Testament. We also see an interest in theological texts and other Christian writings intended for edification and teaching, such as Irenaeus's *Against Heresies,* the *Shepherd of Hermas,* and writings of Melito. We would probably expect that Christians in Alexandria, one of the great centers of trade and culture of the Roman era, would have had a certain breadth of vision and opportunities to benefit from an acquaintance with Christian texts from other quarters of the empire. But these artifacts show a lively readership even in a more modest town like Oxyrhynchus.

There is, to be sure, also some interest shown in writings that came to be categorized as Christian "apocrypha." But the comparative dates and numbers of manuscripts do not justify any notion that these writings were particularly favored. Further, there is scant reason to think that the extant copies of these texts stem from heterodox groups. If, on the other hand, these copies of apocryphal texts do come from particularly heterodox circles, the comparative numbers of manuscripts among extant material suggest that any such circles were likely a clear minority among Christians of the second and third centuries, at least in the provenances from which our manuscript evidence survives. In reaching these judgments I am pleased to find that I echo those of Stephen Llewelyn.[94]

Finally, I want to underscore the translocal nature of the texts in these early manuscripts. As proposed earlier, this suggests an impressive geographical breadth of communication and interchange between the Egyptian-based Christians whose copies of texts we have and Christians in other places, including places at considerable distance from middle Egypt. Without denying the diversity of Christianity in the second and third centuries, we should probably avoid the notion that Christian groups conducted themselves in isolation from others. This means that some of our commonly employed ideas of quite distinct "communities" of Christians may need to be reconsidered, or at least balanced by indications (especially from the artifacts that we have noted here) that early Christian circles, whatever their geographical or religious particularities, also seem to have been keen on exchange of texts and ideas with other Christian circles.

94. Llewelyn, *New Documents Illustrating Early Christianity*, 7, 244-48. It is also worth noting that this judgment is consistent with that reached by Birger Pearson about second-century Alexandrian Christianity, based on his analysis of literary evidence. Pearson concluded that heterodox Christians were very much in the minority (albeit, in their own eyes, an elite minority), and that their writings presuppose the *prior* regard for what became Christian scriptures, writings of the "Old Testament" and "New Testament." See Pearson, "Pre-Alexandrian Gnosticism in Alexandria," in *Future of Early Christianity*, ed. Pearson, 455-66.

CHAPTER TWO

The Early Christian Preference for the Codex

E ven beyond the circles of those scholars acquainted with ancient Christian manuscripts, it is somewhat well known that Christians preferred
the "codex" (plural: codices) book form over the roll, the more traditional
form in the early Roman period.[1] The sort of codex used by Christians was
made up of sheets of writing material (predominantly papyrus in the period of our concern here) folded once so that each sheet forms two leaves or
four pages of writing surface; multiples of these folded sheets were then attached to one another with binding threads.[2] On the other hand, a roll is
constructed by attaching sheets of writing material end on end, forming a
continuous writing surface, the length of the roll depending on the size of
the text to be written on it.[3] As we shall note later in this chapter, codices
could likewise be of varying sizes and shapes, and there are some variations
in the construction, especially in how the folded sheets were arranged. But
essentially the ancient codex preferred by Christians resembles our familiar
book form, the reading of a text done by turning the pages, whereas one
reads a roll column by column, holding the roll in both hands.

---

1. Two essential resources for study of the codex in Roman antiquity are Turner,
Typology, which focuses more on the physical features and questions about the varying sizes
of codices, and Colin H. Roberts and T. C. Skeat, *The Birth of the Codex* (London: Oxford
University Press, 1983), oriented more toward various historical questions about the emergence of the codex and its rise to dominance in late antiquity.
   2. An individual leaf is also called a "folium" (Latin for "leaf") by specialists in manuscript study, a folded sheet (of two leaves) forming a "bifolium."
   3. On the physical features of the roll, see now the essential study by William A. Johnson, *Bookrolls and Scribes in Oxyrhynchus* (Toronto: University of Toronto Press, 2004).

The Christian preference for the codex form is not disputed; but beyond this scholars debate a lot of questions. In this chapter I lay out the relevant evidence, address the key questions, and explore inferences prompted by the physical forms in which Christian texts were transmitted in the second and third centuries.[4]

Ancient Book Forms: Quantitative Data

Before we address the questions, let us first take account of some data that indicate a strong, indeed, remarkable early Christian preference for the codex. In what follows I draw upon data readily available online in the Leuven Database of Ancient Books (LDAB), especially for reviewing the wider pattern of ancient book forms and texts.[5] For the early Christian manuscripts, however, I have supplemented the LDAB data with other sources of information, particularly the files of the Macquarie University project on the Papyri from the Rise of Christianity in Egypt (PRCE). After reviewing the quantitative data, I will offer some observations.

Let us commence with the larger picture. The first thing to note is that we have a reasonably good-sized body of manuscript data on which to draw. The LDAB includes nearly ten thousand items (manuscripts) dated by editors from the fourth century BCE through the eighth century CE.[6]

---

4. In many cases, what survives is as little as a single piece of writing material. But papyrologists can often judge whether it is a portion of a larger manuscript, especially if the top or bottom of the column of writing survives. If the text appears to begin or end abruptly, this suggests that it was part of a larger text. Otherwise, it may simply be a single "sheet" of writing material. If the writing on one side appears to be part of the same text as that on the other side, we probably have a leaf from a codex. If there is writing only on the "recto" (the side with the papyrus fibers running horizontally), then it is likely part of a roll. If we can identify the text, then it is possible to estimate the number of missing lines. If (as is often the case) there is a page number on what remains of a single codex page, it is possible to estimate how many pages the codex may have comprised.

5. This valuable database is accessible via the Internet: http://ldab.arts.kuleuven.ac.be. The focus of the LDAB is on manuscripts containing "literary" texts. A curious feature of the LDAB is that to some extent figures for the number of items in a given century in the graphs that one can produce on the site differ from the totals given if one uses the "search" facility. But in any set of figures the comparative patterns are clear.

6. At the time of the writing of this chapter (November 2005), the LDAB referred to 9,875 items catalogued as of 1 August 2003 (http://ldab.arts.kuleuven.ac.be/database.html).

These are largely copies of "literary" texts, which are the closest analogy to the key Christian texts, such as their biblical writings.[7] Within this period, the number of items varies from one century to another, the manuscripts dated to the earliest centuries (third through first century BCE) forming a much smaller body (see bar graph 2, p. 93). To start with these earliest centuries, the LDAB lists 283 items for the third century BCE, 268 items for the second century BCE, and 449 items for the first century BCE.[8]

Thereafter, however, the number jumps to 1,044 for the first century CE, 2,752 for the second century CE, and 2,267 for the third century CE. It is particularly worth noting that the second and third centuries CE have the largest totals by far, in comparison with the preceding and the following centuries covered in the LDAB.[9] For instance, for the fourth century CE, there are 1,181 items, just a little over half the number for the second century CE. Thereafter, the seventh century CE has the fewest number of manuscripts (1,015).[10] The basic point is that we have a reasonably large body of manuscripts, including a good number from the second and third centuries CE, making the sort of quantitative analyses that I offer in the following paragraphs an interesting exercise.

For our analysis it is also helpful that items in the LDAB are categorized as to their form, the overwhelming number, of course, being either

---

7. Jean Gascou, "Les codices documentaires Egyptiens," in *Les débuts du codex: Actes de la journée d'étude organisée à Paris les 3 et 4 juillet 1985 par l'Institut de papyrologie de la Sorbonne et l'Institut de recherche et d'histoire des textes,* ed. Alain Blanchard (Turnhout: Brepols, 1989), 71-101, noted that the codex was not in much use for "documentary" (i.e., nonliterary) texts in Egypt prior to the fourth century CE, and so this could not account for the Christian usage (79). He ascribed the increase of documentary codices in the fourth century to the efforts of Diocletian and others to effect greater romanization of Egypt (75-77).

8. Figures are those from the LDAB at the time of writing this chapter. Manuscripts continue to be added to the database as they are published, but the basic pattern seems unlikely to alter, the second century CE providing the largest number of items.

9. Paleographical judgments vary, so the specific number of manuscripts for any given century may vary. But such variations do not change the basic pattern of the data. Also, because paleographical dating can rarely be more precise than +/- 25 to 50 years, the proposed dating of many manuscripts will lie across two centuries (e.g., second/third century CE). In such cases, the LDAB includes manuscripts in the number of items for each century. So adding up the number of items for each century will yield a higher total than the actual number of items in the database.

10. At the latest opportunity to consult the database for this book (November 2005), the LDAB lists 1,240 items for the fifth century CE, 1,377 for the sixth century, 1,015 for the seventh century, and 1,609 items for the eighth century.

rolls or codices. In a smaller number of instances, items are categorized as "sheet" or "fragment." Bear in mind that the LDAB simply records the information and judgments given by the editors of published editions of manuscripts. The designation "sheet" often means that an item was judged to have been a complete text on a single piece of writing material, that is, not a portion of a larger manuscript (e.g., a letter, amulet, or some other short text). The designation "fragment" may mean that the editors were unable to judge the original form of the writing from the extant material. In some cases, however, even though it might have been possible to determine the original form of the manuscript, editors appear to have neglected to do so (for reasons not always clear).

This means that a number of items categorized in the LDAB as "sheet" or "fragment" may well be remnants of a larger manuscript, and, in light of the clear general preference for the roll in antiquity, more often the manuscript will have been a roll. So it is likely that the percentage of rolls to codices is even higher than indicated in the LDAB, especially in the early centuries when the roll format was dominant.[11] But we shall simply work with the counts as given in the LDAB, which will be fully adequate for detecting the basic patterns. At several points, however, I will exclude items tagged as "sheet" or "fragment," to calculate simply the balances between items clearly identified as either rolls or codices. In what follows I refer to several pie charts and bar graphs that appear at the end of this chapter.

I begin by noting that the total number of items identified on the LDAB as Christian amount to 35.4% of the aggregate number logged across the entire period of its coverage (chart 1). But it is important to break this aggregate down by century. As shown in chart 4, the earliest identifiably Christian manuscripts are dated to the second century CE, constituting only about 1.9% of the total number for that period, and rising to 10.3% of third-century items logged (chart 5).[12] Thereafter, Christian manuscripts form an increasingly large part of the totals, especially in

11. If a "sheet" or "fragment" has portions of the same text on both sides, it is quite likely a leaf of a codex, whereas writing on only one side (especially if on the recto) may mean a portion of a roll.

12. I note again that many manuscripts have been dated to the second/third century CE, or to third/fourth century CE. So, e.g., the LDAB count of second-century Christian manuscripts includes those dated second/third century as well as those more strictly dated second century, and the total for the third century includes those dated second/third century and those dated third/fourth century.

the fourth century CE (38%, chart 6) and still more thereafter.[13] Obviously, the steeply rising percentage of Christian manuscripts, especially from the fourth century onward, reflects the increasingly prominent place of Christianity in the larger culture, particularly after Constantine's momentous approbation of the religion. But, although Christian manuscripts make up a tiny portion of the second-century total, and a modest slice of third-century items, I submit that we have enough manuscript evidence to allow us to attempt an analysis.

If we now focus on quantitative evidence about the forms of ancient books, the early Christian preference for the codex is demonstrable. Of the total number of items classified in the LDAB as rolls (3,033), only about 81 (2.7%) are identified as Christian (chart 2). But at least 73% of all codices (2,328 out of 3,188) are listed as Christian (chart 3). Moreover, even in the earliest centuries, Christian codices constitute an impressive percentage of the totals. Of the 104 codices dated in the LDAB to the second century CE, at least twenty-nine are Christian (27.9%); and of 397 third-century codices, 134 (33.8%) are Christian.[14] Set alongside the small percentage of Christian items overall for these same centuries, the much larger percentage of early codices identified as Christian is all the more remarkable.

Furthermore, restricting ourselves to items listed as Christian, we get yet another clear indication of the preference for the codex.[15] Of the forty-one second-century Christian manuscripts listed in the LDAB, about 71% (29) are codices, and about 22% (9) may be rolls, whereas codices make up only about 5% of the total number of second-century items (i.e., Christian and non-Christian, chart 8).[16] At least 67% of third-century Christian

---

13. Items identifiable as Christian make up 43% of the total items for the fifth century, 58.6% for the sixth century, 73% for the seventh century, and 88% for the eighth century.

14. Of the 41 second-century Christian items listed in the LDAB (which include those dated second/third century), 9 are rolls, and 4 are identified as "sheet." Of the 199 third-century Christian items, 40 are rolls, whereas 4 are tagged as "fragment" and 23 as "sheet." As mentioned earlier, it is quite possible that some of those listed in the last two categories may be portions of either a codex or (more likely) a roll.

15. The statistics that I provide here differ somewhat from the oft-cited ones offered by Roberts and Skeat (*Birth of the Codex*, 37). They portrayed some 98% of second-century Greek literature as rolls, but they were much more selective in what to count, and I am also able to benefit from the further publication of ancient manuscripts since Roberts and Skeat wrote. Even so, my calculations still demonstrate their basic point that the roll was overwhelmingly preferred generally, whereas Christians overwhelmingly preferred the codex.

16. These include items dated second century and those paleographically dated second/

items registered on the LDAB are codices, and about 20% are rolls, whereas all items identified as codices make up only about 21% of the total number of third-century items (chart 9).[17] We should also observe, however, that about one-third of all third-century codices (134 of 397) are Christian. So one major factor in the increased place of the codex book form in the third-century total is a larger number of Christian codices dated to that century.

Tracing book forms diachronically across the first several centuries CE, one finds some interesting movement from an initial dominance of the roll toward an increasing preference for the codex in the general culture (bar graph 1 and charts 7-10). But there was a marked Christian preference for the codex format from the first, far earlier than in general book preferences of the same time. Of the total number of first-century CE items listed, rolls make up 77.5% (chart 7), and if we omit items tagged either as "sheet" or "fragment," rolls make up 98% of that total.[18] About 73.8% of the total number of 2,276 second-century items are identified as rolls, and 4.9% are codices (chart 8). Restricting the count to second-century items identified as either rolls or codices, however, some 94% are rolls, and 6% codices.[19] Rolls constitute 56% of the total number of third-century items (chart 9), but about 73% of items if we restrict ourselves to items classified

---

third century (i.e., possibly late second or early third century). If we confine ourselves to counting only second-century Christian items tagged on the LDAB either as "roll" or "codex," the 29 codices make up 76%. In a few cases it is difficult to be sure whether we have a portion of a roll or simply a single sheet with writing on one side. For this calculation I have treated all these as rolls. See my more detailed discussion of second-century Christian items later in this chapter, where I include a few additional items in the list to be considered. These additional items, however, do not significantly alter the statistics gained from analysis of the list of second-century Christian items given on the LDAB.

17. Even if we restrict our calculations solely to items identified either as rolls or codices, the percentages show clear differences between Christian preferences and those in the wider cultural environment of the time. For instance, of the 1,784 second-century items listed in the LDAB as either rolls or codices, the latter make up about 5.8%. Codices make up 27% of the total of third-century items identified either as rolls or codices, but, as noted above, about one-third of these are Christian.

18. Many first-century items are categorized by the LDAB either as "sheet" (50) or "fragment" (123), leaving the total number of first-century items listed either as rolls or codices at 648. I list specific instances of putatively first-century codices in the next section of this chapter.

19. Items categorized as "fragment" comprise 317 second-century items, another 150 are categorized as "sheet."

either as rolls or codices.[20] It bears repeating that one factor in the increased percentage of codices in the third century (21%) is the larger number of Christian codices, which make up one-third of the total of third-century codices (134 of the 397 total).

This continues in later centuries. For instance, in the fourth century, Christian manuscripts make up 38% of the total of 1,184 (chart 6), which helps explain why the proportion of rolls to codices begins to shift markedly. Of the fourth-century items listed by book form (chart 10), the LDAB shows about 56% as codices and about 15% as rolls.[21]

At the risk of dizzying readers, I have included all these figures to try to give somewhat greater precision to the familiar judgments previously offered by scholars about Christian book-form preferences. Let us now try to draw some broad conclusions about what we observe in these data.

First, it is clear that ancient Christians preferred the codex, and that this preference is already demonstrated in the earliest artifacts of Christian texts. As noted, the overwhelming majority of all forms of second-century Christian items (over 70%) are codices, whereas among all second-century items rolls amount to about 74% (chart 8). In the third century CE, there is a somewhat larger percentage of codices in the total number of items (about 21%), but the roll remains by far the dominant book form (chart 9). So the early Christian preference also seems at odds with, or at least clearly distinguishable from, general tastes of the time about the preferred form for books, and this justifies further investigation and analysis.

Texts: Non-Christian Preferences

Toward this end, let us look now at the texts copied.[22] Both Christians and others in the early centuries used the codex, but with very different disposi-

20. The LDAB lists 174 third-century items as "sheet" and another 250 items as "fragment."

21. Of fourth-century items, 22% are listed as "sheet" (a curiously high percentage) and 6.5% as "fragment." Again, any adjustments in identifications will not alter the basic conclusion that in the fourth century the codex begins to be the favored book form.

22. Cf. the analysis in Roberts and Skeat, *Birth of the Codex,* 35-37, which involved a much smaller number of non-Christian codices. But they excluded all but what they considered to be proper "books" (i.e., codices used for literary texts). Also, in the years since their valuable study, more early codices have come to light.

tions toward this book form in comparison to the roll. Can we tell anything further from the texts copied in one form or the other? Here again the LDAB makes it much easier to obtain basic information for this question.

Let us first look at what texts are found in early non-Christian codices. As many as thirteen items can be included in a total of codices for the first century CE.[23] One item hardly qualifies for attention (Berl. Aeg. Museum Papyrus Sammlung P. 14283 [LDAB 3850]), a set of wooden tablets and wax writing surfaces with a bit of a literary text, obviously an example of the informal note-taking item used by students, and used by others for making lists of things to do.[24] We know from other artifacts as well (including paintings) that people employed such simple devices. But we are more concerned here with the use of the papyrus or parchment codex for extended texts.

Two others probably must be eliminated as well (P. Hamb. 2.134 [LDAB 4305], and (BIFAO 61 [LDAB 6833]), as they appear to be either portions of reused rolls (opisthographs) or single sheets of writing material, the texts they contain apparently school exercises. Another six are a bit more interesting, as they contain astronomical/astrological tables.[25] With numerous others, these particular manuscripts demonstrate a frequent use of the codex in the earliest Christian centuries for material that was more consulted as manuals rather than read as literary texts. There is at least one further instance of this in the list of first-century codices, P.Ross.Georg. 1.19 (LDAB 3910), apparently a medical text arranged alphabetically.[26]

The remaining items include a parchment codex dated to about 100 CE containing a Latin account of Rome's Macedonian wars (P.Oxy. 30 [LDAB 4472], perhaps the earliest extant parchment codex containing such a literary work), a papyrus codex of some poetic or musical text (Louvre codex AF11357 [LDAB 10361]), and a Psalms codex (Bodl.MS.Gr.bibl.g.5 [LDAB

---

23. For some reason, when one orders a list of first-century CE codices on the LDAB, the eighteen listed include five that do not carry a first-century date, but are dated considerably later. The valid ones carry the following LDAB inventory numbers: 3083, 3850, 3910, 4293, 4305, 4472, 6833, 7242, 7269, 7298, 7299, 8241, 10361.

24. See the discussion in Roberts and Skeat, *Birth of the Codex*, 11-14 ("The Writing Tablet"); and Colette Sirat, "Le codex de bois," in *Débuts du codex*, ed. Blanchard, 37-40, who gives ancient representations of their usage.

25. P.Oxy. 470 (LDAB 4293); P.Oxy. 4174 (LDAB 7242); P.Oxy. 4196a (LDAB 7269); P.Oxy. 4220 frag. 3 (LDAB 7298); P.Oxy. 4231a (LDAB 8241); P.Oxy. 4220 frag. 4 (LDAB 7299).

26. But it is not entirely clear whether this is a codex or a reused roll (opisthograph).

3083]). But it has been suggested that this last one may well be a Christian copy. Its dating (end of first century to end of second century CE) makes this fully plausible, especially if one leans toward a date in mid-to-late second century.[27] We will come back to this item when we consider the texts in Christian codices later in this chapter.

There is a larger body of second-century codices, and these exhibit an interesting inventory of texts/uses. It is not practical here to review in the same depth all 75 non-Christian codices that can be dated to the second (or second-third) century. An overview of their contents will serve well enough. Once again, there are (4) examples of the wooden tablets with wax writing surface. I count 34 with identified literary texts,[28] 5 others with unidentified literary/poetic/musical texts, 2 that appear to contain philological or grammatical texts of some sort, 2 containing some medical or philosophical text, 5 with unidentified rhetorical or oratorical texts, and the largest category by far, as many as 19, astronomical and astrological treatises or manuals. These last ones make up 25% of the total, and confirm that one favorite use of the codex in the earliest Christian centuries was for this sort of "paraliterary" text.[29]

As for the codices containing literary texts, I suggest that at least a number of them were probably prepared for personal study. As a sample, the fourteen codices containing texts of Homer include one example of the wooden tablet devices (BKT 5.1 [LDAB 1515]), and at least some others with annotations ("scholia") probably made by the users (LDAB 1820 and 1847), and others that appear to be excerpt texts (e.g., LDAB 1843 and 2415). That is, it appears that when codices were used for literary texts, it was often to provide workaday copies for annotation and handy aids such as excerpt collections.

To be sure, the Roman writer Martial (ca. 40-104 CE) makes a number of references to the parchment codex as a form in which some literary texts were available, in one place noting in particular what seem to be copies

---

27. See, e.g., VH #151, a judgment reflected also in the LDAB entry for this manuscript (3083).

28. The authors identified are these (the number of copies of each in brackets): Aeschines Socraticus (1), Demosthenes (5), Euripides (2), Hesiod (1), Hippocrates (1), Homer (14), Lollianus (1), Lysias (1), Menander (3), Pindar (2?), Plato (1), Thucydides (1), Xenophon (1).

29. See the valuable online catalogue of paraliterary texts: http://perswww.kuleuven .ac.be/%7Eu0013314/paralit.htm.

sized to be handy for taking along on a trip.[30] Roberts and Skeat aptly characterized Martial as promoting copies of literary works that can be considered as "the Elzevirs, if not the Penguins, of their day."[31] We have actual examples of both parchment and papyrus codices used for literary texts in the early centuries.[32] An interesting second-century CE letter (Egyptian provenance) refers to a bookseller offering several parchment codices *(membranas),* which gives us further confirmation that literary works were becoming available in codex form.[33]

Early Christians were not unique in using the codex for texts intended to be read, not merely consulted. But in their strong *preference* for the codex, they definitely seem to be distinctive. Prior to the fourth century, and especially in the first and second centuries CE, non-Christian use of the codex for serious literary texts seems to have been limited.[34] As illustration of this, of all manuscripts of Homer across the centuries covered in the LDAB, about 63% are rolls, and only 18.5% are codices. About 66% of manuscripts of Euripides are rolls and about 18% codices. Moreover, if we confine our calculations to the period before 300 CE, the number of codices used for these authors is minuscule. For instance, to choose the most

30. Martial, *Epigrams* 1.2. Martial mentions that his own poems were thus available from a local bookshop/copyist, these handy on account of their "small pages" ("brevibus membrana tabellis"). I cite the text as given in Walter C. A. Ker, *Martial: Epigrams,* 2 vols., Loeb Classical Library (Cambridge: Harvard University Press, 1979). Martial's other apparent references to the parchment codex are at 14.184, 186, 188, 190, and 192. It is not clear what size these "small pages" were. For discussion of the Martial references, see Roberts and Skeat, *Birth of the Codex,* 24-29. There is a list of literary-text parchment codices of different sizes and categorized by date in Turner, *Typology,* 39.

31. Roberts and Skeat, *Birth of the Codex,* 27.

32. For example, the oft-cited second-century CE parchment codex of Demosthenes (P.Lit.Lond. 127; LDAB 0651), the pages 16.5 × 19 cm., two columns per page, and what Turner described as a small "sober everyday script" intended "to make the best use of space." For a plate, transcription, and description, see Eric Turner, *Greek Manuscripts of the Ancient World,* ed. P. J. Parsons, 2nd ed. (London: Institute of Classical Studies, 1987), 140-41.

33. The letter, P.Petaus 30, is from a Julius Placidus to his father. It is perhaps worth noting that Julius says that he refused the six parchment codices offered for sale by a bookseller named Dius, but did acquire several other copied items instead (it is not entirely clear whether rolls or other codices). So perhaps the letter shows both that parchment-codex copies of literary works were being produced, and also that there was a certain resistance to this format.

34. In the following figures I do not include items classified in the LDAB as "fragment" or "sheet."

frequently copied classical author in Roman antiquity, of the 789 second-century copies of Homer logged in the LDAB, 16 are codices (2%), and only about 10% (67) of the 647 third-century copies of Homer are codices.[35] These data are consistent with the survey of references to book forms in Roman-era writers by Roberts and Skeat, who concluded that "for a century or more after Martial's experiment our literary sources are silent on the development of the codex."[36]

Even if the general increase in the use of the codex in the third century (bar graph 1) means that second-century Christian preference was simply anticipating a trend that caught on outside Christian circles later, that still leaves us with the questions of *how and why* Christians opted for a book form when it was not yet so favored in the general culture.[37] It is curious that Christians should have anticipated so quickly and successfully a preference that may have developed in the general population much more gradually. As Roberts and Skeat noted, the slow but steady advance of the codex in general usage across the first three centuries CE contrasts sharply with the early and rather wholesale embrace of this book form in Christian usage.[38]

Texts: Christian Preferences

Christians clearly preferred the codex; yet it is also clear that they used rolls. Later in this chapter I explore possible reasons for the Christian pref-

---

35. These statistics give some specific backing for the broad statement by Roberts and Skeat (*Birth of the Codex*, 24), "In the first two centuries of the Empire polite society acknowledged one form and one form only for the book — the roll."

36. Roberts and Skeat, *Birth of the Codex*, 30.

37. Joseph van Haelst suggested that a transition to greater use of the codex was commencing in the late second century, but he grants that the rapidity and extent of the early Christian preference for the codex are unparalleled. See van Haelst, "Les origines du codex," in *Débuts du codex*, ed. Blanchard, 13-36, esp. 32-34. This programmatic essay is essential for any serious study of the Christian use of the codex.

38. Roberts and Skeat, *Birth of the Codex*, 53. They show that in non-Christian usage "the codex emerged as an acceptable form only after a long period of gestation" (32), and that it was "only in the course of the fourth century that the codex obtained a significant share of book-production" (37). As a recent updating of data, in vol. 67 of *The Oxyrhynchus Papyri*, there is a list of about 175 manuscripts of Euripides (one of the most popular literary authors of the Roman period) now identified. They are all rolls, except for one early papyrus codex copy of "Phoenissae" (P.Oxy. 3321), and a handful of other codices all dated to the fourth century CE and later.

erence for the codex. But can we discern any pattern in their use of the one book form or the other?

I order the analysis chronologically, commencing with Christian items that have been dated to the second century CE.[39] The LDAB lists 41 such items, which includes those dated either second century or second/third century (the latter usually meaning a date somewhere between late second and early third century). To these I add another 4 items from my table of early Christian manuscripts, based on the dating of them by experts.[40] But with or without any or all of these 4 items, the pattern of Christian usage is sufficiently clear.

Among the 45 second-century items to consider initially, at least 6 (and quite possibly 7) are cases of literary texts copied on unused rolls, another 4 (possibly 5) are reused rolls (opisthographs), and yet another 3 items may have been either rolls or single sheets containing an extract of a text. One of the items on the list produced by the LDAB (P.Harris 1.55 [LDAB 4599]) is a single sheet of papyrus containing a magical text, probably used as an amulet, and it is not entirely clear whether it is from a Christian or Jewish user. This leaves at least 29 items (including the 4 items that I add to the LDAB list) that are all clearly codices.[41]

I now consider the texts copied, as well as the book form chosen. We may begin by dealing quickly with the opisthographic copies. In the ancient setting, rolls were typically reused, to make personal copies of texts for study purposes, for example. The texts of our five second-century Christian opisthographs are Revelation (P.IFAO 2.31 [LDAB 2776]), Psalms (*PSI* 8.921v. [LDAB 3088]), *Shepherd of Hermas* (P.Mich. 130 [LDAB 1096]), and a couple of otherwise unknown theological treatises or homilies (P.Gen. 3.125 [LDAB 5033], and P.Mich. 18.763 [LDAB 5071]).[42] These five

---

39. For details on specific items see appendix 1.

40. Schøyen Codex 187 (Exodus; dated variously from second through fourth century CE), P.Leip.inv. 170 (Psalms; dated fourth century on LDAB), P.Chester Beatty VIII (Jeremiah; dated fourth century on LDAB), and P.Mich. 130 (*Hermas;* dated third century on LDAB). I have found occasional errors in LDAB entries, and have tended to follow the datings given in scholarly editions and treatments, such as Turner, *Typology.*

41. At the risk of throwing too many figures at my readers, I point out that these codices make up about 84% of the total of second-century Christian items that are either rolls or codices.

42. The text on the recto side has not been identified. It has been suggested, however, that this may be part of the same manuscript as P.Oxy. 1079, which is a portion of an opisthographic copy of Revelation with a copy of Exodus on the recto side. But these two

manuscripts are probably best taken as artifacts reflecting interests of some second-century Christians in having edifying texts for their own reading. In the case of opisthographs, however, the roll format was not chosen, but was simply the form of the writing material capable of being reused (because the outer surface of rolls was left blank).

But seven items in our list of second-century manuscripts must represent a choice to copy texts in the roll book form.[43] The texts in question are these: an unknown homily or perhaps a letter (P.Mich. 18.764 [LDAB 0562]), Irenaeus's *Against Heresies* (P.Oxy. 405 [LDAB 2459]), *Sibylline Oracles* (P.Oslo 2.14 [LDAB 4797]), Esther (P.Oxy. 4443 [LDAB 3080]), Psalms (P.Barc.inv. 2 [LDAB 3082]), an eschatological discourse (*PSI* 11.1200 [LDAB 4669]), and a portion of some Gospel-like text whose identity is disputed (P.Oxy. 2949 [LDAB 5111]).[44]

In the case of two of these items, however, the rolls containing Esther and Psalms, scholars are divided over whether they derive originally from Christian or Jewish copyists. Both are dated to the early second century or perhaps even earlier, which makes it more plausible that they could have come from Jewish hands (the Jewish population of Oxyrhynchus having suffered serious decline after the Jewish revolt of 132-135 CE). Also, the Psalms roll is parchment (and there may have been a Jewish preference for leather or parchment for biblical texts), whereas second-century Christian biblical manuscripts (at least in Egypt) are almost entirely papyrus.[45] The absence of *nomina sacra* forms (e.g., the uncontracted θεος in P.Oxy. 4443) is inconsistent with the usual Christian scribal practice. Finally, the strong Christian

---

manuscripts were edited separately, and the editor of P.Oxy. 1079 dated it third/fourth century CE! So if they are indeed portions of the same opisthograph, the dates for each will have to be reconsidered.

43. In each case the text in question was written on the recto (inner) side of writing material, the verso side blank (or, in the case of the portion of *Sibylline Oracles*, P.Oslo 2.14, there is another text on the verso, indicating a subsequent reuse of the writing material).

44. Dieter Lührmann proposed that both P.Oxy. 2949 and P.Oxy. 4009 constitute fragments of an early stage of the *Gospel of Peter*, but this is now seriously challenged. Cf. Lührmann, "POx 2949"; idem, "POx 4009;" but now also criticism by Kraus and Nicklas, eds., *Petrusevangelium*; and, still more forcefully, Paul Foster, "Are There Any Early Fragments of the So-called *Gospel of Peter*?" *NTS* 52 (2006): 1-28.

45. Tov (*Scribal Practices*, 44-53) shows that the papyrus manuscripts from Judea overwhelmingly contain nonbiblical texts, and that papyrus copies of biblical texts are very few. Judge and Pickering ("Biblical Papyri," 5) noted that leather or parchment rolls are "almost unknown" in Egypt, though predominant in Judea.

preference for the codex, especially for biblical writings (as we will see shortly), is itself a factor that leads some scholars to suspect that these two rolls are Jewish. It is certainly important to note that all the unambiguously Jewish biblical manuscripts from prior to the second century CE are rolls.[46]

But we cannot linger over the matter further, and there is no way to settle the issue conclusively. It is, of course, possible that these items are copies originally made by and for Jewish usage, which then came into Christian hands. For instance, the original Jewish owners/users could have become adherents of a circle of Christians, or Christians might have purchased or been given copies by Jews. But it is also possible that these copies were prepared for use by individuals or circles whose practices and self-identity might have combined features of what we know as "Judaism" and "Christianity." However we imagine that the "parting of the ways" between these two traditions might have taken place, we should presume that for some Jews and Christians the division was neither early nor complete, at least in the second century CE.[47] Although I think that these two manuscripts are likely of Jewish provenance, for the present analysis, I treat these as apparently occasional instances of Christian copies of biblical texts on rolls.[48]

Given the Christian preference for the codex book form, it is not surprising that there is a variety of texts in the second-century Christian codices. In addition to biblical writings (which we will look at more closely a bit later), we have two early codices of *Shepherd of Hermas* (P.Iand. 1.4 [LDAB 1094]; P.Oxy. 3528 [LDAB 1095]), an apparent homily (BKT 9.22 [LDAB 4973]), one of the three copies of the *Gospel of Thomas* (P.Oxy. 1 [LDAB

---

46. Indeed, as Tov observes (*Scribal Practices,* 31), none of the texts from the Judean sites (first century CE and earlier), biblical or nonbiblical, is on a codex. The evidence suggests that Jewish use of the codex may have developed only as part of the wider readiness to use this book form in the third century CE and thereafter.

47. The phrase quoted apparently derives from the title of the book by Abraham Cohen, *Parting of the Ways: Judaism and Christianity* (London: Lincolns, 1954), and has become a topos repeated in numerous academic publications in recent decades, the idea variously affirmed, qualified, and challenged. Cf., e.g., J. D. G. Dunn, *The Partings of the Ways: Between Judaism and Christianity and Their Significance for the Character of Christianity* (Philadelphia: Trinity Press International, 1991); Adam H. Becker and Annette Yoshiko Reed, eds., *The Ways That Never Parted: Jews and Christians in Late Antiquity and the Early Middle Ages* (Tübingen: Mohr Siebeck, 2003).

48. Judge and Pickering proposed ("Biblical Papyri," 5 n. 19) that Berlin Staats.Bib. Cod. gr. fol. 66 I,II (Rahlfs 911), a third-century Genesis codex, may reflect a text copied by a Christian scribe from a roll.

4028], see plate 7, appendix 2), a portion of a Gospel-like text of disputed identity (P.Oxy. 4009 [LDAB 4872]), a text of Philo of Alexandria (P.Oxy. 1173 + 1356 + 2158 + *PSI* 11.1207 and P.Haun. 1.8 [LDAB 3540]), and fragments of the so-called Egerton Gospel (P.Lond.Christ. 1 + P.Köln 6.255 [LDAB 4736]).

The remaining 26 second-century Christian codices in my list are all copies of writings from what became the Christian Old Testament or New Testament. This far greater number of biblical texts in codex form is itself very interesting. But the infrequency of identifiably Christian copies of these writings on rolls (again, excluding opisthographs) is still more notable. Other than the one copy of Esther and the one Psalms roll (whose Christian provenance is disputed, as previously noted), there are no second-century Christian copies of writings that became part of the Christian canon on rolls. Indisputably, in the entire body of Christian manuscripts of the second and third centuries there is no instance of a New Testament writing copied onto the recto side of a roll.[49]

The use of the roll for other Christian texts makes this all the more interesting. Clearly, Christians preferred the codex generally, but they felt free to use rolls sometimes, at least for *some texts.* In particular, in the earliest extant artifacts of their book practice, it appears that Christians strongly preferred the codex for *those writings that they regarded as scripture* (or, at least, writings that were coming to be widely so regarded).

If we broaden our coverage to include third-century Christian items, the same picture holds. The roll seems to have been reasonably acceptable for some Christian texts: theological treatises such as Irenaeus, *Against Heresies* (both early copies), P.Iand. 5.70, P.Ryl. 3.469 *(Epistle against Manichaeans?),* Julius Africanus (P.Oxy. 412), P.Oxy. 2070 (Jewish/Christian dialogue?), P.Med.inv. 71.84 (unidentified text), edifying texts such as *Shepherd of Hermas* (BKT 6.2.1), an unidentified eschatological discourse (*PSI* 11.1200), *Sibylline Oracles* (P.Oslo 2.14), homilies (P.Mich. 18.764), liturgical texts (BKT 6.6.1), the Dura Europos Gospel-harmony fragment

---

49. There are several opisthograph NT texts: 𝔓22 (P.Oxy. 1228; curiously, however, a portion containing two columns of the Gospel of John on the verso side, the recto side blank); 𝔓13 (P.Oxy. 657 + *PSI* 12.1292; portions of Hebrews on verso, Epitome of Livy on recto); 𝔓18 (P.Oxy. 1079; Revelation on verso, Exodus on recto); 𝔓98 (P.IFAO 2.31; portion of Revelation on verso, illegible text on recto, perhaps part of same roll as 𝔓18). As with all opisthographs, however, the (re)use of a roll was dictated by the need/desire to reuse writing material previously used for some other text, the opisthograph usually made for personal study of literary texts or for documentary texts.

(P.Dura 10), and other Gospels (or Gospel-like texts) such as P.Oxy. 655 *(Gospel of Thomas,* see plate 9, appendix 2*),* P.Ryl. 463 *(Gospel of Mary),* and the Fayum Gospel (P.Vindob.G. 2325). By my count, of 58 Christian copies of extrabiblical literary texts dated second or third century CE listed in appendix 1, 18 (31%) are rolls (34% if we exclude opisthographs).[50]

So far as biblical texts are concerned, as noted already, there is no New Testament text copied on an unused roll among second- or third-century Christian manuscripts.[51] As for "Old Testament" texts, in addition to the two manuscripts previously noted whose provenance is uncertain, there are nine more items to consider dated third (or third/fourth) century CE. In the case of at least some of them, however, there are reasons for wondering if they may be Jewish copies.[52] If they are, then their roll form is not evidence of Christian preferences. We cannot, and need not, here engage the matter in sufficient detail to try to argue for some definitive view on all nine manuscripts. For at least three, however, there are good reasons for supposing that they are Jewish. For example, one copy of Psalms (Stud. Pal. 11.114) has the Tetragrammaton written in Hebrew characters, a practice otherwise found in indisputably Jewish copies of Greek Old Testament writings.[53] In two

---

50. I exclude magical texts and a few others whose provenance is uncertain. Roberts and Skeat (*Birth of the Codex,* 43-44) counted 118 Christian copies of extrabiblical texts, extending their coverage to all items dated prior to 400 CE, 83 of these in codex form, the remaining 35 being rolls, including 3 opisthographs. They observed that, along with a clear majority of all these Christian writings in codex form, "an appreciable minority are on rolls," the numbers of rolls significant in certain categories. For documentary and "paraliterary" texts as well, Christians continued to use the roll for a long time. For example, the cache of sixth-century CE carbonized papyri discovered (1993) in a church in Petra comprises 152 rolls, private papers of a prosperous local family, mainly financial documents concerning marriage, inheritance, sales, loans and disputes, and also taxation. Ludwig Koenen ("The Carbonized Archive from Petra," *Journal of Roman Archaeology* 9 [1996]: 177-88) gave an advance overview; and Jaakko Frösén has edited the first volume of the manuscripts: *The Petra Papyri,* American Center of Oriental Research Publications 4 (Amman: American Center of Oriental Research, 2002).

51. I take P.Oxy. 1228 (𝔓22) to be an opisthograph.

52. The key discussions are these: Kurt Treu, "Die Bedeutung des Griechischen für die Juden im römischen Reich," *Kairos* 15 (1973): 123-44 (challenging common criteria for distinguishing Jewish and Christian biblical manuscripts; trans. William Adler and Robert Kraft, http://ccat.sas.upenn.edu/gopher/other/courses/rels/525/2.3%20Greek%20Judaism%20Article%20%28Treu%29. See also Roberts, *Manuscript,* 74-78, answering Treu and clarifying his proposed criteria; and Roberts and Skeat, *Birth of the Codex,* esp. 38-42. Note also Judge and Pickering, "Biblical Papyri," 5-7.

53. Tov, *Scribal Practices,* 218-21.

other rolls, P.Harris 31 (Psalms) and P.Lit.Lond. 211 (Daniel), the word Θεος is written in uncontracted form, whereas we would expect third-century Christian copies of biblical writings to have the *nomina sacra* abbreviation for this key word (the *nomina sacra* are discussed in chapter three below).

P.Oxy. 1166 is a portion of a roll of Genesis dated mid-third century CE and written in an elegant hand; Roberts suggested more tentatively that it too might be a Jewish copy that then came into Christian usage.[54] As for P.Harris 2.166, this may well be an excerpt text and not a regular copy of Exodus. If so, it is not so much direct evidence for Christian preferences in the copying of biblical writings. Another is an opisthograph (P.Lit.Lond. 207), Psalms written on the verso of a roll that was originally used for a copy of a work by Isocrates. As noted already, opisthographs are not really relevant as evidence of book-form preferences.

The two remaining items, however, are notable. These are P.Oxy. 1075, a roll originally used for a copy of Exodus, and P.Alex.inv. 203, a copy of Isaiah. Both have the *nomina sacra* form for Κυριος, a scribal practice usually thought to reflect Christian copying.[55] Thus these two manuscripts may represent exceptions to the general Christian preference for the codex for copies of biblical texts. Alternatively, they may be rare instances of the *nomina sacra* forms being taken up by Jewish copyists, a kind of cross-fertilization in scribal practice among Jewish and Christian circles who were likely in dialogue/debate in the second century.

So, depending on how one judges particular cases, we may have a few instances of Christian copies of Old Testament writings on rolls, perhaps as few as two, perhaps a few more. That is, of approximately 75 manuscripts of Old Testament writings that are dated second and third century CE (including several that may be either Jewish or Christian), perhaps as many as 9 are rolls (not counting opisthographs), about 12% of that total. And if we remove items that are quite arguably Jewish copies from the count, the result is something closer to 4-7%.[56] In any case, it is clear that Christians favored the codex particularly for the writings that they treated as scripture.

54. C. H. Roberts, "The Christian Book and the Greek Papyri," *JTS* 50 (1949): 155-68, esp. 157.

55. Even Roberts and Skeat, who underscored early Christian preference for the codex, were ready to grant that these were "two normal rolls of Christian origin" (*Birth of the Codex*, 39-40).

56. See appendix 1, esp. items numbered 1-90, excluding those marked with a single asterisk (which are rather clearly Jewish manuscripts).

We should not be surprised that Christians used rolls as well as codices for their literary texts, occasionally (so it appears) including biblical texts, given the strong preference for the roll in the general culture of the time. (We are, after all, considering human behavior, for which all experience leads us not to expect uniformity.) The notable and curious phenomenon is that Christians favored the codex so strongly, it appears, especially for their scriptural texts. That is, there are two main features to the pattern of early Christian preferences in book forms: a general Christian preference for the codex, and a particularly strong preference for the codex for the texts that they used as scripture.

This means that early Christian copying preferences cannot be accounted for on the basis of general preferences of that day. It may even mean that the preference for the codex represents a deliberate disposition *counter* to the wider tendencies in book copying of the time. Given the clear regard for the roll as the preferred book form for literary works and also for sacred texts in the second century CE, the Christian use of the codex would have been salient. Neither Christians nor the general public could have been unaware that the strong preference for the codex differentiated Christians from the general book-form preference of the time.

The strong place of the codex in early Christian copying practice may be our earliest extant expression of a distinctively Christian "material culture."[57] Scholarly discussions about how and when early Christianity may be identified and distinguished as such should certainly take adequate account of the body of important artifacts made up by Christian manuscripts of the second and third centuries. Granted, we should not assume that everyone in the second century thought of themselves simply as "pagan," "Jewish," or "Christian," or that every form of Christianity was completely distinct from any form of Judaism.[58] But the material evidence of

---

57. I echo here a point that I made in "Earliest Evidence."

58. Judith M. Lieu, *Neither Jew nor Greek? Constructing Early Christianity* (London: T&T Clark, 2002), is an interesting set of critiques of scholarly assumptions and categories. But she also exhibits the curious tendency among scholars to ignore the artifactual significance of earliest Christian manuscripts. Note, e.g., her confident claim that for the first two centuries CE, "material remains are not available as markers of Christian identity, or/and, if available, they would not be or perhaps are not distinguishable" (171). As appendix 1 shows, however, there are at least ten Christian manuscripts dated to the second century, and another thirty-three dated late second century or early third century. Though in most cases only portions survive, these constitute a rather substantial body of Christian material remains.

Christian book practice indicates that in their *preference* for the codex Christians were apparently distinctive, at least in the second and third centuries.[59] As we shall see in the next chapter, the *nomina sacra* may form another distinguishing feature of early Christian book practice. Moreover, both the preference for the codex and the use of the *nomina sacra* are *conventions,* practices that apparently spread widely and rapidly among early Christian circles and were embraced as emergent Christian customs. We turn next to consider the question of how and why the codex came to enjoy such favor among Christians.

Why Did Christians Prefer the Codex?

Before we examine proposals as to how and why Christians preferred the codex, I have to make one further observation. "In the surviving evidence, we do not see an evolution in Christian preference with incremental stages, but an appropriation of the codex that appears to have been as thorough as it was early."[60] Yet, as just noted, we have to think of this as a rapidly spreading *convention* among Christians, not something legislated or enforced by some ecclesiastical authority. In other words, we are looking at a genuine historical problem, and it is understandable that scholars have proposed various solutions.

Before we examine them, however, I want to consider the view urged by Robert Kraft (expanding upon an argument made several decades ago by Kurt Treu) that the codex and the *nomina sacra* as well are not actually the typical identifying marks of Christian scribal practice, but were adopted from Jewish scribal practice.[61] I agree that early Christianity was "formed in large measure in close relationship (positive and negative) to the types of Judaism present in the Graeco-Roman world," and that there is good reason to think that on some matters Christian scribal practice was influenced by previous Jewish scribal practice (e.g., sense-unit spacing).[62] But proper historical method surely requires us to test hypotheses by the available evidence.

59. Thus occasional/limited use of the codex by others does not efface this distinction.
60. Hurtado, "Earliest Evidence," 272.
61. Robert Kraft, "The 'Textual Mechanics' of Early Jewish LXX/OG Papyri and Fragments," in *The Bible as Book: The Transmission of the Greek Text,* ed. Scot McKendrick and Orlaith O'Sullivan (London: British Library, 2003), 51-72; Treu, "Bedeutung."
62. Kraft, "Textual Mechanics," 68.

As Kraft readily notes, none of the unambiguously Jewish manuscripts dated first century CE and earlier is a codex, nor does any exhibit the *nomina sacra* scheme of abbreviations of certain special words so familiar in Christian manuscripts.[63] This seems rather decisive in my view, and the same judgment has been reached by others as well.[64] Kraft (as did Treu earlier) points to a small number of manuscripts dated variously from the late second century through the fourth/fifth century CE in which we find a curious mixture of features that are most often taken as characteristic of Jewish or Christian scribal practice, claiming (with some cogency and support from other scholars) that at least one or two codices of biblical writings, for example, are likely Jewish.[65]

I have already noted that there are such manuscripts that are difficult to identify as of either Jewish or Christian provenance, and I have proposed that it is entirely plausible that the scribal habits of some copyists (to judge by the evidence, a very small minority) may reflect varying mixtures of influences. I also repeat the points that, after all, we are studying human behavior, so we should not be surprised if it is less than uniform, and that (so far as I know) scribal practices were not legislated or policed by church or synagogue authorities. So we should expect to find some exceptions to any generally followed customs or conventions, and that, I submit, is precisely what the manuscript evidence shows. We have a distinctively strong use of the codex in identifiably Christian manuscripts (especially biblical

63. Kraft refers to his "intuition" (ibid., 51) and "suspicion" (66) that Christian use of the codex came via Jewish usage, but candidly expresses doubts "whether there will ever be sufficient evidence" (66) to validate his stance. I return to the possible connection of the *nomina sacra* with Jewish scribal treatment of the Tetragrammaton in chapter three.

64. E.g., Colette Sirat, "Le livre Hébreu dans les premiers siècles de notre ère: Le témoignage des texts," in *Débuts du codex,* ed. Blanchard, 115-24, who concludes that "the hypothesis of Jewish sources for the Christian codex is not supported by the texts or by archaeology" (124).

65. See Kraft, "Textual Mechanics," 66, where he points in particular to P.Oxy. 656 (a second/third-century CE Genesis codex) as "almost certain" to be Jewish. This judgment is supported by Roberts (*Manuscript,* 76-77, revising his earlier view), and van Haelst (VH 32-33, #13). This is also the position taken in the file on this manuscript in the PRCE project (Macquarie University). Especially significant is the original scribe's tendency to leave a blank space at places where the Tetragrammaton should appear, these spaces filled in with Κυριος (uncontracted) by another hand. If correct, this makes P.Oxy. 656 the earliest Jewish biblical text in codex form, and the earliest instance of a text with the Tetragrammaton replaced by Κυριος.

texts), with a few possible uses of rolls, and a few possible-to-likely uses of a codex in/for Jewish use of the early centuries CE (of which P.Oxy. 656 is a particularly strong instance). But I contend that it is not sound to use these few items to try to overturn the clear weight of the great body of evidence.

In short, I do not consider Kraft and Treu persuasive in contending that Christian use of the codex owes particularly to prior Jewish use. The majority of scholars think otherwise because the comparative weight of evidence seems to require it.[66] There is certainly no indication that Jewish use of the codex was as pronounced as its use in Christian circles. But, whatever the reasons, at a very early point Christians appropriated the codex format, which was already in limited use in the early Roman period, and with impressive speed made it their favored format, especially for their scriptures. Let us turn now to weigh other scholarly proposals about how and why the codex came to be such a characteristic feature of early Christianity.

We may organize the proposals into three categories: (1) those emphasizing one or another alleged practical advantage of the codex, (2) those that explain the preference as reflecting the socioeconomic background of early Christians, and (3) suggestions that early Christian use of the codex may represent a deliberate choice to embrace a book form different from that favored more generally at the time. We may need to allow for more than one factor and perhaps more than one historical step in a process that led to the Christian preference of the codex. But, I repeat, any steps in the process appear to have been taken already by the time of the earliest extant Christian manuscripts. So whatever factors and steps were involved, they had to have been quite early.

Supposed Practical Advantages

Several proposals about the supposed practical advantages of the codex were subjected to a rather rigorous critique by Roberts and Skeat, and I need not do more here than summarize the results and add a few com-

---

66. Responding to a draft version of this chapter, Kraft wrote that the majority of scholars subscribe to this view "by default to certain presuppositions" (which he did not specify). But as I state above, the evidence seems to point toward the inference that the Christian preference for the codex was an innovation. It is not correct to refer to an inference made from data as a "presupposition."

ments of my own.[67] It does seem correct that copying a text in a codex might have been somewhat less costly than copying the same text on a roll. For example, Skeat estimated that there might have been a saving of about 26% between producing the Chester Beatty Codex of the Pauline epistles and copying the same body of texts on a roll.[68] But, as Roberts and Skeat judged, it seems unlikely that any such reduction in cost was sufficient to account for the wholesale preference for the codex form among early Christians.[69] If cost were an important factor, it is curious that early Christian codices do not characteristically exhibit any effort to make maximum use of the writing material. The handwriting is not generally smaller or more compressed than one finds on literary rolls of the day, and the wide margins and generous line spacing further indicate no concern to conserve on writing material. In short, there is scant corroboration for the suggestion that the codex was embraced by Christians for economic reasons.

I want to add that Skeat's analysis included only the likely costs of papyrus and the fee paid to a copyist. But there is another factor. In copying onto a roll, one simply acquired a sufficiently lengthy piece of writing material, and then wrote the text in columns.[70] But a codex required the extra work of construction, a length of writing material (e.g., papyrus) cut into sheets of preferred size, which were then folded to form two leaves each, all the leaves of the codex then attached in one arrangement or another. I describe more specifically the codex-construction measures used by early Christians later in this chapter. For now, my point is simply that the codex book form required the development of additional skills beyond those required for the roll.[71] As William Johnson observed, "Codex production brings in its wake the need for specialty skills, such as the knowledge of how to fashion and plan quires, sew bindings, craft and attach the covers.

---

67. Roberts and Skeat, *Birth of the Codex*, 45-53. Gamble (*Books and Readers*, 54-56) also reviewed these proposals with similar results.

68. T. C. Skeat, "The Length of the Standard Papyrus Roll and the Cost-Advantage of the Codex," *ZPE* 45 (1982): 169-76; repr. in *Collected Biblical Writings*, ed. Elliott, 65-70.

69. Roberts and Skeat, *Birth of the Codex*, 46.

70. I greatly simplify what was involved, particularly in producing a high-quality copy of a text on a book roll. This required careful calculation of column width, and other scribal skills. See Johnson, *Bookrolls*, esp. 86-99. But the codex required a further set of skills.

71. Note, e.g., Johnson's contrast of what was involved in use of a codex or a roll, ibid., 85-86.

Bookroll production, by contrast, is nearly trivial."[72] That is, the choice to use a codex involved some significant extra steps in construction of the finished copy, hence making it all the more interesting that early Christians made such heavy use of this book form.

To consider briefly another putative advantage of the codex, one might assume that it was obviously easier or more convenient to read. But we should beware that such an assumption likely reflects our greater familiarity with the use of the descendant of the ancient codex, the modern book. Indeed, on the basis of a small experiment that he devised, Skeat suggested plausibly that the roll may well have had certain advantages over the codex, at least for ordinary reading of continuous texts.[73] I might add that, if the codex was so obviously a superior book form for reading/use of texts, why did most users of literary texts in the second and third centuries so firmly prefer book rolls? Were the Christians the only ones with sufficient good sense? Much as I admire some things about early Christians, this is somehow counterintuitive.

Or should we imagine that the force of tradition operated so strongly that it prevented most people from appropriating the codex, whereas the Christians were simply more flexible or adaptive? Were this the case, I suggest that we should expect to find some initial Christian experimentation with the codex, followed then by a progressively more confident and consistent use. But this is emphatically not what the artifactual evidence suggests. Instead, we seem to have a wholesale Christian adoption of the codex, even a strong preference for it, so full and so early that it is already well established by the time of our earliest evidence.

Likewise dubious is the suggestion that the codex was preferred because it offered a supposedly greater facility to consult particular passages in texts. As Roberts and Skeat noted, upon close examination this proposal does not persuade.[74] In the absence of chapter and verse divisions, which were introduced only much later, the only way to find a particular passage would have been by searching in its approximate textual vicinity, or per-

72. Ibid., 86-87.

73. T. C. Skeat, "Roll versus Codex — A New Approach?" *ZPE* 84 (1990): 297-98; repr. in *Collected Biblical Writings*, ed. Elliott, 71-72. See also Roberts and Skeat, *Birth of the Codex*, 49-50; and Skeat's note on his experiment in rerolling a papyrus roll in *Collected Biblical Writings*, ed. Elliott, 60-63, arguing further that ancient readers likely did not regard the roll as a particularly difficult form for reading texts.

74. Roberts and Skeat, *Birth of the Codex*, 50-51.

haps by stichometry, that is, calculating the number of lines of text at certain points in a manuscript. The only way this latter method could have operated would have been to indicate a passage by the number of stichoi (lines of text) from either the beginning or the end of the text. But there is scant evidence of any such procedure being used. The page numbers found on some early codices appear more likely to have functioned for keeping pages in the right order for final binding, and to ensure that none was missing.[75]

We might assume that the key attraction of the codex for early Christians was a greater capacity to accommodate a large body of text. Indeed, noting that a number of codices dated second to fourth century CE have fifty or more lines per page, Eric Turner observed that "large holding capacity was a prime recommendation for a papyrus codex in its developmental period."[76] It is all the more important, however, to note that among the twenty-nine early codices listed by Turner that have such large numbers of lines per page, only one is an identifiably Christian item, P.Chester Beatty IX-X, which originally contained Ezekiel, Daniel, and Esther.[77] That is, Turner's suggestion that holding capacity may have been a factor in the early use of the codex does *not* appear applicable to early Christian codex usage. The page layout of early Christian manuscripts (e.g., usual number of lines per page, generous margins, and line spacing) indicates that they were not characteristically prepared for maximum use of writing surface.

Furthermore, scholarly assumptions on this matter have been shaped by inaccurate notions about the size and capacity of ancient book rolls. Johnson's recently published study proves that earlier estimates of typical roll length as 9-10 m. "must be heavily qualified," and that "a normative range of 3-15 metres seems in order," with adequate examples of rolls extending well beyond 15 m.[78] Tov's analysis of Judean evidence basically points in the same direction.[79] We should also note that a book roll ade-

---

75. We do not know this for certain and for all instances, but this is a widely shared view among papyrologists.

76. Turner, *Typology*, 95. See his table 14 (pp. 96-97) for a list of relevant codices.

77. In this single-gathering codex (59 sheets folded to form 118 leaves), Ezekiel occupied the first half, and Daniel and Esther (written in a different hand) formed the second half. For further description see Frederick G. Kenyon, *The Chester Beatty Biblical Papyri, Fasciculus VII, Ezekiel, Daniel, Esther: Text* (London: Walker, 1937), v-xii.

78. Johnson, *Bookrolls*, 148-49. Cf., e.g., Gamble, *Books and Readers*, 47.

79. Tov (*Scribal Practices*, 74-79) projects rolls as great as 25-30 m. long.

quate for a goodly sized text would form a cylinder of more modest dimension than we might imagine. Johnson's calculation of the diameter of book rolls of varying lengths shows, for example, that the diameter of a 10-m. scroll was about 7.4 cm., "roughly the same as a wine bottle," and even a huge 20-m. roll was slightly smaller than a 2-liter container of soft drink (10.45 cm.). Skeat calculated that a roll 18 cm. high and 6 m. long could make a cylinder of 5-6 cm. in diameter, "which could easily be held in the hand."[80] But even if we allow for a significantly larger roll and go by Johnson's calculations of diameters, a 7.5-m. scroll, for instance, would roll up in a cylinder of about 6.4 cm. (about 2.5 in.), an object easily handled.

To my knowledge, the only advantage of the codex referred to in ancient writers is Martial's commendation of the portability of this format (*Epigrams* 1.2). What Martial seems to commend, however, is not simply the codex format as such but, more specifically, *small* parchment codices, perhaps something like modern pocket-sized editions of literary works ("brevibus membrana tabellis").[81] A few scholars have proposed that the codex form, particularly modest-sized codices, may have been more attractive and serviceable for itinerant Christian teachers and evangelists, and that this may account for the Christian preference for this book form. I shall return to this suggestion shortly for further consideration of its merits. At this point I only note that, even if the portability of "modest"-sized codices may have been the initial factor that made this book form attractive to some very early (first-century?) Christian evangelists, the subsequently wide adoption of the codex by Christians requires some further factor(s). There is no basis for thinking that many of our extant Christian codices from the second and third centuries were prepared for itinerant reading/usage. Indeed, it is more likely that they were prepared for use by Christians in settled residence, such as Oxyrhynchus. The Christian preference for the codex format seems to reflect something more than an appreciation for its portability.

In sum, although it is plausible that the potential of the modest-sized codex format may have made it attractive for some very early Christian itinerant use, this does not by itself account for the subsequently strong and widely shared Christian preference for the codex.

---

80. Skeat, in *Collected Biblical Writings*, ed. Elliott, 81. Skeat acknowledges his mistake earlier in estimating the diameter of such a roll as 3-4 cm. (in Roberts and Skeat, *Birth of the Codex*, 47).

81. Turner (*Typology*, 39) gives examples of small, early, parchment-codex copies of literary works.

Socioeconomic Explanation

G. H. R. Horsley proposed that a combination of factors disposed early Christians to favor the codex. Contending that in the early centuries Christians were largely from social levels with limited educational attainment, he suggested that they were more accustomed to the codex because of its use in elementary schooling and in day-to-day business dealings, whereas the roll was the format more used for literature by the "highly educated elite" of the time. He also asserted that in the first two centuries Christians "did not yet look on their newly written texts [he apparently means writings such as those that became part of the NT] as sacred," and so the workaday codex format seemed a thoroughly appropriate form to use.[82] Then, having been favored initially for these reasons, the codex thereafter became the traditional and preferred form for Christian texts. But there are at least a couple of serious problems with Horsley's proposals.

First, his socioeconomic characterization of early Christians is inadequate. In the early centuries there were probably many Christians of limited educational background. But over the last several decades scholars have shown that from the first century onward Christian circles were located characteristically in urban centers, not in rustic and backward locations, and that the converts came from varied social and economic levels, including (especially among leaders of Christian circles) people of economic means and education beyond elementary levels.[83] In any case it was not only members of the "highly educated elite" who had occasion to use texts written on rolls; the format was simply predominant broadly in the early Roman era. There is no reason to assume that people of lower social levels were any less affected by the widely shared preference for the book

---

82. G. H. R. Horsley, "Classical Manuscripts in Australia and New Zealand and the Early History of the Codex," *Antichthon: Journal of the Australian Society for Classical Studies* 27 (1995): 60-85, esp. 81-83. But cf. Horsley's acknowledgment that there were some of higher social and economic status in early Christian circles: *New Documents Illustrating Early Christianity*, vol. 5 (Sydney: Ancient History Documentary Research Centre, 1989), 108-11. (I thank Scott Charlesworth for this reference.)

83. See, e.g., Abraham J. Malherbe, *Social Aspects of Early Christianity* (Baton Rouge: Louisiana State University Press, 1977), esp. 29-59; and Wayne A. Meeks, *The First Urban Christians: The Social World of the Apostle Paul* (New Haven: Yale University Press, 1983). The pioneering and influential work was by Edwin Judge, *The Social Pattern of Christian Groups in the First Century* (London: Tyndale, 1960).

roll and would have been any more ready to turn so freely to the codex in preference to the roll.[84]

Still more crucial against Horsley's proposals is that the early Christian preference for the codex is evident not only in copies of their own texts, such as what became New Testament writings (whose scriptural status was not fully secured in the second century especially), but also in copies of Old Testament writings, whose scriptural significance was rather clearly accepted characteristically by Christians from the earliest years. As noted previously in my analysis of Christian use of the codex and roll book forms, right from our earliest evidence onward Christians preferred the codex especially for those texts that they seem to have esteemed highly as sacred or authoritative. So the general associations of the codex with copies of texts for use in schools or with workaday mercantile/business settings seems irrelevant. The Christian preference for the codex represents something else.

A Deliberate Preference?

Neither putative practical advantages of the codex nor supposed socioeconomic factors are sufficient to account fully for the Christian preference for this book form. That is, to state the results negatively, there seems to be nothing adequate to have made the codex an obvious choice, and nothing to suggest that the Christian preference for the codex could have developed without awareness by Christians that this was a notable orientation, somewhat out of step with the larger culture of the time. Instead, we have to see the early Christian preference for the codex as remarkable and as needing some more adequate explanation. Moreover, given the prominence of the roll in the wider culture (as indicated by pagan and Jewish artifacts), we need to consider whether the Christian preference for the codex may represent not only a characteristic of early Christianity but also a distinguishing mark, a convention that may have carried some semiotic significance.

84. Horsley basically echoes a proposal by Guglielmo Cavallo, *Libri, Editori e Pubblico nel mondo antico: Guida storica e critica* (Rome: Laterza, 1975), 83-86. But Roberts and Skeat showed that the remnants of ancient popular-level reading material are almost entirely from rolls, not codices (*Birth of the Codex,* esp. 68-70).

In attempting to engage the place of the codex in early Christianity, I suggest that we keep in mind two distinguishable matters. In reverse chronological order, there is first the wholesale Christian preference for the codex already exhibited in our earliest extant physical evidence, and what this preference may represent and tell us about early Christianity. Second, the strength of this preference is such that we probably have to posit some prior Christian use(s) of the codex that carried sufficient precedent-setting force to have generated what amounts to an early Christian convention in copying and book production.[85] I emphasize again that the extraordinarily early and widespread place of the codex in Christian scribal practice seems difficult to account for by some incremental process. As Gamble noted, the Christian preference for the codex is "a genuine anomaly that needs an explanation."[86] We have to look for some stimulus, probably some use(s) of the codex sufficiently early and capable of being influential upon subsequent Christian practice.[87] This approach is reasonably well accepted, but there have been several proposals as to what early use of the codex might have been capable of generating the Christian preference for this book form.[88]

Over the course of a number of years of pondering the matter, Roberts and Skeat offered three successive theories about what might have been the initially influential Christian use of the codex. Their first proposal, built in part on the assumption that the papyrus codex was a development from the parchment notebook, and in part on the hypothesis that the Gospel of Mark was the first written Gospel, was that Mark first appeared in the form of such a parchment notebook, and perhaps in Rome (taking a cue from early Christian tradition connecting Mark with Peter in Rome).[89] They fur-

---

85. By "use(s)" I allow implicitly for one or more, anticipating here the criticisms (discussed later) of any "big bang" theory of a single influential use of the codex.

86. Gamble, *Books and Readers*, 54.

87. Turner (*Typology*, 40) observed that the papyrus roll was so "firmly entrenched that a major shock was needed to prompt the experiments that resulted in its eventually being supplanted by the codex," and judged that "There must have been a powerful motive for using the codex form."

88. Roberts and Skeat (*Birth of the Codex*, 53) argued that the Christian motivation for adopting the codex so widely must have been "something overwhelmingly powerful." Although he rejected their proposals about what it was, Gamble (*Books and Readers*, 58) judged them correct that "there must have been a decisive, precedent-setting development" that led to the codex rapidly becoming the dominant book form in early Christianity.

89. See esp. Eusebius, *Hist. eccl.* 3.39.15-16. For discussion see, e.g., C. Clifton Black,

ther proposed that in this parchment-notebook form the Gospel of Mark came to Egypt, where it was copied on papyrus, and in this format became influential for Christian book practice. But, subsequently recognizing that the arguments against this proposal were "formidable," they wisely withdrew it.[90] There is no reason to think that Mark originally appeared as a parchment notebook, or that this writing had an early connection with Alexandria. Also, the manuscript evidence indicates that Matthew and John were much more widely copied and circulated, and gives us no basis for assuming that Mark had an early and influential place in Egypt.

Their second proposal involved the view that the codex and the curious scribal practice known today as the *nomina sacra* (which seems to have arisen parallel with the Christian preference for the codex) had a common origin, and that both of these conventions must have derived from some early Christian center with "sufficient authority to devise such innovations and to impose them on Christendom generally."[91] In their view, only Jerusalem and Antioch qualified, and they indicated a slight preference for the latter, but regarded Jerusalem as another option.[92] But this theory is no more persuasive than their first one. It naively assumes a scheme of ecclesiastical authority and centralization that is seriously anachronistic for the first and early second centuries CE. Also, there is no basis for their suggestion that any Jewish use of wax tablets for taking down notes of teachers of Torah led to a similar use of wax tablets to record teachings of Jesus, which then would have generated the use of the papyrus codex for biblical and other texts. Jesus' followers might have used wax tablets (but this is no more than a possibility), but this in itself scarcely would account for the Christian preference for the codex for larger "literary" texts such as Old Testament writings and those that became part of the New Testament.

Skeat later made a third proposal, that the codex was embraced by

---

Mark: *Images of an Apostolic Interpreter* (Columbia, SC: University of South Carolina Press, 1994), 82-94.

90. Roberts and Skeat, *Birth of the Codex*, 54-57. The proposal had been made by Roberts in "The Codex," *Proceedings of the British Academy* 40 (1954): 187-89 (169-204).

91. Roberts and Skeat, *Birth of the Codex*, 57-58.

92. Ibid., 58-61. Previously, Roberts had proposed Jerusalem as the point of origin of the *nomina sacra*, believing that only "the circle of the apostles or their immediate successors" had sufficient authority "to lay down the guidelines for Christian scribes" (Roberts, *Manuscript*, 44-45 n. 4, 46).

early Christians initially as a means to produce within one set of covers an edition of the four canonical Gospels.[93] Apparently accepting that previous attempts by Roberts and him to find an adequate stimulus for the Christian appropriation of the codex involved anachronisms and other serious problems, Skeat now proposed trying to identify "something which the codex would easily do, but which the roll could not, in any circumstances, do."[94] Granting that the Gospels at first circulated individually on papyrus rolls, Skeat argued that sometime early in the second century "the Church" fastened upon the idea of "the Four-Gospel codex" as a physical means of expressing that these particular Gospels had a unique "authority and prestige."[95]

It is perhaps congruent with Skeat's proposal that many of our earliest Christian codices contain Gospel texts, which evidence certainly shows that early Christians embraced the codex form with notable use for these writings. But the key problem with Skeat's theory also comes precisely from the artifactual evidence. The earliest unambiguous four-Gospel codex is $\mathfrak{P}$45 (P.Chester Beatty I), now usually dated around 250. Further, if we consider all the Gospel codices dated second or second/third century (i.e., no later than ca. 250), most of them appear to have contained only one Gospel writing: $\mathfrak{P}$52 (P.Ryl. 457; John), $\mathfrak{P}$66 (P.Bod. II; John), $\mathfrak{P}$77 (P.Oxy. 2683 + 4405; Matthew), $\mathfrak{P}$90 (P.Oxy. 3523; John), $\mathfrak{P}$103 (P.Oxy. 4403; Matthew), and $\mathfrak{P}$104 (P.Oxy. 4404; Matthew). Even if we accept Skeat's proposals that $\mathfrak{P}$75 (P.Bod. XIV-XV; portions of Luke and John) originally included Matthew and Mark as well, that $\mathfrak{P}$4 (portions of Luke) is part of the same codex of which $\mathfrak{P}$64 and $\mathfrak{P}$67 (portions of Matthew) are remnants, and that this (reconstructed) codex originally included all four canonical Gospels and should be dated to the late second century, it remains clear that the far more common second-century use of the codex for Gospel writings was to accommodate individual Gospels.[96] If the key impetus and original rationale for the Christian use of the codex was to accommodate and promote the fourfold Gospels, why is it that

93. Skeat, "The Origin of the Christian Codex," *ZPE* 102 (1994): 263-68; repr. in *Collected Biblical Writings*, ed. Elliott, 79-87, which I cite here.

94. *Collected Biblical Writings*, ed. Elliott, 79.

95. Ibid., 84-86. Interestingly, Skeat returned to the notion that the choice to use the codex suggested that the Roman church played a leading role in the matter (86).

96. Skeat, "The Oldest Manuscript of the Four Gospels?" *NTS* 43 (1997): 1-34; repr. in *Collected Biblical Writings*, ed. Elliott, 158-92.

most of the extant Gospel codices of the second century were single-Gospel manuscripts?

We have other good reasons for thinking that the four canonical Gospels were linked in some special regard among at least some influential Christian circles by the early decades of the second century.[97] But the physical evidence gives no reason for the notion that the codex was initially appropriated by Christians to accommodate all four writings between one set of covers. Instead, it seems more likely that combining four Gospels in the same codex (apparently, late in the second century) was a *result* of their having come to be regarded as a charmed circle of "Jesus books," and was not the *vehicle* adopted to accomplish this.[98]

I regard Harry Gamble's proposal as more plausible. Agreeing with Roberts and Skeat that "there must have been a decisive, precedent-setting development in the publication and circulation of early Christian literature that rapidly established the codex in Christian use," Gamble proposed that an early collection of the Pauline epistles in codex form fits the bill best.[99] As Gamble noted, Paul's letters are the earliest New Testament writings, the earliest extant Christian literary texts circulated translocally, and apparently the earliest to be collected and treated like scripture (as reflected in 2 Pet. 3:15-16, dated variously 70-110).[100] In short, Gamble contended, Paul's letters had the religious re-

---

97. E.g., Stanton, *Jesus and Gospel*, 63-91.

98. The term "Jesus books" designates Gospels as artifacts of devotion to Jesus, and the Gospels collectively (canonical and extracanonical) represent a remarkable cluster of literary efforts expressive of devotion to such a figure. See my discussion in *Lord Jesus Christ*, 259-347, 427-85.

99. Gamble, *Books and Readers*, 58-65 (quotation, 58). Gamble posited prior Christian uses of codices (more as notebooks) for collections of biblical proof texts ("testimony books," 65), but contended that these items would not have had sufficient impact to serve as the catalyst to establish the codex format as the preferred Christian book form.

100. Gamble (ibid., 271, n. 71) cites Andreas Lindemann, *Paulus im ältesten Christentum: Das Bild des Apostels und die Rezeption der paulinischen Theologie in der frühchristlichen Literatur bis Marcion* (Tübingen: Mohr, 1978); and Ernst Dassmann, *Der Stachel im Fleisch: Paulus in der frühchristlichen Literatur bis Irenaeus* (Münster: Aschendorff, 1979). To these I add Andreas Lindemann, "Der Apostel Paulus im 2. Jahrhundert," in *The New Testament in Early Christianity: La Réception des écrits Néotestamentaires dans le Christianisme primitif*, ed. Jean-Marie Sevrin, BETL 86 (Leuven: Peeters, 1989), 39-67. Unfortunately, the recent discussion by Calvin J. Roetzel shows no familiarity with these works and repeats the earlier fancy that Paul was avoided in proto-orthodox Christian circles till late in the second century: "Paul in the Second Century," in

spect and a breadth of circulation that, if copied in codex form in/by the late first century, could have established the codex as the preferred book form quickly thereafter.[101]

But Gamble's proposal has been rejected by two more recent contributors to the debate. In an informative review essay focused on Gamble's book, Eldon Epp complained about the "speculative aspects" of Gamble's proposal, and Epp argued that the relatively fewer number of codices of Pauline epistles in comparison to Gospel codices among Christian manuscripts of the second and third centuries made it unlikely that a codex edition of Pauline letters was the key influence that Gamble alleged.[102] Moreover, Epp faults all of the proposals by Roberts, Skeat, and Gamble for resting on an assumption that there had to be one particular early use of a codex that generated the Christian preference for this book form, a criticism echoed by Graham Stanton.[103] But, although both Epp and Stanton offer a good deal of stimulating analysis that is based on some commendable attention to relevant data, I am not sure that either of their own proposals is more persuasive or escapes the charge of being speculative. Moreover, although they cite each other as allies in rejecting previous theories, their own proposals seem to me to differ from each other notably, which requires us to deal with them individually.

I consider first Epp's theory. He suggests that it was not any particular *text* issued in codex form, but instead use of codex-type books by traveling Christian leaders containing writings important in their mission, "whatever those writings might have been," that was influential in making the codex favored among Christians.[104] Taking a cue from an essay by Michael McCormick, who proposed that the initial attraction of the codex was its portability in first-century Christian missions, Epp argued that such a "travelling codex" may have been "visibly displayed . . . and employed . . . in heart-stirring proclamation, in compelling paraenesis, or in urgent de-

---

The Cambridge Companion to St. Paul, ed. J. D. G. Dunn (Cambridge: Cambridge University Press, 2003), 227-41.

101. See Gamble's discussion of evidence of early collections of Paul's epistles, *Books and Readers*, 59-61.

102. Epp, "Codex and Literacy," esp. 18, 22-24.

103. Both Epp and Stanton refer to various "big bang" theories derisively: Epp, "Codex and Literacy," 21; Stanton, *Jesus and Gospel*, 167-69.

104. For example, these writings might have included collections of Jesus' sayings and/or of biblical passages used in proclamation and teaching ("testimonia").

bate" by itinerant Christian leaders. Then, in "the highly charged setting of evangelism and edification in pristine Christianity," such use of the codex had a "galvanizing" effect upon hearers/converts, and this is the key factor.[105] The codex then "quickly became a trademark of Christian teachers and preachers and was rapidly adopted as the format for writings used in the worship and life of the Christian community."[106]

But Epp's theory raises some questions that make it less than compelling.[107] For instance, although it is in principle plausible that Christian itinerant teachers and preachers *may* have taken along on their travels copies of texts such as biblical writings or collections of biblical excerpts or sayings of Jesus, how do we know *that* they did so, or that doing so was as common as Epp suggests? Further, even if traveling Christian leaders did often take along copies of certain writings, what reason is there for assuming that they were characteristically employed so prominently that they would have had the impact that Epp proposes?[108]

Also, what particular reason do we have for assuming that writings taken on their missions by Christian leaders would have been codices? Christian "testimony collections" are likely enough, but it is significant that none of the known instances of Jewish biblical excerpt texts from the first century CE or earlier (from Qumran) is a codex.[109] Stanton points to

---

105. Epp, "Codex and Literacy," 20-22; Michael McCormick, "The Birth of the Codex and the Apostolic Life-Style," *Scriptorium* 39 (1985): 150-58. McCormick's essay was occasioned by publication of Roberts and Skeat, *Birth of the Codex*.

106. Epp, "Codex and Literacy," 24.

107. In fairness to Epp, he stops short of rejecting Gamble's theory outright, urging more modestly that other explanations be considered, including his ("Codex and Literacy," 24).

108. Billy Graham famously holds a Bible in one hand as he preaches, giving it a virtually iconic association with his ministry, but did first-century Christian preachers use copies of Epp's undefined texts in such a manner? Epp does not invoke this analogy; I do so simply to register a concern that we avoid unconscious anachronism. In comments on an earlier draft of this chapter, Scott Charlesworth pointed to references to public reading of texts in early Christian circles (e.g., 1 Thess. 5:27; Col. 4:16; 1 Tim. 4:13; Rev. 1:3; 22:18) as offering credibility for Epp's proposal. But public reading of texts is not the issue. The question is whether itinerant teachers/preachers carried about and displayed publicly *codices*, which then generated a Christian preference for the codex bookform.

109. For example, 4QTestimonia (4Q175) seems to be a one-page sheet, and 4QFlorilegium (4Q174, also known as 4QMidrEschata) and other texts are portions of rolls. On the relevance of Qumran items for theories of early Christian testimony collections, see Joseph A. Fitzmyer, "'4QTestimonia' and the New Testament," *Essays on the Semitic Background of the New Testament* (Missoula, MT: Scholars Press, 1974), 59-89.

P.Ryl. 460 as an instance of a Christian testimony collection in codex form, but this fourth-century CE manuscript is hardly probative for mid-first-century CE Christian practice.[110] Given the status of the roll as a "cultural icon" in the first and second centuries CE, is it not more likely that earliest Christian leaders would more readily have had their texts in roll form, especially if they sought to use these texts visibly and with the aim of securing respect for them? Epp rightly notes that in the earliest years the possible use of codices as a prominent item in the accoutrement of Christian leaders would have been noticed as contrasting with "the expected roll."[111] But this comes close to begging the question. Were codices used in this manner? *Why* would itinerant Christian leaders have preferred the codex, which had little status in the culture, over against the roll, which had prestige value and long association with religious and literary texts? Would not such a characteristic and public use of codices by Christian leaders logically require as a prior basis the very "sentimental" and "symbolic" significance of the codex form that Epp seeks to account for by suggesting the practice?

Epp cites McCormick's essay as influential for his proposal about a connection of the codex and itinerant Christian mission, but on a couple of matters McCormick's otherwise helpful discussion seems to me somewhat more open to objection than Epp judges. McCormick offers 2 Timothy 4:13 as crucial, with its very interesting appeal by "Paul" to bring to him items left at Troas: "the cloak . . . , and also the books, especially the 'parchments.'"[112] "Parchments" translates τὰς μεμβράνας, a loanword from Latin, which is now widely thought to refer to parchment notebooks, or perhaps even parchment codices.[113] McCormick prefers the lat-

---

110. Stanton, *Jesus and Gospel*, 183-84. P.Ryl. 460 was first identified by C. H. Roberts, "Two Biblical Papyri in the John Rylands Library, Manchester," *BJRL* 20 (1936): 241-44; and restudied by Alessandro Falcetta, "A Testimony Collection in Manchester: Papyrus Rylands Greek 460," *BJRL* 83 (2002): 3-19.

111. Epp, "Codex and Literacy," 21.

112. I agree with McCormick ("Birth of the Codex," 155) in rejecting Skeat's proposal that τὰς μεμβράνας here is synonymous with τὰ βιβλία. Cf. T. C. Skeat, "'Especially the Parchments': A Note on 2 Timothy 4:13," *Collected Biblical Writings*, ed. Elliott, 262-66, originally in *JTS* 30 (1979): 173-77.

113. See, e.g., BAGD s.v. μεμβράνα; and esp. Roberts and Skeat, *Birth of the Codex*, 22. It is interesting that two Latin loanwords are used in 2 Tim. 4:13, the other one being τὸν φαιλόνην (see BAGD s.v.). I distinguish here "notebooks," used for "notes, memoranda, or rough drafts" (Skeat, "Especially the Parchments," 262) from "codices," i.e., full texts copied

ter sense of the word, and suggests that this passage shows that "the author of 2 Timothy expected his audience to identify writings in the novel format [codex] with St. Paul." But then, without further ado, McCormick claims the passage as showing that by about 100 CE Christians were associating the codex with "apostolic tradition."[114] Especially if 2 Timothy is pseudepigraphical, 4:13 may well show that *Paul* was associated with the codex (for whatever reason), but the passage is hardly a basis for thinking that the codex was associated more generally with apostolic leaders and missionaries in particular.

As an illustration of the alleged impact of early Christian missionaries' use of books that they supposedly carried with them, McCormick cites Acts 17:2, where Paul is pictured as arguing the truth of the gospel from the scriptures. But the passage is set in a synagogue, where readers might expect that a copy of at least some biblical writings was at hand. Neither this passage nor any other that I know of in early Christian writings refers to Paul or any other missionizing leader using "books he had lugged with him."[115] Indeed, one might even take 2 Timothy 4:13 as indicating quite the opposite. Why would "Paul" ask for his books to be brought to him if he were known to lug them about with him?

On the other hand, McCormick is right to suggest that the relatively modest page size of many Christian codices of the second and third centuries may be significant. But does it so readily signify that the early Christian codex was literally shaped by an initial, influential usage of modest-sized codices in itinerant missionizing? In his important analysis of codex sizes and dimensions, Turner offers no support for this explanation, observing only that from one period to another scribes generally seem to reflect particular preferences.[116] We simply do not know why. We might take the sizes of earliest Christian codices as indicating an original association of the format with Christian missionizing if there were corroborative evidence, and that is precisely what we lack. It is also possible that the goodly percentage of early "modest"-sized codices containing Old Testament or New Testament writings may reflect a significant demand by Christians for

---

in codex format. There may well be a historical connection of the two types of items, but there is also a significant distinction between use of a simple codex device for informal note taking and more ambitious use of a codex for a copy of a full literary text.

114. McCormick, "Birth of the Codex," 155.

115. Ibid., 157.

116. Turner, *Typology,* 25. See his table of papyrus codices grouped by dimensions, 14-22.

copies for personal usage, the sizes of many codices intended to make then handy for such reading.[117] In the final chapter of this book, I discuss further the importance of the sizes of codices.

I turn now to Stanton's proposal. Although he approvingly cites Epp's emphasis on the putative impact of the use of the codex by respected Christian missionaries and teachers, Stanton denies that any one factor caused a shift toward the codex. Instead, he proposes that from the earliest years "the followers of Jesus would almost certainly have made use of more than one kind of notebook" (e.g., wax tablets, wooden leaf tablets, papyrus or parchment notebooks) for varied purposes (e.g., sayings of Jesus, testimony collections). Then, these early uses may have prompted "more substantial notebooks, i.e., codices, for their more permanent writings." So there was no big move from roll to codex. Instead, Stanton urges "a gradual evolution from 'notebook' to 'codex'" as much more likely, and he sees this theory as "simple and elegant," and "more plausible than any of the alternatives."[118]

Stanton's discussion is richly informative on such things as the use of various types of "notebook" devices in the early Roman era.[119] But his theory as to why and how the codex became so prominent among Christians is less free of problems than he claims. The assumption that from the earliest years Jesus' followers used one or more "notebook" devices is entirely plausible, largely because they were so much a part of ordinary life generally in that time. This, however, actually makes it more difficult to explain why a supposed transition from these notebook devices to more ambitious use of codices took place so rapidly among Christians, but not among the larger population.

Moreover, Stanton notes that the speed of the putative transition is "astonishing," and he even proposes that "use of the codex in the middle of

117. This might also be reflected in the simplicity of the scribal hands of many or even most early Christian biblical manuscripts. That is, they may be codices prepared for Christians, including those of modest financial means, who wanted their own copies of texts. More elegant copies (hence more expensive to produce) might have been preferred for use in corporate worship, and more affordable if paid for by a group. But as a single such copy served the liturgical needs of a circle of Christians, there would have been fewer copies made, and hence fewer remnants of these in what survives.

118. Stanton, *Jesus and Gospel,* 181. A somewhat similar view is advanced (more briefly) by H. Gregory Snyder, *Teachers and Texts in the Ancient World* (London: Routledge, 2000), 212-14.

119. The section of his discussion entitled "Predecessors of the Codex" (173-78) is particularly useful, including an informative reference to the Vindolanda leaf tablets.

the first century is perfectly possible."[120] He claims that "once Christian scribes discovered how useful the 'page' format was, it very quickly became the norm for copies of Paul's letters and of the gospels, and for Christian copies of scripture."[121] But what precisely were the putative advantages of the "page format," and why were Christians the only groups of the time to perceive them and to embrace the codex so readily?

The only explanation he gives is that Christians were "minority, partly counter-cultural groups with limited literary pretensions," and so the codex was not so much "a major shift in mind-set" for them.[122] This "generally counter-cultural stance" made them readier to "experiment with the unfashionable codex."[123] But as already noted, even "popular" levels of literature were overwhelmingly copied in roll format, which means that ascribing "limited literary pretensions" to early Christians does not explain their fascination with the codex. As to early Christianity being "counter-cultural," which was expressed particularly, of course, in refusing to worship the gods and in sexual ethics, it seems to have been entirely deliberate and invested with great significance. So, if the Christian use of the codex represents another differentiation from the larger culture, this means that it is less a "gradual evolution" and something more invested with semiotic significance.

To sum up at this point, it is not clear that either Epp or Stanton has succeeded in producing a fully satisfactory explanation for early Christian use of the codex. With due appreciation for attributes of simplicity and elegance, an adequate theory must also account for all the relevant phenomena. Certainly, the early Christian appropriation of the codex is notable and requires some explanation. But we may be better placed to deal with this matter if we keep before us the full picture of early Christian book practices, and that means, once again, that we must take account of all identifiable Christian texts, not only their biblical writings.

Most early Christian manuscripts by far are codices, but certainly not all. Early Christians overwhelmingly preferred the codex for copies of their scriptures and those writings that were acquiring usage as scriptures, and

---

120. Ibid., 190. He suggests that the Gospel of Mark may have been released in codex form, and that, even if the autograph of the Gospel of Luke was a roll, by the time copies were made "Christian addiction" for the codex was already in effect. It is not clear how something of "astonishing" speed can also be described as a "gradual evolution."

121. Ibid., 189.

122. Ibid., 181.

123. Ibid., 171-72.

early Christian use of the codex also extended beyond biblical texts. But, as noted earlier, about one-third of the copies of other Christian texts of the second and third centuries CE are rolls. Christians clearly retained a significant level of use of the book roll, a format that they continued to regard as appropriate for copies of *some* texts. In short, the evidence indicates something a bit more complex than a general Christian "addiction" for the codex. So what we require is a theory adequate to the full picture of early Christian copying preferences and practices.

Indeed, we need to address several questions. Why did Christians use the codex so heavily and so early? Why did they prefer the codex so strongly for copies of biblical texts in particular? What are we to make of the continued use of the roll as well, which constitutes a significant minority of Christian manuscripts, especially those containing nonbiblical Christian texts? Does the particularly strong early Christian preference for the codex format for biblical texts reflect a desire to differentiate copies of Christian scriptures from other texts of somewhat equivalent significance in other religious groups? It is certainly the case that contemporary religious texts of pagan or Jewish usage were characteristically rolls, especially Jewish copies of scripture and pagan texts with any cultic usage. Whatever the Christian intention(s) in the firm preference of the codex for their scriptures, it is very plausible that such a differentiation would have been an effect.

Although one should probably not exclude altogether such factors, it still seems to me that alleged practical advantages of the codex, some supposedly greater readiness by early Christians to experiment with different forms of books, and a familiarity with various notebook devices do not suffice. Epp's emphasis on the possible emotional impact of inspiring Christian leaders using codices as part of their traveling kit brings questions of its own, as I have noted. But at least it reflects a recognition that one or more rather powerful stimuli must have been responsible for the strong place of the codex in early Christianity.

It is not my primary purpose here to argue for a particular answer to the questions involved. I will admit, however, that I still find cogent Gamble's suggestion that an early edition of Paul's epistles in codex form could have provided the influential precedent that helped generate a subsequent appropriation of the codex by early Christians. The early high regard for Pauline epistles reflected in 2 Peter 3:15-16 could explain why, in particular, Christians so strongly regarded the codex as preferable for the texts that they used as scripture.

In any case, my main emphasis in this discussion is that the early Christian use of the codex is an important matter worthy of attention by all scholars concerned with Christian origins. From the second and third centuries, we not only have fascinating early Christian texts, we also have remnants of the physical forms in which these texts were copied, transmitted, and used in Christian circles. Given the significant place that texts occupied in early Christianity, it is surely important to take note of the physical forms of these texts, which may give us further clues about how the texts were regarded and actually used. We should, however, be wary of simplistic conclusions. For example, in light of the clear Christian preference for the codex generally, it would be unsound to assume that if a text was copied in a codex this signals that the text was used as scripture. On the other hand, given this general Christian preference for the codex, particularly for scriptures, plus a noteworthy readiness to use the roll for a variety of other Christian texts, it is reasonable to judge that the use of a roll to copy a text signals that the copyist and/or user for whom the copy was made did not regard that text (or at least that copy of that text) as having scriptural status.

I offer by way of illustration a very brief case study involving the remnants of the three copies of the collection of Jesus' sayings that we now call the *Gospel of Thomas*.[124] Surprisingly, in the large body of scholarly literature on these fragments, there is not much discussion about the possible import of the physical forms in which the texts in question were copied.[125] We begin with P.Oxy. 654, a portion of text written on the verso of a roll originally used for a land register (plate 8, appendix 2). This both allows us to date the text later than the land register (i.e., mid-third century CE) and also indicates that, as usual with reused rolls, this copy was probably prepared for personal study of the text. The horizontal paragraph signs in this manuscript after each of

124. These are P.Oxy. 1, P.Oxy. 654, and P.Oxy. 655, originally published by Bernard P. Grenfell and Arthur S. Hunt, *The Oxyrhynchus Papyri. Part 1* (London: Egypt Exploration Fund, 1898); and idem, *The Oxyrhynchus Papyri, Part IV* (London: Egypt Exploration Fund, 1904). The scholarly literature on these items is vast, and need not all be cited here. For a detailed analysis see Joseph A. Fitzmyer, "The Oxyrhynchus Logoi of Jesus and the Coptic Gospel according to Thomas," *Essays on the Semitic Background*, 355-433. Also essential is the more recent contribution by Harold W. Attridge, "Appendix: The Greek Fragments," in *Nag Hammadi Codex II, 2-7, together with XIII, 2*, Brit.Lib.Or. 4926(1), and P.Oxy. 1, 654, 655*, vol. 1: *Gospel According to Thomas, Gospel according to Philip, Hypostasis of the Archons, and Indexes*, ed. Bentley Layton, NHS 20 (Leiden: Brill, 1989), 95-128.

125. Even the recent discussion of these fragments by Lührmann (*Apokryph gewordenen Evangelien*, 144-81) includes no consideration of the possible import of their physical forms.

the preserved sayings are consistent with such usage (somewhat similar to how a reader might underline or otherwise mark up a personal copy of a text today). As true of any opisthographic text, it is not possible to tell whether the text of P.Oxy. 654 was held as scripture, only that someone wanted his/her own copy for perusal. The particular importance of P.Oxy. 654 is that its first lines preserve the opening of the text, where it is designated as "words . . . [which] the living Jesus spoke," and where Thomas is named.[126]

P.Oxy. 1 is a single leaf from a papyrus codex, paleographically dated to the early third century CE. The page number on the verso side of the leaf (Ｉ Δ) tells us that ten pages preceded it, and we are also able to judge that this was probably a single-gathering codex.[127] Grenfell and Hunt's proposal that the original full leaf was much taller than the 14.5 × 9.5 cm. fragment has been widely accepted, but we cannot be sure how much more of the original leaf there was.[128] Accepting that the original page held about thirty-eight lines, however, Fitzmyer has noted that some other text probably preceded this sayings collection in the codex.[129] With its codex form, wide margins, and "informal literary hand," P.Oxy. 1 is visually very similar to most of the Christian biblical manuscripts from the second and third centuries. Certainly nothing about the manuscript forbids us to wonder what status the text may have enjoyed, even whether it may have been used as scripture. Yet we should also recall the generally wide use of the codex in early Christian circles for a variety of texts, which means that, by itself, the codex format of P.Oxy. 1 does not necessarily indicate the status of the text(s) that it contains.[130]

126. The damaged lines are usually now restored to make a "Judas who is also Thomas" the one who wrote the sayings. It is, however, curious that the Greek word for "Thomas" here lacks the normal final *sigma* of the Greek form of the name.

127. In the following section of this chapter, I discuss different types of codex construction. In the first half of a single-gathering codex (the papyrus sheets typically first stacked with their recto sides facing up, the sheets then folded), the text is copied first on the verso side of a leaf and then on the recto. In the latter half of the codex, it is the reverse. Thus, as the verso side of P.Oxy. 1 is page 11 of the codex, it is probable that page 1 was likewise the verso side of the bottom sheet in the stack.

128. Note, e.g., that Turner simply gives "?" for the page size and the size of the written area on the page (*Typology*, 143).

129. Fitzmyer, "Oxyrhynchus Logoi," 355-56 n. 2. This also assumes that we can guess basically the extent of the rest of the text of P.Oxy. 1 on the basis of the Coptic *Gospel of Thomas* from Nag Hammadi.

130. The recto side (i.e., horizontal fibers) has a 3-cm.-wide patch of vertical fibers running the full page length on the left-hand margin. In a direct examination of P.Oxy. 1, I was

P.Oxy. 655 comprises several fragments of a roll, whose estimated height was about 16 cm. The hand is dated to 200-250 CE, and is a "well-written specimen" of a slightly right-sloping, small majuscule type.[131] In short, this particular copy of the text seems to have been prepared with some care. The format chosen for this copy, however, likens it to a number of other Christian texts of this period, such as theological treatises and other texts read/studied for edification and instruction (see appendix 1). The choice to use a roll for this text suggests strongly that it (or at least this copy) was not prepared for use as a scripture, but perhaps more as a text for edifying reading or study.

On the basis of this brief case study of the remnants of three Oxyrhynchus copies of what appears to be basically the text that we call the *Gospel of Thomas,* we can say that there are strong reasons to hesitate to ascribe the text a scripture-like status, at least among those Christians whose usage is reflected in these artifacts. But whether or not one is persuaded by these results, I hope to have shown that the physical forms in which texts were copied comprise important data that must be considered as part of engaging the question.

The Production of Codices

Before I conclude this chapter, it is important to give further attention to the ways in which the early Christian codices were constructed.[132] This is not only something of antiquarian interest, and the issues involved go beyond historical questions about Christian use of the codex format. I con-

---

able to verify that the lines of text in the hand of the original scribe commence *on* the patch and continue onto the horizontal fibers of the rest of the page. After conversation about this with Dr. Nick Gonis (Sackler Library, Oxford, a papyrologist/paleographer working on the Oxyrhynchus material), I infer that the repair was made to the papyrus writing material *before* the copyist did his/her work, i.e., the damage to the leaf must have happened during the manufacturing process or in cutting the sheet for use in the codex, and did not arise from frequent use of the codex after it was copied. This means that the strip was not added as a result of the outer edge of the page being worn through usage, contrary to the suggestion by Bernard P. Grenfell and Arthur S. Hunt, *ΛΟΓΙΑ ΙΗΣΟΥ: Sayings of Our Lord from an Early Greek Papyrus* (London: Egypt Exploration Fund, 1897), 7. I thank the Bodleian Library for access to P.Oxy. 1, and Dr. Gonis for access to other Oxyrhynchus material now held at the Sackler Library.

131. The phrase is from Grenfell and Hunt, *Oxyrhynchus Papyri, Vol. IV,* 22-23. (See plate 9, appendix 2, for a photo.)

132. The best discussion is in Turner, *Typology,* 55-71, which I draw upon here.

tend that the subject also throws further light on wider historical issues pertaining to early Christianity.

In principle, a codex can be made up of a single sheet, but more characteristically it has multiple sheets of writing material, each sheet folded in half once to form two leaves (a "bifolium"), or four pages. A "single-gathering" (sometimes also called a "single-quire") codex is constructed of a single stack of folded sheets of writing material.[133] A codex could also be constructed by attaching two or more "gatherings" of folded sheets, each gathering composed of one or more sheets. By the late Byzantine period, it was becoming conventional for each gathering typically to comprise four sheets, or eight leaves/sixteen pages, and from the Latin word *quaternio* (designating a set of four) came our word "quire."[134] All the leaves of a single-gathering codex were attached to one another by thread run through holes made in the fold of the sheets. In multiple-gathering codices, each gathering (quire) is stitched together as above, and next a thread is stitched through all the gatherings horizontally to hold them all together, forming the spine of the codex. Then, whether a single- or multiple-gathering codex, a cover was attached. This basic procedure is still followed today in the construction of high-quality books.

As nearly all the earliest Christian codices are made of papyrus, it is also important to note some basics about this material.[135] To manufacture papyrus for writing, one layer of strips cut from the papyrus stalk was laid on top of another, the fibers of one layer running perpendicular to the fibers of the other. When the two layers were pressed together, the juices of the papyrus formed a natural adhesive, and, when dried, the overlaid strips formed a sheet that could be used for writing. So, on one side of the finished writing material the fibers ran vertically, and on the other side horizontally. Papyrologists often refer to the side with horizontal fibers as the "recto" and the other side as the "verso."[136] The size of manufactured

---

133. According to Turner (*Typology*, 58), "no example of a single-quire codex of parchment has yet been identified." This is one reason for Turner's view that the papyrus codex did not simply evolve from the parchment codex.

134. Modern-day books are still constructed of "quires" of folded sheets.

135. Again, I refer to Turner, *Typology*, 43-54, for more detailed discussion.

136. In studies and editions of papyri today, one often sees the following signs: → for the recto, and ↓ for the verso. Typically, in a scroll only the recto side of the papyrus (horizontal fibers) was used for writing, which was the inner surface when the text was rolled up for storage or carrying. The scroll written on both sides in Rev. 5:1 is unusual, the description

sheets depended on the length of the papyrus stalks used, or perhaps the preferences of the manufacturer. Sheets of the same size were then glued together end on end (the fibers of the recto side running continuously) to form a large roll of the manufactured material, from which lengths were cut and sold for use in writing and copying. For a small text, a modest-length piece would do; it could either be rolled to form a small scroll or folded to form a single-sheet codex.

For a larger text, one would have to estimate the amount of writing material needed, and purchase the required length to be cut from a seller's stock, similar to the way one estimates the amount of fabric needed for making an item of apparel, the required length of fabric then cut from a seller's stock roll. The purchased length of papyrus was then cut into sheets by the copyist, and folded as indicated previously to construct either a single-gathering or a multiple-gathering codex. It appears that at least in some cases the scribe wrote/copied the text on the individual folded sheets, thereafter joining them together to form the codex.[137]

This required some planning. For example, in preparing a single-gathering codex (e.g., P.Chester Beatty II, 𝔓46), the text began on the left-hand leaf of the outermost folded sheet in the gathering, and ended on the right-hand leaf of the same sheet. So one began writing/copying on the left-hand leaf (or half) of this sheet, but then immediately continued the text on both sides of the left-hand leaf of another folded sheet, and so on until the left-hand leaves of all the sheets were used. Then one continued copying on both sides of the right-hand leaves, beginning with the most recently used sheet, and continuing successively on the right-hand leaves of the remaining sheets in the reverse order in which their left-hand leaves were used. If the calculation of the number of sheets needed was correct, the end of the text was reached by/before the bottom of the final page, which would be on the right-hand leaf of the same sheet on which the copying was begun.

In the case of a codex formed of two or more gatherings, the process was a bit different. P.Chester Beatty I (𝔓45) was constructed entirely of single folded sheets sewn one to another to form a codex of some 224 pages (56 folded sheets). In such a construction, the scribe wrote in succession on both

---

probably influenced by Ezek. 2:8-10. For a recent discussion of this passage see G. K. Beale, *The Book of Revelation*, NIGTC (Grand Rapids: Eerdmans, 1999), 339-47.

137. As noted earlier, the page numbers sometimes found on codex leaves are now thought to have functioned to identify the order of the folded sheets for final assembly as a codex.

sides of the two leaves of each folded sheet until the end of the text was reached. One advantage of this type of codex was that if the initial estimate of the amount of papyrus needed was wrong, the scribe could either add additional folded sheets readily, or omit any not needed, to complete the text. Curiously, it appears that this type of construction and the single-gathering type compete with each other to be judged the earliest form of the codex.[138]

In other cases codices were made up of gatherings that could comprise three, four, or more folded sheets, and sometimes gatherings of varying numbers of sheets in the same codex.[139] In using gatherings of multiple sheets, the copyist had to commence using the leaves of one gathering in proper sequence, and then the leaves of another gathering, continuing on until the text was completely copied.

It is also important to note that codices were of different sizes in breadth and height of the pages. We have remarked already that many early Christian manuscripts are of what some have described as a "modest" page size. But we should remember that the height of the codex page was probably determined by the size of the writing material available (i.e., from the seller of the rolled-up papyrus material), and that this seems to have depended on such things as fashion and even the size of the papyrus stalks used in the manufacturing process. The early Christian codices are within the spectrum of commonly used page sizes of their time. Early Christians may exhibit a certain appreciation for books sized to make them handy to use. But we would need much more analysis of all the evidence of early codex sizes to make any more definitive conclusions. In the final chapter, I discuss the matter more fully.

I have not gone into these specifics merely to entertain readers with quaint curiosities. My point, again, is that these matters are relevant for wider issues. To cite one, the use of the codex was not as easy and simple as we might at first assume. As noted earlier, it required forethought and a particular set of skills in addition to the regular ability to copy a text. Earliest Christian codices exhibit the differences in construction that I have sketched here. Indeed, the differences in construction of codices are such that the specific copying work involved varied significantly, much more than references to Christian use of the codex might suggest.

To cite another matter for which the specifics of roll and codex construction can have implications, let us consider briefly suggestions that

138. So Turner, *Typology*, 60.
139. Turner (ibid., 58-64) lists actual codices of various constructions.

some part of a given text may have been lost in the process of its copying and transmission. I contend that any such proposal should indicate specifically the book form involved in the putative damage to the text, and should demonstrate the particular possibilities of the specific type of damage more likely with that book form.

By way of illustration, let us consider the frequent suggestion that the ending of Mark reflects loss of some other material here. With a book roll, the loss of the final portion of a text is less likely than damage to the initial part of the text, as the end of the text is most protected by the rest of the book roll when it is rolled up. On the other hand, with a single-gathering codex (very common among earliest Christian manuscripts), the end of a text would be on the final leaf, which forms one half of the outermost sheet, whose exposure might make it more subject to damage or loss. But in a single-gathering codex, loss of either the initial or the final leaf makes it much more likely that the other one will be lost too. So one would need either to suggest how the final leaf was lost but not the first one, or consider whether *both* ending *and* beginning of the text may have suffered damage.

Christian codices made up of multiple-sheet gatherings (such as $\mathfrak{P}45$) are equally early, however, and pose still other possibilities for text damage. In these the most exposed parts, which are the initial or final two leaves, form one sheet, attached to the rest of the codex by thread. So it is more likely that the entire sheet would be lost rather than a single page, and this would comprise a much more substantial body of text at the opening *or* closing of the writing.

Also, on any codex the outer edge of a page was subject to greater damage through usage and handling. Damage to the outer margin of codex leaves could extend to the loss of parts of lines of text (the final part of lines on one side of a leaf, the initial part of lines on the other). The potential for such damage may be one reason why the margins of many papyrus codices are so wide.

Moreover, the differences between papyrus and parchment/leather make certain kinds of damage and loss more likely for one material than the other. For instance, the joins where sheets of papyrus are connected in the manufacturing process provide the particular possibility of damage by the writing material separating at these points.[140] In principle, this could

---

140. Papyrologists call the join where two sheets of papyrus were gummed together a

happen in a papyrus roll or codex, but it may be that the way pages of a codex were handled could have made this kind of damage more likely. If there was a join in the writing material where a column of text was to be copied, the scribe simply wrote across the join. This means that a break at the join would have involved the loss of *parts of all lines of text on two successive pages of a codex,* a very different type of text damage in comparison to the loss of a whole leaf or double leaf.[141]

To repeat for emphasis, in order to be granted plausibility, a proposal about the putative loss of some portion of a text should include an indication of a particular book form and should show its specific potential for the kind of damage/loss proposed.

I want to add a couple of further observations. First, although serious Christian use of the codex had probably begun at least several decades earlier, the different forms of Christian codices evident in those dated in the second and third centuries indicate that Christians were still experimenting with different ways of producing them. The main aim in this experimentation was probably to find the best way(s) to construct codices of sufficient size to accommodate progressively larger bodies of texts. More specifically, by the end of the second century (and perhaps earlier) Christians were seeking to place in one codex *multiple* texts, especially texts that they wished to link in some common regard and usage as scripture. The key examples of this noted earlier are the linking of Gospels exhibited in 𝔓45, and 𝔓75, and perhaps also in 𝔓4 + 𝔓64 + 𝔓67, and the linking of Pauline epistles in 𝔓46. That is, the second- and third-century manuscripts show that early Christian "codex technology" was driven particularly by the regard for writings that came to form the heart of the New Testament canon.

Second, I also contend that the different forms of codex construction evident in Christian manuscripts of this period confirm that the level of serious use of the codex format among early Christians was just as unprecedented as the artifact record indicates. Had there been some well-developed use of the codex format, whether in Jewish scribal tradition or

---

kollēsis (κόλλησις), and the sheet of papyrus a *kollēma* (κόλλημα). These sheets tended to be about 20 cm. or less in width, but could be as wide as 34 cm. or so. See Turner, *Typology,* 51.

141. Turner (ibid.) suggested that one reason why early papyrus codices tended to have a narrow width in comparison to their height may be that scribes sought to avoid having a join, or at least more than one join, running down the sheets of the codex. Parchment codices tended to be squarer in dimensions.

in the general book culture of the time, it is difficult to imagine why Christians were still struggling to develop more effective ways of constructing codices that would be able to bear the weight of increasingly large bodies of text.

In the following chapters, I introduce other important features of early Christian manuscripts. I hope that this lengthy chapter has succeeded in showing that the physical forms used for Christian texts, and especially the codex form, are themselves important data for the study of early Christianity.

Chart 1: Total Manuscripts by Religion

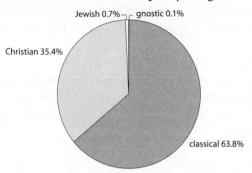

Chart 2: Total Rolls by Religion

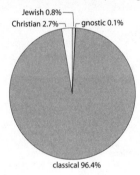

Chart 3: Total Codices by Religion

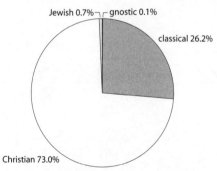

Chart 4: Second-Century Manuscripts by Religion

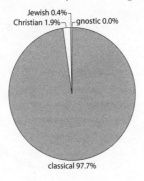

Chart 5: Third-Century Manuscripts by Religion

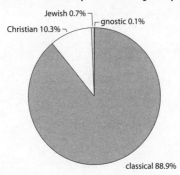

Chart 6: Fourth-Century Manuscripts by Religion

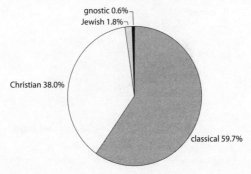

Chart 7: Book Forms, First Century CE

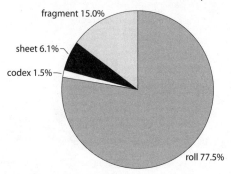

fragment 15.0%

sheet 6.1%

codex 1.5%

roll 77.5%

Chart 8: Book Forms, Second Century CE

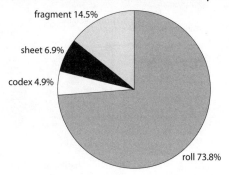

fragment 14.5%

sheet 6.9%

codex 4.9%

roll 73.8%

Chart 9: Book Forms, Third Century CE

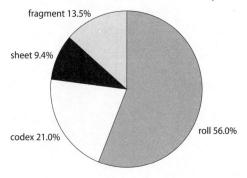

fragment 13.5%

sheet 9.4%

codex 21.0%

roll 56.0%

Chart 10: Book Forms, Fouth Century CE

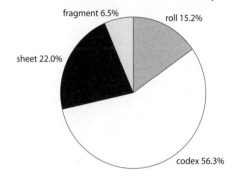

Bar Graph 1: Rolls and Codices by Century

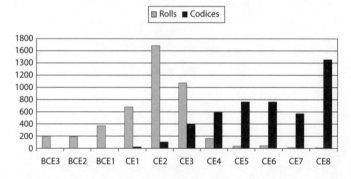

Bar Graph 2: Manuscript Totals by Century

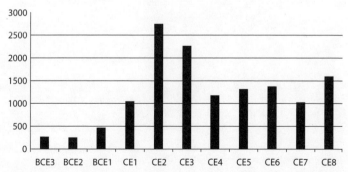

CHAPTER THREE

The *Nomina Sacra*

In addition to the codex format, the other strongly characteristic feature of early Christian Greek manuscripts that has received considerable notice, especially in recent years, is the interesting way that certain words are written in special abbreviated forms (see the list at the end of this chapter).[1] Since the pioneering study by Ludwig Traube, scholars have referred to these curious abbreviations by the Latin term *nomina sacra* ("sacred names").[2] Typically, these abbreviations comprise the first and final letter of the words, and in some cases one or more medial letters as well.[3] This is referred to as abbreviation by "contraction." As we will note shortly, however, in some early manuscripts the name of Jesus is abbreviated by "sus-

---

1. In this chapter I draw upon my earlier study, "The Origin of the *Nomina Sacra*: A Proposal," *JBL* 117 (1998): 655-73, which includes a rather full citation of relevant scholarly literature to that point. The most stimulating discussion remains that of Roberts, *Manuscript*, 26-48. For a brief introduction to the *nomina sacra*, see Bruce M. Metzger, *Manuscripts of the Greek Bible: An Introduction to Palaeography* (New York: Oxford University Press, 1981), 36-37.

2. Ludwig Traube, *Nomina Sacra: Versuch einer Geschichte der christlichen Kürzung* (1907; repr. Darmstadt: Wissenschaftliche Buchgesellschaft, 1967). Traube gave a listing of *nomina sacra* forms and the manuscripts in which they appear, but he did his work well before the great body of early Christian papyri had been published. A. H. R. E. Paap produced a valuable study updating Traube's data, *Nomina Sacra in the Greek Papyri of the First Five Centuries A.D.: The Sources and Some Deductions*, Papyrologica Lugduno-Batava 8 (Leiden: Brill, 1959). Further updates include José O'Callaghan, *"Nomina Sacra" in Papyris Graecis Saeculi III Neotestamentariis*, Analecta biblica 46 (Rome: Biblical Institute Press, 1970).

3. The final letter in the abbreviation may vary, depending on the ending of the inflected form of the word, e.g., ΘΥ = Θεου (genitive form of Θεος).

pension," this particular *nomina sacra* form comprised of the first two letters, I H. Also, however they are abbreviated, with very few exceptions there
is a horizontal stroke written just above the *nomina sacra* forms of all the
words in question.

The *nomina sacra* are so familiar a feature of Christian manuscripts
that papyrologists often take the presence of these forms as sufficient to
identify even a fragment of a manuscript as indicating its probable Christian provenance. *Nomina sacra* forms are also often found later on Christian icons, and sometimes on other Christian objects, but our focus here is
on their earliest known usage, which is in Christian manuscripts. Likewise,
although the scribal practice was also taken up in early Christian manuscripts in Latin, Coptic, and some other languages, it is rather clear that it
began in Greek, and so we shall confine our attention here to this linguistic
expression of it.[4]

As the case with the early Christian preference for the codex, the two
main questions about the *nomina sacra* are what might be the origins of
this scribal practice, and how we should understand its function or significance. All scholars acquainted with the data agree that the questions are
important, but there remain competing proposals as to the answers. In
this chapter my main aims are to familiarize readers with the scribal practice, to evaluate the various scholarly proposals, and, most crucially, to
underscore the importance of the *nomina sacra* for the study of Christian
origins.

The Scribal Practice

I begin by noting that in the earliest observable stage of this Christian scribal practice, four words in particular are written as *nomina sacra* with far

---

4. For example, Jesus' name is treated in *nomina sacra* fashion in the Coptic text of the
Gospel of Thomas from Nag Hammadi. David C. Parker compared *nomina sacra* forms in the
Greek and Latin columns of Codex Bezae (*Codex Bezae: An Early Christian Manuscript and
Its Text* [Cambridge: Cambridge University Press, 1992], 97-106). Paap briefly notes the
nomina sacra forms found in Christian Latin, Coptic, Gothic, and Armenian translations of
biblical writings (*Nomina Sacra*, 120). For a still-valuable study of Latin evidence, see C. H.
Turner, "The *Nomina Sacra* in Early Latin Christian MSS," in *Miscellanea Francesco Ehrle,
Scritti di Storia e Paleografia*, vol. 4: *Paleografia e Diplomatica* (Rome: Biblioteca Apostolica
Vaticana, 1924), 62-74.

greater regularity.[5] I cite these with their more typical *nomina sacra* forms in parentheses: ΘΕΟC (ΘC, ΘY, etc.), ΚYΡΙOC (ΚC, ΚY, etc.), ΧΡΙCΤOC (ΧC, ΧY, etc., sometimes ΧΡC), and ΙΗCOYC (ΙC, ΙY, etc., or ΙΗC, etc., sometimes ΙΗ). As Schuyler Brown pointed out, these four nouns are "not simply *nomina sacra* but rather *nomina divina*."[6] That is, these terms are all key, direct designations of God and Jesus (also typically regarded by early Christians as bearing divine significance),[7] an important matter to which I return a bit later. By the late second century, however, some copyists were extending the practice to additional words in the early Christian vocabulary as well. For instance, in P.Egerton 2 (the so-called Egerton Gospel fragment), in addition to ΚC (ΚYΡΙOC), ΘC (ΘΕOC, plus one probable instance of ΘY = ΘΕOY), and ΙΗ (ΙΗCOYC), we find ΠΡΑ (ΠΑΤΕΡΑ), ΜΩ (ΜΩYCΗC),[8] ΗCΑC (ΗCΑΙΑC), ΠΡΟΦΑC (ΠΡΟΦΗΤΑC), and ΕΠΡΟΦCΕΝ (ΕΠΡΟΦΗΤΕYCΕΝ).[9] By the Byzantine period, some fifteen words came to constitute those more regularly and frequently treated as *nomina sacra*. In addition to the four *nomina divina* already noted, these include YΙOC ("son," especially in references to Jesus), ΠΝΕYΜΑ ("spirit," references to the Holy Spirit), CΩΤΗΡ ("savior"), CΤΑYΡOC ("cross"),[10] ΠΑΤΗΡ ("Father," especially in references to God), ΑΝΘΡΩΠOC ("man," especially in references to Jesus, e.g., "the Son of Man"), ΜΗΤΗΡ ("mother," especially in

5. I use here unaccented majuscule Greek characters (capital letter forms, sometimes referred to as "uncial" letters, which applies more correctly to the Latin alphabet), and the "open" *sigma* characteristic of early Greek papyri.

6. Schuyler Brown, "Concerning the Origin of the *Nomina Sacra*," *SPap* 9 (1970): 19 (7-19).

7. Christopher Tuckett has questioned whether it is appropriate to call Χριστός a "divine" name/epithet, and whether Κύριος "always refers to a 'divine' figure": "'Nomina Sacra': Yes and No?" in *The Biblical Canons*, ed. J.-M. Auwers and H. J. de Jonge, BETL 98 (Leuven: Peeters, 2003), 449 n. 76 (431-58). But for at least most Christians of the second century and thereafter, when applied to Jesus, Χριστός and Κύριος obviously designated a divine figure. Κύριος could have other referents (e.g., a master of a slave), of course, but in these cases was not typically written as a *nomen sacrum*.

8. It is interesting (though I am not sure what the significance is) that in P.Egerton 2 Moses' name is abbreviated by suspension (the first two letters), similarly to the way that Jesus' name is treated.

9. For discussion of the *nomina sacra* forms in P.Egerton 2, see H. Idris Bell and T. C. Skeat, *Fragments of an Unknown Gospel and Other Early Christian Papyri* (London: Trustees of British Museum, 1935), 2-4.

10. In the next chapter I discuss the interesting use of the *tau-rhō* device as part of the abbreviation of σταυρος and σταυρoω in a few early Christian manuscripts.

references to Jesus' mother), OYPⲀNOC ("heaven"), ICPⲀHⲀ ("Israel"), IЄPOYCⲀXHM ("Jerusalem"), and ⲀⲀYЄIⲀ ("David").

It will be important later in considering what the *nomina sacra* may signify about early Christianity to note here that these forms appear not only in Christian manuscripts of biblical texts (both OT and writings that came to form the NT), but also widely in copies of other Christian literary texts, such as the *Gospel of Thomas* (e.g., P.Oxy. 1, P.Oxy. 654), *Acts of Peter* (P.Oxy. 849), and *Acts of John* (P.Oxy. 850), and even (though less frequently) in Christian "documentary" texts (e.g., letters). There are cases in what appear to be some private copies of Christian writings (e.g., some letters, prayers, magical texts) where the words are not written as *nomina sacra*, but for copies of Christian *literary* texts *nomina sacra* forms are more typical.[11] The prevalence of this scribal practice suggests another curious instance of a convention widely spread and followed among various Christian circles (the preference for the codex being the other key instance) at a remarkably early point.

Because we are dealing with a convention, we should expect occasional variations in the ways that some of these words are abbreviated in Christian manuscripts, and that some words were much more regularly treated as *nomina sacra* than others.[12] Later we will consider what we might infer from such variations, with particular attention to the variation in the way Jesus' name is handled, and also inferences from the general pattern of the words that are and are not treated as *nomina sacra*. Let us now turn, however, to various possibilities about the derivation of the scribal practice.

---

11. For example, P.Oxy. 3.407 (a third-century Christian prayer text) does not have *nomina sacra* forms. Likewise, in the cache of private documentary texts of a Christian family from Petra, the *nomina sacra* forms do not appear; see J. Frösèn, ed., *The Petra Papyri*, vol. 1, American Center of Oriental Research Publications 4 (Amman: American Center of Oriental Research, 2002).

12. Roberts drew attention to some unusual forms of *nomina sacra* (*Manuscript*, 83-84; and see also his addenda, n. 5). Also, P.Bod. VII and VIII have rare instances of Μιχαήλ, Νῶε, Σάρρα, and Ἀβραάμ with a horizontal stroke written above them, and P.Bod. XIII has a stroke above Ἀδαμ. In addition, in this manuscript we have δνιν, δυιν (abbreviated forms of δυναμιν), and Ἀβρμ (Ἀβραάμ), with the typical horizontal stroke.

Origins

We can begin by observing that abbreviations of various types and for various purposes were a familiar feature in the larger historical environment of earliest Christianity. For people in the first Christian centuries, the most frequent encounter with Greek or Latin abbreviations would probably have been on coins. Roman-era coins typically feature the particular emperor in whose reign they were stamped, along with his various honorific titles. On account of the very limited space available on a coin, these titles are given in standard abbreviations, for example, "Imp" *(Imperator),* and "Cos" *(Consul).*[13] Likewise, on Roman-era inscriptions (Latin or Greek), abbreviations are frequent for the titles of governmental figures and even for a number of other commonly used terms and expressions.[14] So there is a certain phenomenological similarity between these sorts of abbreviations of honorific titles and the *nomina sacra,* especially the four names and titles for God and Jesus, the so-called *nomina divina.*

But it is also important to note the dissimilarities. The abbreviations on coins, for example, are largely required by the need to crowd a number of honorific titles onto the very limited space available. Likewise, abbreviations on inscriptions seem often to be required by the need to accommodate a body of text onto a limited, preset amount of space. Moreover, the titles are standard protocol for referring to the figures in question. A mod-

13. Kevin Herbert, *Roman Imperial Coins: Augustus to Hadrian and Antonine Selections, 31 BC–AD 180,* John Max Wulfing Collection in Washington University 3 (Wauconda, IL: Bolchasy-Carducci, 1996). See also Larry J. Kreitzer, *Striking New Images: Studies on Roman Imperial Coinage and the New Testament World,* JSNTSup 134 (Sheffield: Sheffield Academic Press, 1996).

14. See esp. Michael Avi-Yonah, *Abbreviations in Greek Inscriptions (The Near East, 200 B.C.–A.D. 1100)* (London: Humphrey Milford, 1940; repr. in *Abbreviations in Greek Inscriptions, Paypri Manuscripts and Early Printed Books,* ed. Al. N. Oikonomides [Chicago: Ares, 1974], 1-125); and Lawrence Keppie, *Understanding Roman Inscriptions* (London: B. T. Batsford, 1991), which includes a table of common abbreviations used in Latin inscriptions (138-39), and a discussion of titles of emperors (42-51) and of other officials (52-69); P. Bureth, *Les titulatures imperiales dans les papyrus, les ostraca et les inscriptions d'Egypte* (Brussels: Fondation égyptologique reine Elisabeth, 1964). Ernst Nachmanson, "Die schriftliche Kontraktion auf den griechischen Inschriften," *Eranos* 10 (1910): 100-141, pointed to similarities, but the possibility of derivation of the *nomina sacra* practice from inscriptions has not won much support. See also Gunnar Rudberg, "Zur paläographischen Kontraktion," *Eranos* 10 (1910): 71-100; idem, *Neutestamentlicher Text und Nomina Sacra* (Uppsala: Humanistika Vetenskapssa fundet Skrifter, 1915 [1917]).

ern analogy is the standard way of attaching "HRH" before the names of high-ranking members of the British royal family. With the *nomina sacra*, however, it is usually the case that limitations of space are not a factor. As noted previously, the wide margins, generous line spacing, and usual size of the characters all indicate no concern whatsoever about conserving space or having to crowd text into a limited amount of space. Thus the *nomina sacra* are not really abbreviations, at least in the sense that they do not function to save space or writing effort. Nevertheless, it may be that the sort of abbreviations of honorific titles that feature on Roman-era coins and inscriptions made for a climate in which Christians did not find the abbreviated forms of their *nomina sacra* so strange.[15]

Another setting for frequent abbreviations is in manuscripts of what are called "documentary" texts, such as land registers, contracts, and a variety of other purely utilitarian writings.[16] There is a variety of such devices in these sorts of texts, but when one looks at specifics it is difficult to posit documentary practice as the origins of the Christian *nomina sacra*. For instance, as Blanchard noted, in documentary texts the abbreviation practices do not feature use of contractions; and, except in the representation of numbers by alphabetic characters, we do not find the horizontal stroke over the abbreviations, which is characteristic in Christian *nomina sacra*.[17] More importantly still, the most regularized use of the *nomina sacra* is in copies of Christian biblical texts, which, as already noted, are hardly to be compared to documentary texts.

In Greek literary texts, on the other hand, abbreviations are rare, particularly in manuscripts prior to the third century CE, except for copies rather clearly made for personal study.[18] There is certainly no observable system of abbreviation. There are occasional contractions and, a bit more

15. But abbreviation by contraction, the dominant practice with the *nomina sacra*, is different from the usual technique of abbreviation on Roman coins and inscriptions, which involved "suspension" (using the first, or first few, letters of the word).

16. Alain Blanchard, *Sigles et abbréviations dans les papyrus documentaires grecs: Recherches de paléographie*, BICSSup 30 (London: Institute of Classical Studies, 1974).

17. Ibid., 2 (on contractions), and 3 and 21 (on the horizontal stroke). Later in this chapter I return to the use of the horizontal stroke over alphabetic characters that serve as numbers.

18. See esp. Kathleen McNamee, *Abbreviations in Greek Literary Papyri and Ostraca*, Bulletin of the American Society of Papyrologists Sup 3 (Chico, CA: Scholars Press, 1981). She gives an appendix of what occasional abbreviation forms that we do find (118-19). She notes the "exceptional" instances of abbreviations by contraction (xiii).

frequently, the omission of the final character or two from a readily recognizable word that ends a line. In these cases a horizontal stroke is often written above the last character in the word, extending slightly out into the right margin to signal to readers that one or more characters have been omitted.

The differences from the *nomina sacra* are obvious. The latter forms are found regardless of where the words in question appear in the line of text. Even in the mechanics there are differences. With the *nomina sacra* the horizontal stroke is usually placed directly over the shortened form, not attached to the final letter. Paleographers generally view the placement of this horizontal stroke as a curious and distinctive feature of the *nomina sacra*. A bit later in this chapter, I explore the possible derivation of this mark. More generally, the Christian practice is much more conventionalized, whereas in classical literary texts abbreviations are far less frequent, are more varied in technique, and seem to reflect the practices and preferences of individual scribes. Most significantly, however, the words that are treated as *nomina sacra* with greatest regularity are not the sort that are occasionally abbreviated in literary texts, such as καὶ ("and"), but instead comprise central terms in the religious vocabulary of Christian faith.

In short, although it is likely that the mechanics of the Christian *nomina sacra* practice (e.g., suspension and contraction) were adapted from pre/non-Christian techniques of abbreviation, the pervasiveness of the Christian convention is remarkable, and its likely function seems distinctive.

A Jewish Origin?

This last observation points to another possibility suggested by a number of scholars, that the Christian *nomina sacra* may owe something to Jewish scribal practice, particularly the scribal treatment of the Tetragrammaton. A variety of evidence indicates that, by the first century CE, at least many devout Jews exhibited a concern about oral and written treatment of the divine name. For instance, the LXX translation of Leviticus 24:16 invokes punishment upon the pronunciation of God's name (ἐν τῷ ὀνομάσαι αὐτὸν τὸ ὄνομα κυρίου τελευτάτω; whereas the Masoretic text forbids "blaspheming" [בקנ] the name), and both Philo (*Vit. Mos.* 2.114, 205) and

Josephus (*Ant.* 2.276) reflect a concern about uttering God's name inappropriately.[19]

Most significant for the present discussion is the rich artifactual evidence of the ways that the Tetragrammaton was handled in the copying of Jewish texts, from ancient times and on through centuries later.[20] Note particularly that in extant pre-Christian Jewish manuscripts the divine name is often handled in one or another special way intended clearly to distinguish it from the surrounding text.[21] In his recently published comprehensive study of scribal practices in Jewish manuscripts from Roman Judea, Emanuel Tov reviews the multiple methods followed.[22] These include use of Paleo-Hebrew characters in some texts that are written in regular ("square") Hebrew letters, in other manuscripts four dots or four diagonal strokes written in place of the Tetragrammaton, and in some other manuscripts the systematic writing of a colon-shaped device (:) before the Tetragrammaton (written in the "square" Hebrew script). Some Qumran texts also show a concern about writing the Hebrew word "God" *(elohim)*. For instance, in one manuscript designated 11Qpaleo-Unidentified Text (11Q22) לאלהיך ("to/for God") is written in a different color of ink (possibly red).[23]

19. See H. Bietenhard, "ὄνομα," *TDNT* 5:242-83, on divine names generally. On rabbinic traditions about the Tetragrammaton, see E. E. Urbach, *The Sages* (Cambridge: Harvard University Press, 1987), 124-34. Frank Shaw gathered a large body of evidence, however, concerning the use of Ἰάω as a designation for God among Roman-era Jews: "The Earliest Non-Mystical Jewish Use of ΙΑΩ" (Ph.D. diss., University of Cincinnati, 2002).

20. See M. Delcor, "Des diverses manières d'écrire le tétragramme sacré dans les anciens documents hébraïques," *Revue de l'histoire des religions* 147 (1955): 145-73. Jacob Z. Lauterbach ("Substitutes for the Tetragrammaton," *Proceedings of the American Academy for Jewish Research* 2 [1930-1931]: 39-67) listed numerous ways in which the Tetragrammaton is handled in Hebrew texts available at the time of his writing, which were mainly medieval and later.

21. Metzger (*Manuscripts of the Greek Bible,* 33-35) gives an introductory discussion. On the Qumran manuscripts see Hartmut Stegemann, "Religionsgeschichtliche Erwägungen zu den Gottesbezeichnungen in den Qumrantexten," in *Qumrân: Sa piété, sa théologie et son milieu,* ed. M. Delcor, BETL 46 (Leuven: Leuven University Press, 1978), 195-217; Patrick W. Skehan, "The Divine Name at Qumran, in the Masada Scroll, and in the Septuagint," *BIOSCS* 13 (1980): 14-44; and now Tov, *Scribal Practices,* 218-21, 238-46.

22. Tov, *Scribal Practices,* 218-19.

23. Tov (ibid., 239) also notes an avoidance of the Tetragrammaton and *elohim* in the Qumran *pesharim* texts, "which by way of circumlocution often refer to God in the third person."

In still other cases, Hebrew *el* was used in place of the Tetragrammaton (e.g., 4QpPsb = 4Q173; 4QHosb = 4Q167; 1QHa).[24] Tov judges that the "overwhelming preponderance" of *el* and "the rare use of the Tetragrammaton" in Qumran community writings (*pesharim, Hodayot,* prayers, blessings, rules) give further evidence of an avoidance of the divine name. This textual avoidance of the Tetragrammaton may also have served to alert readers to avoid pronouncing it.[25]

Tov has also given a good deal of attention to the scribal treatment of the divine name in Jewish biblical manuscripts in Greek, and this body of data is perhaps still more directly relevant, given that the Christian *nomina sacra* seem to have been first manifested in Greek.[26] In the Greek biblical manuscripts of undeniable Jewish provenance, as with the Hebrew and Aramaic manuscripts, the precise practice varies, but the common factor seems to be a concern to distinguish the Tetragrammaton from the surrounding text. In some cases, for example, 8HevXIIgr (first/second century BCE, Minor Prophets) and P.Oxy. 3522 (first century CE, Job), the Tetragrammaton is written in Paleo-Hebrew characters.[27] In P.Fouad 266b (first century BCE, Deuteronomy) the Tetragrammaton is written (by a second hand) in square Hebrew script.[28] In the Qumran manuscript 4QpapLXXLevb (4Q120, first century BCE, Leviticus), we have the Greek characters ΙΑΩ used to represent the Tetragrammaton. In this last case, the

24. See ibid., 239, for further details and discussion.

25. Ibid. In table 1 (242-43) Tov lists the nonbiblical and biblical Qumran manuscripts that employ Paleo-Hebrew characters for the Tetragrammaton.

26. Emanuel Tov, "Scribal Features of Early Witnesses of Greek Scripture," in *The Old Greek Psalter: Studies in Honour of Albert Pietersma,* ed. Robert J. V. Hiebert, Claude E. Cox, and Peter J. Gentry, JSOTSup 332 (Sheffield: Sheffield Academic Press, 2001), 125-48, esp. 146-47; idem, "Greek Biblical Texts"; idem, *Scribal Practices,* esp. appendix 5 (303-15). By Tov's calculation, only about 3% of the texts at Qumran and Wadi Daliyeh are Greek, whereas at the several other Judean sites the percentage varies from 23% to 56% (*Scribal Practices,* 299-300).

27. Note also the following manuscripts that are probably Jewish or show Jewish scribal influence: P.Oxy. 1007 (third-century CE parchment codex, which has two Paleo-Hebrew *yods* with a horizontal stroke through both, but also has an instance of ΘΣ for θεος); and P.Vindob. gr39777 (third/fourth-century CE parchment roll, with Paleo-Hebrew Tetragrammaton and uncontracted θεος).

28. It seems that the scribe copying the Greek text left a blank space sufficient to accommodate the Tetragrammaton, and someone else then wrote it in. Tov notes the suggestion that the person who filled in the Tetragrammaton may have held a higher stature within the Qumran community than the original scribe (*Scribal Practices,* 245).

divine name is distinguished from the rest of the text in being transliterated phonetically rather than translated.[29]

I cannot here go into the details of scholarly discussion of how these various practices for handling the Tetragrammaton may have originated and developed at Qumran and elsewhere in ancient Jewish circles.[30] For instance, did the practice of using Paleo-Hebrew characters originate in the Qumran community texts and then spread to copies of biblical texts? Did the Qumran scribes follow an established practice of employing Paleo-Hebrew characters for the Tetragrammaton, or did each scribe exercise some initiative and freedom according to his own preferences? The key observation is *that* Jewish scribes often appear to have been concerned to handle the divine name in a special manner.

For further comment a bit later, I observe here that the particular method for doing so varies. For instance, use of Paleo-Hebrew characters and substituted dots or strokes is not consistent across all Qumran Hebrew and Aramaic manuscripts.[31] Likewise, as noted already, in Jewish Greek biblical manuscripts, there are different practices. But all these various ways of according special scribal treatment to the Tetragrammaton and (somewhat less consistently) *elohim* reflect a view that these words have a "special status."[32] That is, these various devices all express the piety of the copyists.

I contend that this Jewish reverential attitude reflected in the scribal handling of the Tetragrammaton and key related designations of God has a

29. Shaw ("Earliest Non-Mystical Use of IAΩ") discusses various indications of the vocalization of the Tetragrammaton in early Jewish circles. For an earlier valuable, and often overlooked, discussion of various early Greek transcriptions of the Tetragrammaton, see Adolf Deissmann, *Bible Studies*, trans. Alexander Grieve (1901 [German 1895]; repr. Peabody, MA: Hendrickson, 1988), 321-36.

30. See now Tov's review of this discussion, *Scribal Practices*, 238-46.

31. Tov (ibid., appendix 1, 277-88) includes tables of texts indicating the various scribal features in manuscripts from the Judean desert sites. I note that the various special scribal handling of divine names is less consistent in Qumran biblical manuscripts than in the community texts. Tov (244) lists 36 Qumran manuscripts (8 biblical and 28 nonbiblical texts) in which the Tetragrammaton and *el* are written with the same square characters as the text in which they occur.

32. Ibid., 245. Delcor ("Diverses manières," 147 n. 2) and Skehan ("Divine Name," 17) cite instances where *el* (with reference to God) is written in Paleo-Hebrew characters as well (e.g., 1QH 1:26; 2:34; 7:5; 15:25). Josephus (*Ant.* 12.89) refers to Hebrew biblical manuscripts with the Tetragrammaton in gold ink, also probably cited in *Let. Aris.* 176.

counterpart in the early prominence of the four *nomina divina* (*Theos, Kyrios, Christos,* and *Iēsous*) in the Christian manuscripts. That is, the four early *nomina sacra* may reflect a somewhat similar reverence for God and Jesus expressed in the special way that these key terms were written in early Christian texts.[33] Moreover, because these terms are written as *nomina sacra* with far greater consistency and earlier than other words, it seems likely that the whole Christian scribal practice of these curious abbreviated forms originated in such a religious motive. Thereafter, in less consistent fashion, further words in the early Christian religious vocabulary were accorded similar treatment, apparently as individual scribes felt more or less free to do so.

But we must also note what appear to be distinctively Christian developments. In contrast to the more varied measures and somewhat less consistent practice of Jewish scribes, a more consistent Christian special handling of the four terms for God and Jesus is indicated surprisingly early and quickly. Moreover, whereas there is some variation in Jewish scribal practice with reference to terms for God in biblical manuscripts, the *nomina sacra* appear with *greater* consistency in Christian *biblical* manuscripts.

Also, of course, the specific scribal mechanics differ. In Jewish manuscripts of pre-Christian date, as noted, various scribal tactics are employed to mark off reverentially the key words for God. The Christian *nomina sacra,* however, are both different in form from any of the Jewish scribal devices and comparatively more consistent in form. For instance, among the pre-Christian Jewish manuscripts, there is no use of contracted forms, and no use of the curious horizontal stroke that characterizes the *nomina sacra.*

Most significantly, the four earliest Christian *nomina sacra* are the two key words for God (*Theos* and *Kyrios*) and key designations for Jesus (*Iēsous, Christos,* and *Kyrios*).[34] If, therefore, as is usually believed, the *nomina sacra* practice represents an expression of piety and reverence, it is a striking departure from pre-Christian Jewish scribal practice to extend to these designations of Jesus the same scribal treatment given to key desig-

33. This view of the *nomina sacra* as expressive of early Christian piety is long-standing, as reflected, e.g., in Paap, *Nomina Sacra,* 123. This has been challenged recently by Christopher Tuckett, whose argument I will address later in this chapter.

34. In Christian OT manuscripts, *Kyrios* (esp. without the definite article) usually refers to God (translating the Tetragrammaton), but in NT writings the title usually designates Jesus. In all these cases equally, Christian scribes treated the word as a *nomen sacrum.*

nations for God. That is, the four earliest Christian *nomina sacra* collectively manifest one noteworthy expression of what I have called the "binitarian shape" of earliest Christian piety and devotion.[35]

As I shall note shortly, some scholars have proposed that the Christian *nomina sacra* originated in a similar (but no longer evidenced) Jewish scribal manner of writing *Theos* and/or *Kyrios*. Even if this were granted (and I shall indicate why I do not think this view is persuasive), the Christian inclusion of *Iēsous* and *Christos* among their earliest *nomina sacra* would still constitute a remarkable further innovation marking off Christian scribal practice, and it signifies a momentous religious development.

In sum, although there is at least a certain broad phenomenological similarity between the *nomina sacra* and Jewish reverential treatment of the divine name, it seems most likely that the specific *nomina sacra* scribal practice represents something distinctive. As there have been proposals that the *nomina sacra* sprang more directly from prior Jewish scribal practice, however, I turn to consider these claims now.

In the study that gave the modern scholarly name to the phenomenon, Traube proposed that the *nomina sacra* derived from a supposed practice among Greek-speaking Jews of writing Θεός in a contracted form without the vowels, their alleged intention being to imitate the Hebrew consonantal writing of the Tetragrammaton.[36] Then, Traube further proposed that from this contracted form of Θεός these Jews also began writing other Greek words in contracted forms, including Κύριος, Πνεῦμα, Πατήρ, οὐρανός, ἄνθρωπος, Δαυειδ, Ἰσραήλ, and Ἰερουσαλήμ. All these contractions were also appropriated by Christians, who then added to the list Ἰησοῦς, Χριστός, υἱός, σωτήρ, σταυρός, and μήτηρ. In his valuable updating of manuscript occurrences of the *nomina sacra*, Paap agreed that Θεός was the initial *nomen sacrum*, and that the practice had probably begun among Greek-speaking Jews. But with much more papyri evidence available to test Traube's theory, Paap argued that all the other *nomina sacra* were devised by Christians.[37]

---

35. For example, Larry W. Hurtado, "The Binitarian Shape of Early Christian Worship," in *The Jewish Roots of Christological Monotheism: Papers from the St. Andrews Conference on the Historical Origins of the Worship of Jesus,* ed. Carey C. Newman, James R. Davila, and Gladys S. Lewis, Journal for the Study of Judaism Sup 63 (Leiden: Brill, 1999), 187-213; idem, *At the Origins of Christian Worship* (Carlisle: Paternoster, 1999; Grand Rapids: Eerdmans, 2000), 63-97; idem, *Lord Jesus Christ,* esp. 134-53.

36. Traube, *Nomina Sacra,* 36.

37. Paap, *Nomina Sacra,* 119-27. In Paap's proposal, however, those Greek-speaking Jews

Schuyler Brown, however, identified serious problems in the theories of Traube and Paap. For instance, he noted evidence that among Greek-speaking Jews Κύριος, not Θεός, was the preferred vocalization/substitute for the Tetragrammaton. Brown proposed, therefore, that Κύριος was the initial *nomen sacrum,* written in contracted form and first used by Christian scribes as a reverential way to render this Greek substitute for the Tetragrammaton in Christian copies of the Greek Old Testament writings. Then, he suggested, from the Christian practice of using Κύριος to refer both to God and to Jesus, the practice of reverential contraction was "rapidly extended in one direction to Θεός and in the other direction to Ἰησοῦς and Χριστός."[38] I shall return to the question of which might have been the originating *nomen sacrum* shortly. For now, I simply note that Brown's criticisms of the theories of Traube and Paap are valid.

The respected papyrologist Kurt Treu also registered a theory that the *nomina sacra* began among Greek-speaking Jews prior to Christian usage. Treu proposed that in these circles both Θεός and Κύριος were written as contractions with a horizontal stroke over them to distinguish these words in Greek biblical texts where they served as translation equivalents for the Tetragrammaton. In Treu's view Christians then took up this practice and quickly extended it to include "the remaining persons of their Trinity" and, thereafter, a still wider list of religious vocabulary.[39]

I noted earlier Treu's related proposal that the codex likewise was adopted by Christians from prior Jewish usage. More recently, Robert Kraft has expressed strong support for Treu's position on both matters, urging that "the debt of early Christianity to its Jewish heritage is even greater in these areas of 'textual mechanics' and transmitted scribal craft than our scholarly traditions and approaches have permitted us to recognize."[40] For my part, I second strongly the historical connection of early Christianity and its Jewish religious matrix. But on the specific questions of how to account for the Christian preference for the codex and the ori-

---

who became Christians introduced the initial contraction, ΘС, which then led to further words being accorded a similar scribal treatment.

38. Brown, "Concerning the Origin of the *Nomina Sacra,*" 18.

39. Treu, "Bedeutung des Griechischen," 141 (I quote here from the English translation by Adler and Kraft). In chapter two I noted Treu's view that Christians also appropriated the codex from a supposedly prior Jewish use of this book form.

40. Kraft, "Textual Mechanics," quotation from 68. See also Kraft's Web site, which has much fuller discussion of matters: http://ccat.sas.upenn.edu/rs/rak/papyri.html.

gins of the *nomina sacra*, the evidence seems to me very much against Kraft and Treu.

Essentially, both of these scholars focus on a few biblical manuscripts that are dated to the second to fourth century CE and later, and that exhibit curious combinations of what are widely thought to be characteristic and distinguishing features of Jewish or Christian scribal practices. Treu and Kraft point to these few manuscripts as indicating that such distinctions in scribal practice are invalid, and, in particular, that what are usually thought of as Christian scribal innovations actually originated in Jewish scribal practice. For instance, Kraft contends that "Jewish scribes sometimes may have used contractions of Θεός, and perhaps a few other frequently used words, in the development of their scribal traditions," citing as evidence three biblical manuscripts dated third-fourth century CE, two of which are rolls and may also feature abbreviated forms of Κυριος and Θεος.[41] More precisely, Kraft appears to contend that contracted forms of Θεός originated in Jewish scribal practice and that Christian *nomina sacra* forms derive from this. But even if we grant Kraft's proposal that these few particular manuscripts are from Jewish scribes (and that is by no means equally clear in every case), for reasons that I shall present shortly, I regard this as a very dubious basis on which to make the large claim that the *nomina sacra* originated in Jewish scribal practice.

As I argued with reference to the proposal of Treu and Kraft about the codex, so also with reference to the *nomina sacra*, surely the correct way to proceed is to start with undeniably Jewish biblical manuscripts, especially those dated early enough to reflect pre-Christian Jewish practice. Among these, both those in Hebrew and those in Greek, as we have seen already, there is no instance of any of the *nomina sacra* forms.[42] The

41. Kraft, "Textual Mechanics," 67. The manuscripts that he cites as key instances of Jewish scribes exhibiting features usually associated with Christian scribal practice are these: P.Oxy. 1007 (= P.Lit.Lond. 199, a third-century CE parchment codex of Genesis, with contracted Θεος and the Tetragrammaton represented as a Paleo-Hebrew double *yod*), P.Oxy. 1166 (= P.Lit.Lond. 201, a third-century CE papyrus roll, possibly with [reconstructed] abbreviations of Κυριος and Θεος), and P.Alex. 203 (third/fourth-century CE papyrus roll, reconstructed abbreviations of Κυριος). See Kraft's notes on these and other manuscripts in ibid., 54-65.

42. So also Flavio Bedodi, "I 'nomina sacra' nei papyri greci veterotestamentari prechristiani," *SPap* 13 (1974): 89-103, who judged that the unambiguously pre-Christian Greek biblical manuscripts do not throw direct light upon the scribal practice of *nomina sacra*, but confirm that it must have originated in Christian circles (esp. 103).

108

Jewish copyists of these manuscripts gave a variety of special treatment to the key divine names, but among this variety there is no direct precedent to the *nomina sacra* forms that are such a familiar feature in undeniably Christian manuscripts. I think that it is rather telling that Tov, who has devoted so much attention to the scribal characteristics of pre-Christian Jewish manuscripts, firmly points to differences between Jewish and Christian scribal practice in the handling of the divine names, and he identifies the *nomina sacra* abbreviations as clearly a Christian scribal convention.[43]

In a recent article Christopher Tuckett finds it questionable to regard the *nomina sacra* as a Christian scribal innovation, however, because there are a few instances (which I have noted previously) of manuscripts dated to the third century and much later whose provenance is uncertain and that exhibit abbreviations of Θεος or Κυριος.[44] But, as noted already, the dominant pattern of evidence is not as unclear as he implies. There *may* be a very few instances of Jewish scribes also occasionally using a *nomina sacra* form (e.g., P.Oxy. 1007), but no instance he cites is certainly Jewish and early enough to be relevant for the question of how the practice originated.[45] I am puzzled as to how Tuckett can imply that it is insufficiently "circumspect" to judge that the *nomina sacra* were an early Christian innovation.[46]

43. Tov, *Scribal Practices*, e.g., 314-15.

44. Tuckett, "Nomina Sacra," 433-35.

45. Tuckett (ibid., 435) alleges "clear evidence of a Jewish scribe using a *nomen sacrum* for the divine name" in a fragment of a sixth-century CE manuscript of Kings (Aquila version) from the Cairo Genizah, which has a single instance of ΚΥ (with a supralinear stroke) at the end of a line. Contra Tuckett, Roberts did not "write off" this case, but discussed it and other evidence of Jewish scribal practice, showing that this isolated use of a contracted form of Κυριος was likely due to "exigencies of space" (*Manuscript*, 33). A suspended abbreviation of a word at the end of a line is not remarkable. It would be more interesting to have regularly abbreviated forms of Κυριος in the middle of lines in a Jewish biblical manuscript.

46. Cf. Tuckett, "Nomina Sacra," 434. He (435 and n. 25) accuses Roberts of "dismissing pieces of evidence that do not fit his overall theory." But in considering Roberts's views, we are dealing with the scholar who literally wrote the book on Greek paleography (*Greek Literary Hands, 350 B.C.–A.D. 400* [Oxford: Clarendon, 1955]). Roberts's knowledge of other matters can be criticized, but his judgments that this or that scribe was "amateur or careless," "unskilled or ignorant," etc., rested upon having closely examined at least a few hundred Greek manuscripts firsthand across several decades. Moreover, it is certainly clear that ancient scribes exhibit a considerable variety in skill and consistency, and that one can inductively identify regular scribal practices and deviations from this regularity (e.g., irregular let-

As for the small number of manuscripts highlighted by Treu and Kraft (and cited also by Tuckett), it seems to me more reasonable to take them as interesting instances of occasional "cross-fertilization" of Jewish and Christian scribal practices. Unless we imagine that Jews and Christians had no contact with one another, it should not be difficult to imagine occasional scribal influences in both directions. For example, this or that Jewish scribe could have chosen (or could have been commissioned, by a Jew, a Christian, or someone not exclusively identified as either the one or the other) to produce a copy of a biblical text in codex form. Or, having noted contracted forms of Κυριος or Θεος in biblical manuscripts (produced by Christians), a Jewish scribe might have judged them to be a useful way of reverentially writing these words, and so appropriated (or experimented with) the practice.

Likewise, as noted already, one can readily imagine a (Christian?) scribe familiar with *nomina sacra* forms and ready, at least occasionally, to use a roll for making a copy of an Old Testament text. Moreover, of course, there may well have been some scribes who did not see themselves exclusively as Christian or Jewish, and who therefore easily combined features of what were becoming more typically the distinguishing features of Jewish and Christian scribal cultures.

In short, surely sound scholarly method requires us to understand a smaller body of ambiguous data in the light of much larger bodies of unambiguous data, not vice versa, and to recognize the probative difference between patterns of evidence and occasional exceptions to these patterns. I contend that the unambiguously pre-Christian manuscript evidence gives no basis for the supposition that any of the *nomina sacra* originated in very early Jewish scribal practice and were then appropriated and added to by Christians. The small number of second- to fourth-century CE manuscripts highlighted by Treu and Kraft, though interesting artifacts, are too late to justify their claims.

---

ter forms, spelling, general skill). Also, it must be noted that Roberts's work on the *nomina sacra* received endorsement from other knowledgeable figures in the field, such as Turner, *Greek Manuscripts*, 15. In short, Tuckett's allegation seems misguided.

A Christian Innovation?

The result of this review of possible derivations of the *nomina sacra* is to make it more likely that the specific practice originated among early Christian circles. As we have seen, there is no direct precedent in general Greek or Latin abbreviation practices or in Jewish scribal traditions for the pattern of words or the precise mechanics of how these words are treated. So it looks as if we are dealing with a Christian scribal innovation. Moreover, it appears that this innovation came about very early and spread rather quickly among Christian copyists. In any account of Christian origins, therefore, surely the *nomina sacra* should figure as a fascinating, and potentially significant, feature of Christian textual culture.

George Howard proposed that Κύριος and Θεός were the initial *nomina sacra*, both "first created by non-Jewish Christian scribes who in their copying the LXX text found no traditional reason to preserve the Tetragrammaton," and may have developed the contracted forms of these words as "analogous to the vowelless Hebrew Divine Name."[47] But Howard's proposal is unsatisfactory as an explanation for the *nomina sacra*. For one thing, all Hebrew words, not only the Tetragrammaton, were written as consonants, and the more frequent *nomina sacra* form of Κύριος, KC, involves the omission of vowels *and a consonant!* More seriously still, Howard's proposal does not seem to offer an adequate motivation for the origin of a scribal practice that became so widely followed in Christian circles.[48] As I have demonstrated elsewhere, the conviction that Jesus shares God's name and glory and the devotional practice of treating him as the worthy recipient of worship arose early, among Jewish Christian circles, and cannot be accounted for in the way Howard proposes.[49]

---

47. George Howard, "Tetragrammaton in the New Testament," *ABD*, 6:392-93; idem, "The Tetragram and the New Testament," *JBL* 96 (1977): 63-68.

48. Another problem in Howard's proposal is that it is linked to his unpersuasive idea that early Christian reverence for Jesus as having divine stature/significance sprang initially from the gentile Christian practice of using Κύριος for the Tetragrammaton in copying the Greek OT writings. Howard argued that, as the term had already been applied to Jesus (but initially with the connotation of "Master"), reading Κύριος in their biblical texts led gentile Christians to blur the distinction between God and Jesus. I give a critique of Howard's ideas in *Lord Jesus Christ*, 182-83.

49. See, e.g., Hurtado, *Lord Jesus Christ*, esp. 155-216.

But more precisely when and how did the practice that we call the *nomina sacra* originate? As I argued in 1998, in working toward an answer it is useful to pay careful attention to the details of the scribal devices involved.[50] There are several features to keep in mind, and an adequate theory should account for them all. Indeed, I propose that these features may point us toward the right answer to our questions about origins.

We may begin with the curious, characteristic use of the horizontal stroke placed over the abbreviated forms. This supralinear mark is not derived from any regular abbreviation technique in pre-Christian Greek or Latin tradition.[51] Yet, with only a very few exceptions, it is standard in the words treated as *nomina sacra* in Christian manuscripts. It may be significant, however, that a similar mark was placed over Greek letters when they were used to represent numbers, a feature more typical in documentary than formal literary texts.[52] In the latter type of texts, numbers are more usually written out as words.[53] But the use of letters (with this horizontal stroke) for numbers is often found in Christian literary texts, including copies of biblical writings, which shows that Christian scribes were well aware of the device.[54] As I will explain shortly, this pre/non-Christian use of the supralinear stroke to signal that letters represent numbers may be a clue to the origin of the *nomina sacra*.

Another curious matter that I regard as also significant is that in the case of Jesus' name (Ιησους) two early approaches were taken in treating it

50. Hurtado, "Origin of the *Nomina Sacra*," esp. 664-71.

51. Avi-Yonah (*Abbreviations*, 29-39) lists and discusses numerous abbreviation marks found on inscriptions, including several sorts of horizontal strokes (33-35), which are most commonly placed over the final letter of the abbreviation, occasionally over the penultimate letter, sometimes under the final letter, or over several letters in the abbreviation.

52. See esp. Blanchard, *Sigles*, 3, who notes the difference between this use and placement of the stroke and the placement of a stroke over the final letter of an abbreviation (p. 21 n. 20). For example, P.Oxy. 108, a food bill from the late second or early third century CE, contains numerous examples of alphabetic characters used to represent numbers, in each case with a horizontal stroke over the letter(s).

53. Turner indicated that he knew of only one Greek literary manuscript in which numbers were not written out but represented by alphabetic letters, and noted that Christian texts were "quite different in this respect" (*Greek Manuscripts*, 15).

54. For example, in P.Chester Beatty III (𝔓47), the many numbers in the text of Revelation are characteristically written as letters with the supralinear stroke. So, e.g., in 13:18, the 666 is written as ΧΞC, and the 144,000 (in 14:1) as ΡΜΔ.

as a *nomen sacrum*.[55] Whereas in most manuscripts the name is written in a contracted form (the first and final letters of the inflected form of a word, e.g., Ι C, Ι Υ), in several manuscripts Ιησους was written in a "suspended" form, just the first two letters, Ι Η. The latter technique appears particularly in some comparatively early Christian papyri, for example, the Egerton fragment (P.Lond.Christ. 1) and 𝔓45 (P.Chester Beatty II).[56] A third abbreviation scheme is used for Jesus' name in a number of manuscripts, particularly some dated third through fifth century, involving the first two letters and the final letter, e.g., Ι ΗC. But this form must reflect an acquaintance with the suspended and the contracted forms of Jesus' name, and is a conflation of these other abbreviation forms. As Paap put it, this three-letter abbreviation seems to originate in the suspended form of Ιησους, which was then "fertilized" by the final letter of the contracted form.[57] The suspended form seems basically to have gone out of usage soon after about 300. The contracted forms (Ι C, etc.) are attested about as early and became by far the most favored way of writing Jesus' name.[58]

In light of the clear evidence of a certain amount of variation, even experimentation, in scribal practice with reference to the *nomina sacra* (more on this a bit later), one might wonder if this suspended form of Je-

55. In a few cases Χριστος or Κυριος is written in a two-letter suspended form (e.g., one instance of XP in 𝔓45, and one use in P.Oxy. 1079; nine cases of KY in Berlin Staats.Bib. Cod. gr. fol. 66 I,II). But both the comparative infrequency of this and the dating of the manuscripts in which it appears suggest that these are isolated cases, and likely influenced by the more frequently used suspended forms of Ιησους.

56. In addition, according to Aland, *Repertorium, I,* the ΙΗ writing of "Jesus" appears also in P.Oxy. 1079 (𝔓18, third/fourth-century CE copy of Revelation), Mag.Coll.Gr. 18 (𝔓64, second/third-century CE copy of Matthew), and P.Oxy. 1224 (early-fourth-century CE copy of sayings of Jesus). I am able to confirm the instance in P.Oxy. 1224 (main fragment, verso, line 5) through my own examination of the fragments in the Bodleian Library.

57. Paap, *Nomina Sacra,* 109.

58. For example, in Paap's survey (ibid., 108), the three-letter forms of Ιησους appear 159 times in 24 manuscripts (mainly dated third through fifth centuries CE), and the contracted forms appear 823 times in 56 manuscripts (dated from second through sixth centuries CE, but his dating of P.Chester Beatty V to the second century is incorrect). The suspended form appears 48 times in 7 sources (36 occurrences in P.Chester Beatty II [𝔓45]), the latest of which is P.Oxy. 1224 (VH #587), an early-fourth-century CE unknown text of sayings of Jesus. (In "Origin of the *Nomina Sacra,*" 666 n. 36, my citation of P.Oxy. 210 as having an instance of ΙΗ failed to note that there is a lacuna after the *eta,* which means that we cannot actually be sure whether the scribe wrote ΙΗ or ΙΗC. I note that Paap did not treat this manuscript as a witness to the suspended form.)

sus' name is simply another instance of this experimentation. But there are early Christian comments on IH as representing Jesus' name, which indicate that this particular abbreviation had a reasonable currency and, more importantly, had a religious meaning, at least in its earliest usage. Two important second-century sources, the *Epistle of Barnabas* (9.7-8) and Clement of Alexandria (*Strom.* 6.278-80), refer to this form, and specifically note its numerical value (IH = 18), in commenting on the 318 servants of Abraham in Genesis 14:14.[59] Both of these writers were familiar with Greek copies of Genesis in which the number was written as TIH, and they both see in this letter compendium a foreshadowing of Jesus and his cross: T (= 300) = his cross, and IH (= 18) = Jesus' name.

This is a very interesting instance of early Christian use of the ancient technique of "gematria," which involves ascribing religious significance to the numerical value of alphabetic characters, a practice particularly associated with ancient Jewish exegesis.[60] Other instances of this technique are more familiar to readers of the New Testament, probably the best known being the mysterious number of "the Beast" in Revelation 13:18 and 15:2, which is commonly taken as alluding to the numerical value of the name of Nero Caesar written in Hebrew characters.[61] Likewise, it is widely accepted by scholars that the number fourteen emphasized in Matthew's genealogy of Jesus (Matt. 1:17) alludes to the numerical value of the name "David" in Hebrew characters (דוד).[62]

In short, IH seems to have been a way of representing Jesus' name that was reasonably well known and very early in origin, and that must have

59. These texts were cited by Roberts (*Manuscript*, 37 n. 2). Gershom Scholem mentions a rabbinic interpretation of the 318 servants as referring to Eliezer (Abraham's trusty servant), the numerical value of whose name in Hebrew characters is 318 ("Gematria," *EncJud* 7:370); and see also Louis Ginzberg, *Legends of the Jews*, 7 vols. (New York: Jewish Publication Society, 1909-38), 5:224 n. 93. Scholem cogently proposed that the rabbinic interpretation may have originated as a reply against the Christian interpretation of Gen. 14:14 reflected in *Barnabas* and Clement.

60. For further explanation see, e.g., Joshua Trachtenberg, *Jewish Magic and Superstition* (New York: Atheneum, 1982), 262-63; F. W. Farrar, *History of Interpretation*, Bampton Lectures 1885 (1886; repr. Grand Rapids: Baker, 1961), 98-100. Farrar (99 n. 1) also cites the Christian use of the technique in the comments on Gen. 14:14 in *Barnabas*.

61. See, e.g., Richard Bauckham, *The Climax of Prophecy: Studies on the Book of Revelation* (Edinburgh: T&T Clark, 1993), 384-88.

62. See, e.g., the discussion in R. E. Brown, *The Birth of the Messiah* (Garden City, NY: Doubleday, 1977), 74-81, esp. 80 n. 38.

arisen among Christians familiar with Jewish exegetical techniques.[63] It is improbable that writing Jesus' name as I H was derived from the curious exegesis of the number in Genesis 14:14. Instead, writing the 318 in that passage as the Greek characters T I H almost certainly presupposes and derives from the *prior* Christian use of I H for Jesus' name (and the Christian use of the *tau* as a symbol for Jesus' cross).[64] In these conclusions, I am simply providing further support for views expressed previously by other scholars familiar with the data.[65] Can we, however, say more?

I propose that this suspended form of Jesus' name (I H) was likely the originating device from which the whole scribal practice of the *nomina sacra* then developed. Moreover, my argument involves the suggestion that I H originated in Jewish Christian circles (or among Christians sufficiently acquainted with relevant Jewish traditions) as a gematria, the numerical value of eighteen, perhaps an allusion to the numerical value of the Hebrew word for "life" (חי).[66] In early Christian views of Jesus, he can be thought of as the embodiment of resurrection life, indeed, himself the life-giving Lord (e.g., Rom. 8:1-2, 10-11; 1 Cor. 15:20-23, 45; Phil. 3:20-21; John 1:3-4; 11:25; 14:6; 20:31!), and so an allusion to "life" in a suspended form of Jesus' name would certainly have resonated profoundly with Christian piety. As for the allusion requiring some acquaintance with the numerical value of Hebrew characters, I have already noted parallel phenomena in the other early instances cited in first-century Christian texts from the New Testament that reflect this knowledge.[67]

63. Note that Clement (*Strom.* 6.278 [ANF 2:499]) begins his exegesis of Gen. 14:14 with "φασιν ουν ειναι" ("They say, then"), which, as Roberts observed (*Manuscript*, 37 n. 2), "suggests that ιη was no longer current [as the usual abbreviation of Jesus' name] in Clement's day."

64. Indeed, it is widely accepted among papyrologists that any copy of Greek Genesis in which the 318 in Gen. 14:14 is written as T I H can be taken as likely coming from Christian hands. Note, e.g., that in P.Chester Beatty IV (Rahlfs 961, fourth-century CE codex of Genesis) the 318 of this passage is written as T I H (with the supralinear stroke that in this instance signals that these letters are to be read as numbers). In the next chapter I explore early Christian cross symbolism.

65. See esp. Roberts, *Manuscript*, 37. Note also Bell and Skeat, *Fragments of an Unknown Gospel*, 3, who judged it likely that I H appeared in "the Apostolic age" and "may actually have been the first to be adopted."

66. I reiterate here in abbreviated form the position I set forth in "Origin of the *Nomina Sacra*," esp. 665-69.

67. For further discussion of early Jewish and Christian evidence of the religious signif-

It is an advantage of this proposal that it accounts well for features often not otherwise explained. In particular, we have a cogent explanation for the puzzling supralinear stroke that became characteristic in Christian *nomina sacra*. According to the view advocated here, this mark began its special Christian usage with the writing of Jesus' name as IH, and originally functioned in its more familiar capacity as a signal to readers that this two-letter compendium could also be read as a number, eighteen. Then, however, as Christian piety quickly sought to extend a similar scribal treatment to other key designations of God and Jesus (a development that I return to for further comment shortly), this supralinear stroke came to function as a distinctively Christian device that functioned simply to highlight *nomina sacra* forms, signaling readers that these various compendia were abbreviations of these special words.[68] In none of the other *nomina sacra* forms (other than IH), however, does the numerical value of the letter combinations appear to have been significant.

Also, this proposal accounts for the early currency, and subsequent atrophy in use, of the suspended form of Ιησους. This suspended form of Jesus' name is certainly very early, but was superseded by other ways of writing Ιησους as a *nomen sacrum*. This suggests that the suspended form arose before what became the favored *nomina sacra* conventions were developed, and also that the initial rationale for the suspended form ceased to be sufficiently known and meaningful. If IH originated as a gematria that alluded to the Hebrew word for "life," it is understandable that, as direct widespread familiarity with and appreciation of such trappings of Jewish tradi-

---

icance of numbers, see Reinhart Staats, "Ogdoas als ein Symbol für die Auferstehung," *VC* 26 (1972): 29-52 (dealing esp. with the number 8); O. H. Lehmann, "Number-Symbolism as a Vehicle of Religious Experience in the Gospels, Contemporary Rabbinic Literature and the Dead Sea Scrolls," in *Studia Patristica*, IV, ed. F. L. Cross (TU 79; Berlin: Akademie-Verlag, 1961), 125-35; François Bovon, "Names and Numbers in Early Christianity," *NTS* 47 (2001): 267-88.

68. Tuckett's judgment that my suggestion is "not fully convincing" seems to rest upon a misunderstanding of it. As I have stated here, I do not claim that the supralinear stroke continued to function subsequently in the way that I propose it did initially in the IH compendium. Of course, as used with the other *nomina sacra*, the stroke quickly became simply the standard way of marking these forms as abbreviations of special words. Nor do I claim that IH was ever to be "read" simply as δεκα οκτω (18). Instead, I propose that in its initial usage the IH compendium was read as "Jesus" written in a manner designed *also* to allude to his significance as the divine vehicle of "life" for believers. Cf. Tuckett, "Nomina Sacra," 444-45. I interact further with him at a couple of subsequent points in this discussion.

tion declined in Christian circles, the particular significance of the IH compendium was lost.[69] So the suspended form of Ιησους as IH was eclipsed by the emerging popularity of the technique of contraction also used for the other *nomina sacra.*

In further support of my proposal, of course, the high importance of Jesus' name in early Christianity, both in religious discourse and in devotional practice, means that Christians were certainly ready to revere the name.[70] Marking off Jesus' name visually and writing it in a way that alluded to Jesus' life-giving status and power unquestionably fit with what else we know of early Christian attitudes and practices. That is, Jesus' name is an unsurpassed candidate in early Christian piety as a factor capable of generating the sort of special treatment that is represented in the scribal practice that we call *nomina sacra.* Granted, traditional Jewish reverence for the name of God provides something of the broader religious background, and also a relevant precedent for according special scribal treatment to divine epithets. But the name of Jesus uniquely marked off Christians and their piety from other forms of religion in the earliest period, whether Jewish or "pagan." Indeed, very early evidence indicates that Christians could view Ιησους as itself a *divine* name, and thus worthy of the sort of reverence that Jewish tradition reserved for God's name and closely related epithets.

For instance, Matthew 1:21 likely shows knowledge of the meaning of the Hebrew form of Jesus' name (יהושע, "Joshua," "he [Yahweh] saves"), and perhaps the author reflects a reverence for Jesus' name as theophoric. In Justin Martyr we even have the direct claim that "the name of God

69. Tuckett found it difficult to envisage readers of Christian Greek texts "using cryptic references to numbers which depend for their significance on a Hebrew word" (ibid., 445). But he ignores the indications (such as the other NT references that I have cited again here) that there were certainly early Christians sufficiently acquainted with the numerical values of the Hebrew alphabet to devise and recognize the sort of gematria that I propose. Also, we have to adjust ourselves to a setting in which the only way to represent numbers (other than writing them out) was by alphabetic characters, and so numbers were regularly written simply as letters or letter combinations. In such a setting, readers were much more able than we to "read" alphabetic characters as words or numbers, or as both. See also Bovon's exhortations to fellow scholars in "Names and Numbers."

70. For instance, Paul can refer to Christians simply as "all those who in every place call upon (ἐπικαλεῖν) the name of our Lord Jesus Christ" (1 Cor. 1:2), referring to the characteristic devotional action of appealing to/invoking Jesus in Christian worship. See, e.g., my discussion of early Christian worship practice in *Lord Jesus Christ,* 134-53.

Himself, which, He says, was not revealed to Abraham or to Jacob, was Jesus" (*Dial.* 75).[71] I am strongly inclined to think that Justin here echoes a Christian exegetical tradition that goes back much earlier.

Jesus' name clearly functioned with such divine significance, for example, in the early Christian ritual/devotional practice of appealing to/invoking him. Indeed, the biblical (OT) formula for worship given to God (to "call upon the name of the Lord") was appropriated to refer to this practice of invoking *Jesus'* name (e.g., Acts 2:21; Rom. 10:9-13).[72] To cite important settings for this practice, we have references indicating that Jesus' name was invoked in the initiation ritual of baptism (e.g., Acts 2:38) and in exorcism.[73]

Thus strong considerations make it entirely reasonable to posit that the abbreviation of Jesus' name as IH arose from early Christian piety directed toward Jesus, a piety also reflecting acquaintance with the techniques of Jewish gematria. Indeed, I submit that it is also quite likely that this particular compendium appeared independently of, and prior to, the other *nomina sacra*.[74] Further, I suggest that we can posit that from the IH

71. In Justin's argument in *Dial.* 75, two biblical texts are crucial: Exod. 23:20, where God promises to send his special "angel/messenger" (ἄγγελος) who bears God's name, and Num. 13:16, where Moses renames Hoshea as "Joshua/Jesus" (Ιησους). For Justin, this Joshua/Jesus is the figure who bears God's name and is sent to conduct Israel into their promised land, and the renaming signals that "Jesus" is the divine name. See my fuller discussion of early Christians "finding Jesus in the Old Testament" in *Lord Jesus Christ*, 564-78.

72. Adelheid Ruck-Schröder, *Der Name Gottes und der Name Jesu: Eine neutestamentliche Studie*, WMANT 80 (Neukirchen-Vluyn: Neukirchener Verlag, 1999); William Q. Parkinson, "'In the Name of Jesus': The Ritual Use and Christological Significance of the Name of Jesus in Early Christianity" (Ph.D. diss., University of Edinburgh, 2003); Silva New, "The Name, Baptism, and the Laying on of Hands," in *The Beginnings of Christianity*, ed. F. J. Foakes Jackson and Kirsopp Lake, 5 vols. (1920-33; repr. Grand Rapids: Baker, 1966), 5:121-40; C. J. Davis, *The Name and Way of the Lord*, JSNTSup 129 (Sheffield: JSOT Press, 1996).

73. Lars Hartman, *"Into the Name of the Lord Jesus": Baptism in the Early Church* (Edinburgh: T&T Clark, 1997); Otto Böcher, *Christus Exorcista: Dämonismus und Taufe im Neuen Testament*, BWANT 96 (Stuttgart: Kohlhammer, 1972). Also, note Paul's directions about the ritual expulsion of an unrepentant sinner from the Corinthian church (1 Cor. 5:1-5), which involves "the power of the Lord Jesus" and the invocation of Jesus' name (whether by Paul or by the Corinthians is a matter of exegesis here).

74. Although he is critical on some other points, I note that Tuckett agrees that "an original suspension preceded contracted forms" ("Nomina Sacra," 445). But he then errs in citing a few isolated instances of suspended forms of other words (e.g., XP in Acts 16:18 in P.Chester Beatty II/𝔓45; ΜΩ in P.Egerton 2) as evidence of a broader practice of early sus-

compendium as precedent, Christians were moved by their religious outlook to extend a related scribal treatment to other words. In this view the
circle of terms was first widened by the three other divine epithets that,
along with Ιησους, feature incomparably regularly and so very early as
nomina sacra.[75] The much firmer place of these four words in *nomina
sacra* treatment by early Christians surely indicates their greater antiquity
and significance in this scribal practice.

But, as noted already, none of the other words, including the other divine epithets, either in abbreviated or fully written forms, seems to have
offered to Christians the sort of numerical significance that we know was
seen in Jesus' name (both fully written and as IH).[76] Perhaps this is at least
partly why at a very early point Christian scribes judged that it would be
better to abbreviate these other words by "contraction." One obvious advantage of contraction is that the case of the noun (e.g., nominative, genitive, dative, accusative), and thus its syntactical role in a sentence, is better
signaled because the final letter of the inflected forms is retained, which
would have been a service to readers.[77] This abbreviation system had the
additional advantage of being a relatively standardized way of handling all
the words, thereby giving readers one basic system with which to familiarize themselves.[78]

---

pension of *nomina sacra.* These two instances are rather easily accounted for as influenced
by the much better attested practice of writing Jesus' name as IH. For example, the one instance of XP in 𝔓45 immediately follows the writing of Jesus' name as IH.

75. One has only to scan O'Callaghan's table, for instance, which shows how all fifteen
of the familiar words were treated in third-century CE manuscripts, to see that Ιησους, θεος,
κυριος, and χριστος form a group unto themselves: O'Callaghan, "Nomina Sacra," esp. 72,
and his own observations, 72-73, 80.

76. See, e.g., Bovon's discussion ("Names and Numbers," 282-83) of early Christian references to the numerical value of Ιησους (= 888) in *Sib. Or.* 1.324-31, and in Irenaeus,
Adversus haereses 1.12.4.

77. I proposed this basic idea in "Origin of the *Nomina Sacra,*" 669; and Tuckett subsequently offered some similar suggestions ("Nomina Sacra," 446). Curiously, however,
Tuckett accuses me of bypassing the issue (445).

78. Alan Millard has pointed to first-and-last letter contractions of proper names in
some Phoenician and Palestinian coins of the Hellenistic period and graffiti from Punic sites
in North Africa, and has proposed that early Christian scribes may have drawn the system of
abbreviation by contraction "from a Semitic habit" (*Reading and Writing in the Time of Jesus,* BibSem 69 [Sheffield: Sheffield Academic Press, 2000], 71). Perhaps, but derivation is
one thing, and function/significance is another. Again, abbreviations on coins and graffiti
are space-saving devices, clearly not a factor in the Christian manuscripts. The technique of

In sum, it seems to me that the best reading of the evidence is that the *nomina sacra* represent a Christian innovation. Granted, the practice was, in all likelihood, indebted in some sense to the varied ways that Jewish scribes tried to mark off the divine name (more on this in the next section), but the particular scribal techniques differ. For instance, the Christian innovation appears to include the standardized use of the supralinear stroke to mark off the words treated as *nomina sacra,* and the characteristic use of contracted abbreviations of these words seems likewise to be a distinctively Christian scribal convention.

Moreover, the evidence indicates that Iησους, Κυριος, Θεος, and Χριστος were treated as *nomina sacra* much more consistently, and probably earlier, than any of the other words in question. Finally, there are reasons to suspect that the whole scribal tradition may have begun with a distinctive writing of Iησους as IH, and that this first happened among Jewish Christians or Christians sufficiently acquainted with Jewish traditions to devise and appreciate the gematria involved in this way of writing Jesus' name.

Significance

We now turn to the other key question, the function and historical significance of the *nomina sacra.* As we have seen, the more technical question about how the scribal convention arose has received a variety of proposed answers, and hence the rather lengthy and intricate discussion of the preceding pages. But the question that we now address is obviously of wider import for all scholars concerned with the origins and early history of Christianity. Fortunately, until recently, there has been far more of a broad consensus about the answer to this question, which will permit me to treat the matter in comparatively briefer space.

From Traube's influential study onward the dominant view by far has been that the *nomina sacra* arose from, and reflect, early Christian piety. Although scholars have differed over whether the practice originated in an abbreviated writing of one or more of the words Κυριος, Θεος, or

---

abbreviation by contraction might have been adapted from the sorts of phenomena that Millard identifies, but this does not explain *why* early Christians developed the *nomina sacra* practice and what it represented for them.

Ιησους, they have tended to agree that the impulse was a high regard among early Christians for the referent(s) of these key words. Also, as noted, there has been widespread agreement that this Christian scribal convention has some historical relationship to Jewish scribal practices that involved according special treatment to the Tetragrammaton (and, less regularly, to *elohim*). Thus particularly the four words that are likely earlier in use and are certainly the most consistently written as *nomina sacra* are widely taken to be a notable indication and expression of Christian devotion.

Moreover, even those scholars (e.g., Treu and Kraft) who have proposed that Jewish scribes began the practice of writing Κυριος or Θεος in abbreviated forms, and that the early Christian innovation was to extend the practice to Ιησους, grant that this latter move in particular constitutes a notable historical development. That is, whether the practice of regularly writing Ιησους in abbreviated form developed in imitation of a previous Jewish or Christian scribal treatment of Κυριος or Θεος, or (as I think more likely) was the originating scribal move that generated the whole subsequent *nomina sacra* convention, it is remarkable for early Christians to have treated Jesus' name and key epithets for God in the same, apparently reverential, manner. To repeat a claim that I made earlier in this chapter, the four early *nomina sacra* represent a particularly striking expression of the binitarian shape of early Christian devotion, with reverence for Jesus patterned after, and uniquely linked with, reverence for God.

I have also urged that, along with the codex, the *nomina sacra* should be counted among our earliest extant evidence of a visual and material "culture" that can be identified as Christian.[79] Reiterating a judgment I have offered in previous publications, although the *nomina sacra* perhaps seem less impressive than other early Christian artifacts such as catacomb paintings, these curious abbreviations are also visual and physical expressions of religious devotion. Indeed, the *nomina sacra* can be thought of as hybrid phenomena that uniquely combine textual and visual features and functions; these key words were written in a distinctive manner that was intended to mark them off visually (and reverentially) from the surrounding text.

---

79. Hurtado, "Origin of the *Nomina Sacra*," esp. 672-73; idem, "Earliest Evidence," esp. 276-79, echoing a point made much earlier by Dinkler, "Älteste christliche Denkmäler," 134-78, esp. 176-78.

Christopher Tuckett has recently called all of this into question, however, in a bold discussion that calls for serious consideration.[80] In this substantial essay, Tuckett has two positions in his sights. First, he criticizes David Trobisch's claim that the *nomina sacra* form one feature of a second-century Christian "edition" of the New Testament (and OT),[81] and I have to say that I too have some reservations about Trobisch's claims.[82] But Tuckett also weighs in against what has been a much more widely shared view, which I have summarized and advocated in the preceding paragraphs, that the *nomina sacra* are expressive of early Christian religious devotion.[83] Rejecting any such idea, Tuckett proposes that, instead, the scribal practice originated simply as " '*reading aids*' [emphasis his] to assist some who were perhaps not as proficient as others to read the text [of biblical writings?] more easily."[84] That is, he suggests that the *nomina sacra* forms were somehow intended only as orientation points on the pages for

80. Tuckett, "Nomina Sacra," esp. 444-58.

81. David Trobisch, *Die Endredaktion des Neuen Testaments*, NTOA 31 (Göttingen: Vandenhoeck & Ruprecht; Freiburg: Universitätsverlag, 1996), esp. 16-31; English translation: *The First Edition of the New Testament* (Oxford: Oxford University Press, 2000), esp. 11-19. Cf. Tuckett, "Nomina Sacra," esp. 441-43.

82. Trobisch seems to me correct to point to indications of second-century Christian efforts toward marking off Christian faith and practice, and also toward identifying texts to be treated as scripture. But in my view this process was more extended, and took much longer to complete, than in Trobisch's theory. But I also think that Tuckett errs in asserting that unless one can show that the *nomina sacra* are "uniquely Christian" (i.e., never found in non-Christian manuscripts, or "not used by non-Christians for some time at least"), then one cannot validly claim that the scribal practice served "in relation to group identity" ("Nomina Sacra," 443). Here and at other points in his discussion, Tuckett imposes a curious and unhistorical criterion. In the first and second centuries CE, we can certainly see Christian group identity emerging, but a significant number of people can still be identified as both "Christian" and "Jewish," and they felt no need or desire to identify themselves *exclusively* as one or the other. So we should not be surprised that some manuscripts exhibit a mixture of features that more typically distinguish Jewish and/or Christian scribal practices. Moreover, to say that something *characterizes* a given group does not require that there is no instance of the phenomenon outside that group. As I observed in discussing the claims of Treu and Kraft, the occasional use of abbreviated forms of Θεος or Κυριος in a few putatively Jewish manuscripts of the third century CE and later hardly counts against the massively greater and more consistent use of *nomina sacra* in unquestionably Christian manuscripts, and scarcely refutes the view that the *nomina sacra* were typically a Christian scribal practice, and likely originated among Christian scribes.

83. Tuckett, "Nomina Sacra," esp. 449-58.

84. Ibid., 455.

readers. Because of the importance of the issue of what the significance and original function of the *nomina sacra* may have been, I now consider his theory, which does not seem viable to me.

Essentially, Tuckett's approach is to focus on variations and a lack of absolute consistency in the behavior of scribes, and he tries to use this to refute the notion that the *nomina sacra* had some sort of religious significance. It is not entirely clear to me how the logic works, but let us examine his data. Undeniably, there are a comparatively small number of interesting variations such as those that Tuckett reviews, all of which have been known among students of the evidence for some time.[85] What Tuckett tries to make of these variations, however, is both curious and unconvincing. If I understand him aright, he seems to come perilously close to arguing that, because there are a comparatively small number of cases where a few scribes did not consistently follow a convention otherwise widely attested, there was no convention. Obviously, if "exceptions" are numerous enough, and if practices are not sufficiently regular, frequent, and widely distributed, then one could challenge a claim that something is a "regular" or "characteristic" practice. But, to anticipate the direction of the following discussion, the problem for Tuckett's argument is that the undeniable variations and exceptions that he underscores simply do not amount to much over against the rather clear preponderance of evidence concerning how the *nomina sacra* were handled in Christian manuscripts.

For instance, Tuckett points to some exceptional cases in Christian texts where words usually treated as *nomina sacra* are written in full, his aim being to question the notion that the four "primary" words (Ιησους, Κυριος, Θεος, Χριστος) were "regularly and consistently abbreviated."[86] These include an unidentified prayer or amulet text (P.Oxy. 407, #216 in

85. See, e.g., Roberts, *Manuscript,* 27 n. 6, 83-84, and #5 in his "Addenda," for "eccentric forms" of *nomina sacra;* and Paap, *Nomina Sacra,* 113-15, as well for a list of words other than the more familiar ones, written in abbreviated form and/or with the supralinear stroke. Roberts also discussed P.Oxy. 656 and P.Oxy. 1007, as peculiar cases of biblical manuscripts (both Genesis) in which Κυριος and Θεος are not treated as *nomina sacra.* To cite yet another instance of variation in scribal practice, PSI 7.757 (a papyrus codex fragment of *Barn.* 9:1-6, dated fourth/fifth century) has both Κυριος and Θεος abbreviated by the initial letter (only once with a supralinear stroke over the *kappa*). This manuscript also has a number of other curious scribal irregularities, however. See R. A. Kraft, "An Unnoticed Fragment of Barnabas," *VC* 21 (1967): 150-63.

86. Tuckett, "Nomina Sacra," 436-39 (words quoted from 436).

appendix 1, all *nomina sacra* words consistently written in full), fragments of the *Gospel of Mary* (P.Oxy. 3525, #235 in appendix 1, one uncertain instance of an uncontracted Κυριε), the Michigan fragment of the *Shepherd of Hermas* (P.Mich. 130, #182 in appendix 1, one instance of Θεῳ written in full), and 𝔓72 (P.Bodmer VIII, ##166, 168 in appendix 1, in addition to numerous other instances where it is treated as a *nomen sacrum,* three unabbreviated instances of Κυριος in 1 Pet. 3:12; 2 Pet. 1:2; 2:9; plus one more case at 2 Pet. 2:20, where the scribe put a supralinear stroke over Κυριου). Tuckett also cites 𝔓52 (P.Ryl. 457, #126 in appendix 1) as possibly having a couple of instances of Ιησους in full, and P.Oxy. 656 (#4 in appendix 1, portions of a papyrus codex of Genesis with unabbreviated Θεος and Κυριος), and a few instances in 𝔓45 (P.Chester Beatty I, ##105 et al. in appendix 1) and in 𝔓46 (P.Chester Beatty II, ##137 et al. in appendix 1) where Κυριος is "left unabbreviated."[87]

Unfortunately, however, at some points Tuckett seems to have misunderstood the scholars he engages. Consequently, the data that he rehearses do not have the effect that he seems to suppose. For instance, Tuckett chides Roberts for dismissing certain of these data as exceptions to the "rule," and Tuckett then observes (rightly) that "a large number of non-'biblical' texts do use the [*nomina sacra*] system."[88] This implies that Roberts made some sort of near-absolute distinction between the occurrences of *nomina sacra* in biblical versus nonbiblical texts. But what Roberts actually claimed was that "the [*nomina sacra*] contractions occur in [Christian] documents as well as in literary manuscripts and where exceptions to the rule — rare even in documents — are listed they will be found on examination to occur in private letters or prayers or in e.g., magical texts, often the work of an amateur or careless scribe."[89] That is, Roberts's "rule" was that the *nomina sacra* are characteristic of the overwhelming mass of Christian manuscripts, whether "literary" (which includes biblical and nonbiblical ones) or "documents" (i.e., sub/nonliterary texts such as let-

---

87. For Tuckett's argument that 𝔓52 likely did not have Jesus' name in *nomen sacrum* form, see his article, "𝔓52 and *Nomina Sacra*," *NTS* 47 (2001): 544-48. But cf. refutations by Charles E. Hill, "Did the Scribe of 𝔓52 Use the *Nomina Sacra*? Another Look," *NTS* 48 (2002): 587-92; and my own study, "𝔓52 (P.Rylands Gk. 457) and the Nomina Sacra: Method and Probability," *TynBul* 54 (2003): 1-14. Color images of both sides of 𝔓52 are available online: http://rylibweb.man.ac.uk/data1/dg/text/fragment.htm.

88. Tuckett, "Nomina Sacra," 437 n. 34.

89. Roberts, *Manuscript,* 27.

ters). So Tuckett's observation that *nomina sacra* forms are found in many nonbiblical texts, while correct, is simply misdirected.[90] It is important, therefore, to be clear on what is usually claimed today about the *nomina sacra* by those who ascribe some sort of historical significance for the practice.[91] I itemize matters for greater clarity.

First, across the body of Christian manuscripts of all types and from the earliest date, the four key epithets for Jesus and God mentioned several times already are all treated as *nomina sacra* earlier and much more consistently than any of the other words given such treatment. There were certainly other words written as *nomina sacra,* but they appear not as early, and definitely not as frequently or as consistently, as the four *nomina divina.*

Second, in Christian texts these four words are much more consistently treated as *nomina sacra* when their referents are Jesus and God (as I shall illustrate shortly), and are more consistently *not* treated as *nomina sacra* (even in the same manuscripts) when the words have other referents. This suggests strongly that the special forms for these four words first emerged as reflections of early Christian reverence for Jesus and God.

Third, *nomina sacra* forms are characteristic of Christian texts generally, but appear much more typically and consistently in some texts (especially biblical texts) and somewhat less regularly and consistently in some examples of some other types of texts (e.g., private letters, magical texts, prayer/liturgical texts).

Fourth, in biblical or nonbiblical texts, some Christian scribes exhibit more consistency than others in following the scribal convention (or seem more familiar with the convention), but the dominant pattern is clear and indicates a scribal practice that was appropriated impressively quickly and widely.

Measured against these more specific claims, the data that Tuckett cites fit quite readily and do not falsify anything substantial. For example, neither P.Oxy. 407 nor P.Oxy. 3525 is a biblical text, and so it is not so remarkable that they have unabbreviated forms of the key words in question. Indeed, they exhibit just the *comparative* differentiation between Christian

90. See also Tuckett, "Nomina Sacra," 442-43, where he cites *nomina sacra* forms in copies of texts such as *Hermas, Gospel of Thomas,* and P.Egerton 2 (more effectively here) against Trobisch's claim that the scribal practice is indicative of a second-century "edition" of the NT.

91. In particular, the following are the claims made and reflected in the key studies by Roberts and me that Tuckett seeks to engage in his essay.

biblical and *some* copies of nonbiblical texts that Tuckett hesitates to accept.[92] One could point to other examples of unquestionably Christian manuscripts of nonbiblical texts as well in which the *nomina sacra* are either written out fully or are rather inconsistently abbreviated, although these are comparatively rare, as Roberts noted several decades ago.[93]

Likewise, it is not particularly remarkable to find instances where a given scribe wrote the key words in question as *nomina sacra* when the referents are God and Jesus, but then also occasionally failed to do so in the same manuscript, or other instances in which a given scribe occasionally treated words as *nomina sacra* even in cases when the referents were not the usual "sacred" ones. In the last instances especially, the scribe often appears to have been either somewhat imprecisely acquainted with the convention of writing the words as *nomina sacra,* and consequently did so rather woodenly without a thought for the referents, or at certain points was simply not paying close attention to what he was copying.[94] Especially

---

92. Cf. Tuckett, "Nomina Sacra," 437 n. 34. I emphasize *comparative,* which is what the data show. Tuckett's argument, however, seems to presume that the distinction must be absolute in order for there to be one. But this just is not to be expected in the case of a scribal practice that was not legislated but rather spread (and developed) as a convention, and among copyists with varying degrees of skill, familiarity with the convention, and readiness to experiment with it.

93. For example, in a number of Christian letters from the fourth century, the *nomina sacra* are either not abbreviated at all or irregularly. Usually, other features of the manuscripts suggest scribes of limited abilities, which tallies with Roberts's judgment. Texts and discussion in H. Idris Bell, *Jews and Christians in Egypt: The Jewish Troubles in Alexandria and the Athanasian Controversy* (London: British Museum, 1924), 45-120.

94. For example, in P.Chester Beatty VI (Numbers–Deuteronomy), there are instances where πνευμα is written as a *nomen sacrum* (the basic practice obviously deriving from use of the word with reference to the Holy Spirit), even though the referent is something other, such as in Num. 5:14 ("spirit of jealousy/zeal"), Num. 27:16 ("the God of all spirits"), and Num. 27:18 ("Joshua, a man who has spirit in himself"), as cited by F. G. Kenyon, "Nomina Sacra in the Chester Beatty Papyri," *Aegyptus* 13 (1933): 6 (5-10). Tuckett ("Nomina Sacra," 450-51 n. 82) cites other instances of scribes writing words as *nomina sacra* where they do not have "sacred" referents. On the other hand, the treatment of Ιησους by some scribes (e.g., P.Chester Beatty VI; cf., e.g., P.Chester Beatty II/𝔓46 at Heb. 4:8) as a *nomen sacrum* in references to "Joshua" has to be seen in the context of early Christian belief that, as a divinely ordained prophetic move, this figure had been given the name of God's Son. See my reference to Justin, *Dial.* 75 in n. 71 above (and also *Lord Jesus Christ,* 564-78). Cf. Tuckett, "Nomina Sacra," 452. Tuckett's accusation that Roberts "assume[d] offhand" that the scribal treatment of Jesus' name likely reflected early Christian piety seems unfair. Roberts expressed an inference that most scholars have held who have examined the data, and all that Tuckett does is to

in those manuscripts in which the *nomina sacra* are usually handled in the more customary fashion, one is surely obliged to take any occasional instances where the scribe does otherwise as simply cases where he lapsed from his usual practice.

Unless we set unrealistic expectations of ancient scribes (or fail to take account of the variation in skills among them), it ought not to be terribly strange to find some variation and inconsistency in their practices.[95] The question is not whether there is absolute consistency, but whether one can detect rather clear *patterns* and more characteristic scribal practices. A comparatively small number of variations and inconsistencies in scribal practice are certainly not probative against the conclusion that there was a scribal convention from which these are variations.

To cite another curious matter, Tuckett focuses on scribal treatment of ἄνθρωπος as crucial for his case, citing its appearance as a *nomen sacrum* in a few reasonably early manuscripts: P.Chester Beatty VI (second/third century CE, #24 in appendix 1), P.Oxy. 1 (ca. 200, #228 in appendix 1), and P.Chester Beatty II (𝔓46, ca. 200, ##137 et al. in appendix 1).[96] As he notes, there is, however, greater inconsistency in the way this word is handled, even by the same scribe, and it never acquired the wide frequency among the *nomina sacra* that characterized Ιησους, Κυριος, Θεος, and Χριστος.

This is usually seen as signaling that ἄνθρωπος was probably taken up comparatively later than these *nomina divina*, and in any case simply never

---

plead that we do not "know" this for certain. But, one might also ask, how much of anything in history do we "know" in the absolute sense that he seems to require? In any case, the only "early evidence" that Tuckett offers against the common view is the occasional treatment of Ιησους (Joshua) as a *nomen sacrum* in OT texts. For the reasons given, however, this scarcely has sufficient force to justify Tuckett's reluctance to accept what most other scholars see as the most compelling inference.

95. The ancient manuscripts themselves demonstrate a spectrum of scribal training and abilities in forming characters, spelling, copying errors (then corrected by the same scribe or another hand), and other related matters. Likewise, we must imagine copying being done in a variety of circumstances. It is not special pleading (as Tuckett unfortunately seems to imply more than once) to judge as exceptions to a dominant practice the sorts of occasional or less frequent variations that he cites. One can test any such judgment by the manuscript evidence.

96. Tuckett, "Nomina Sacra," 450-52. I could also note instances in P.Chester Beatty III (𝔓47, ca. 200 CE), P.Bod. II (𝔓66, ca. 200), the Freer Minor Prophets codex (third century), and single instances in P.Ryl. 463 (*Gospel of Mary*, third century), P.Oxy. 1228 (third century), P.Ryl. 469 (treatise, third/fourth century).

held the kind of place in Christian scribal practice (and piety) that these words so obviously had. But Tuckett urges, instead, that these data may show that at the earliest stage of the *nomina sacra,* scribal practice was "*not so regulated at all but displayed considerable variation.*"[97] In particular, Tuckett points to cases (but in only a few manuscripts) where ἄνθρωπος is written as a *nomen sacrum,* even though its referent in these instances is not "sacred."[98]

Clearly, the data for ἄνθρωπος show that there was no complete "system" (covering all fifteen or so words that were, with varying consistency, treated as *nomina sacra*) that was "regulated" for uniformity and consistency.[99] Instead, as I have indicated at several points already, we are dealing with a Christian scribal practice that appears to have spread among scribes as they saw copies of Christian writings with *nomina sacra,* who then may have inferred what was involved as best they could, or *may* have had some limited instruction passed to them from other Christian scribes as to the basics of the practice. My own impression is that at least in some cases scribes may have noted only that certain words pointed out to them were to be written in these abbreviated forms and with a supralinear stroke, and some scribes may well not have understood fully either the function or even the technique involved.[100]

The manuscript evidence suggests that scribes were unevenly familiar with the practice, and unevenly skilled in the intelligent handling of the words in question, and also that the words to be treated as *nomina sacra* varied, and remained somewhat flexible for at least the first few centuries. But the same body of evidence rather clearly shows that there was a much greater consistency in some matters, most of all in the treatment of the four key epithets of God and Jesus as *nomina sacra.* Indeed, the variation

---

97. Tuckett, "Nomina Sacra," 450.

98. Ibid., 450-51.

99. To reiterate a point made earlier, Roberts can be faulted for proposing that the scribal practice represented in the *nomina sacra* may have been promulgated by some authoritative center of the early church, such as he imagined Jerusalem to have been (*Manuscript,* 44-45). In the first two centuries CE, however, there was no center with the sort of translocal authority and the means of enforcing it that Roberts imagined when he proposed this.

100. A similar view is shared by some others with whom I have discussed the matter, and who have more paleographical expertise than I, such as Don Barker and Malcolm Choat (Macquarie University). Judge and Pickering ("Biblical Papyri," 7-8) concluded that, although "reverence for certain words played a part" in the origin of the scribal practice of *nomina sacra,* "it gathered its own esteem and was followed for its own sake."

and relatively greater inconsistency in some other matters makes all the more significant the demonstrably greater regularity and consistency in the way that these four words were treated by Christian scribes. One has only to consult the tables of usage in the studies by Paap and O'Callaghan to confirm these points.[101]

If the practice of writing any of the *nomina sacra* (including the four "divine" epithets) had begun simply as a means of orienting those with limited reading skills, and then afterward came to acquire a religious connotation, we would expect the data to show a movement from greater inconsistency to greater standardization in the early centuries.[102] But instead what we see is the impressive *consistency* with which particularly Θεος, Κυριος, Ιησους, and Χριστος are handled by scribes *from the earliest instances onward.* There are certainly interesting variation and some apparent experimentation (the latter particularly suggested in the number of words written in abbreviated forms and with supralinear strokes in P.Egerton 2, several of which are not typically treated as *nomina sacra* in other Christian manuscripts). But there is also a clear *pattern,* a core practice of great regularity, that has to do especially with the four words noted above.

Because this is a rather important matter, I take the space to set out a few representative examples. Note, for instance, how the scribe of 𝔓46 (P.Chester Beatty II, ca. 200) regularly treats Ιησους as a *nomen sacrum* when the referent is the figure whom Christians revere as Lord and Christ, but writes the same name in full in places where the referent is someone else (a "Jesus called Justus," Col. 4:11; Joshua, Heb. 4:8). Likewise, the scribe writes the name fully in 2 Corinthians 11:4, where Paul uses the expression "another Jesus." It is also significant that the scribe of 𝔓4 (Paris Supp. Gr. 1120, #107 in appendix 1) writes out "Ιησους" fully in the genealogy (Luke

---

101. Paap, *Nomina Sacra,* 6-75, and analysis, 75-127; O'Callaghan, *"Nomina Sacra,"* e.g., 71-81. Stuart Pickering's analysis of several NT papyri published subsequently to the studies by Paap and O'Callaghan exhibits essentially the same pattern: *Recently Published New Testament Papyri:* 𝔓89-𝔓95 (Sydney: AHDRC, Macquarie University, 1991), esp. 58-60.

102. Tuckett suggests that "as one moves back earlier in time, the 'system' may become more haphazard rather than less" ("Nomina Sacra," 453), pointing to P.Egerton 2. But, I regret to say, in this matter Tuckett seems to me to use evidence selectively, preferring here to emphasize this one manuscript over against the greater body of evidence, which shows that from the earliest manuscripts onward some words *are* treated with great regularity and are much more widely attested. P.Egerton 2 simply will not bear the load that he tries to place upon it.

3:29) where it designates "Joshua," but consistently writes the same name as a *nomen sacrum* when Jesus is the referent (e.g., see Luke 3:21, 23). Likewise, as Paap shows, the scribe of 𝔓66 treats Θεος as a *nomen sacrum* (virtually all cases referring to "God"), but writes in full the plural forms of the word, which refer to other deities. The same differentiation is reflected also in P.Chester Beatty VI (Numbers–Deuteronomy), and P.Chester Beatty VII (Isaiah, third century CE, #67 in appendix 1). In the Chester Beatty Gospels codex (𝔓45) and the Pauline codex (𝔓46), the scribes typically distinguish similarly between cases where Κυριος refers to Jesus and the plural forms of the word (which refer to other figures/deities). As a striking instance of this, note how the scribe of 𝔓46 handles these terms in 1 Corinthians 8:4-6, where different referents are in view. (I set the *nomina sacra* forms in majuscule to facilitate easy notice of them.)

οὐδεὶς ΘC εἰ μὴ εἷς. καὶ γὰρ εἴπερ εἰσὶν λεγόμενοι . . . θεοὶ πολλοὶ καὶ κύριοι πολλοί, ἀλλ' ἡμῖν εἷς ΘC ὁ ΠΡ ἐξ οὗ τὰ πάντα καὶ ἡμεῖς εἰς αὐτόν, καὶ εἷς ΚC ΙΗC ΧΡC δι' οὗ τὰ πάντα καὶ ἡμεῖς δι' αὐτοῦ.

These are not exceptional instances, as anyone can verify by checking published editions of Christian manuscripts, or by reviewing carefully the data compiled by Paap and O'Callaghan.[103] And I repeat for emphasis that the question is not whether there are some exceptions and occasional instances of this or that variation, but whether we see clearly dominant *patterns* in scribal practices.

Over against all this, Tuckett proposes that the abbreviations of certain words originated simply as readers' aids. But this would have been a strange move, especially if the concern was for people with limited reading ability. Why increase the difficulty of texts by introducing these peculiar abbreviations, which would have required readers to decode them?[104] Also, if the aim was to help readers get their bearings on the page, it would seem to have been more sensible to select words that occur more predictably on any given page, and more frequently, such as καὶ. There are numerous

103. See, e.g., Paap, *Nomina Sacra*, 100-113.
104. Cf. Tuckett, "Nomina Sacra," 456-57. He acknowledges as "a possible difficulty" (!) in his theory that these abbreviations would actually have made reading more difficult rather than less, but counters this by claiming that with the supralinear stroke the abbreviated forms may not have been so difficult (456 n. 96). But why would scribes have created the difficulty for readers that these abbreviations posed in the first place?

pages in Christian literary texts where none of the *nomina sacra* appear, which means that they do not reliably serve to orient readers.[105]

Moreover, we do not need to speculate about what devices might have been used to help Roman-era readers of limited abilities. We know what was done, and abbreviations such as the *nomina sacra* simply do not feature at all.[106] We have actual artifacts, including school texts, student exercises, and copies of literary works marked up to assist readers. The devices used to make texts read more easily include large, carefully written script, word groups (e.g., articles and nouns, prepositional phrases) marked with oblique strokes (which look like large acute accents) or sometimes with spaces, breathing marks, accents (sometimes placed over every word), sometimes dots to separate words, apostrophes, and even marginal notations.[107] In some literary prose texts, scribes used paragraph marks and punctuation to signal shorter or longer pauses in reading aloud.[108] Also, we have personal copies of literary texts that were made by professional scribes and then marked up by the readers.[109] Among all these devices, there is nothing like the *nomina sacra*.

These artifacts provide a valuable context for assessing the scribal features of early Christian manuscripts, and it does appear that many, especially biblical, texts were prepared with a view toward ease of reading. For example, the wide margins, large writing, generous line spacing, spaces separating sense units, and diaeresis over initial vowels all rather clearly are the sorts of devices used in non-Christian manuscripts as well to facilitate the reading of them. But there is no basis for taking the abbreviations called *nomina sacra* as having anything to do with this. Of course, anything is possible, but the historical task is to judge what is most likely, and what comports most adequately with the extant evidence.

---

105. A quick and limited scan of 𝔓45 (P.Chester Beatty I), for instance, shows many pages without *nomina sacra*.

106. See Raffaella Cribiore, *Gymnastics of the Mind: Greek Education in Hellenistic and Roman Egypt* (Princeton: Princeton University Press, 2001), esp. 127-59, which builds upon her previous work, *Writing, Teachers, and Students in Graeco-Roman Egypt* (Atlanta: Scholars Press, 1996). More briefly, see Italo Gallo, *Greek and Latin Papyrology* (London: Institute of Classical Studies, 1986), esp. 90-93.

107. See Cribiore, *Gymnastics*, 138-39, 140-41, and the photographs of artifacts, 135, 150.

108. William A. Johnson, "The Function of the Paragraphus in Greek Literary Prose Texts," *ZPE* 100 (1994): 65-68.

109. Examples in Turner, *Manuscripts*, e.g., plates 14, 16, 22.

Even Tuckett's proposal would make the *nomina sacra* a significant Christian innovation. The scribal practice would be a novel scribal device, signaling a concern for the reading of texts in Christian circles. But all indications are that the *nomina sacra* are a scribal practice that reflects something of early Christian faith and piety. As Paap concluded from his exhaustive analysis of the ways all the words in question are handled in Christian manuscripts of the first five centuries, the special scribal treatment of them shows that they typically are "technical terms of Christianity and spring from a common spiritual background."[110]

Also, as I have stated already, the *nomina sacra* seem to be particularly (perhaps exclusively) a *visual* phenomenon. Roberts's suggestion that lectors of biblical texts may have made some gesture of "obeisance" where the *nomina sacra* appear has no corroboration in anything that I know of early Christian reading and worship practices.[111] Moreover, this would not at all explain why these abbreviations spread so widely and rapidly in all sorts of texts that were almost certainly not intended for public reading in churches. Instead, so far as we can tell, the *nomina sacra* were registered only by those who copied and had sight of the texts in which they appear. This is why I have emphasized that the *nomina sacra* properly belong in the history of early Christian visual culture. Indeed, this scribal practice is arguably the earliest evidence in such a history, and is thus of singular significance.

Also, even if only limited numbers of Christians could read well enough to handle the demands of the biblical texts, we should not assume that the circle of those who encountered *nomina sacra* was restricted to them.[112] In a culture in which reading and writing were as important as they were in the Greco-Roman period, even marginally literate and illiterate people would have a high appreciation for texts, and also for those who could write and read them.[113] Indeed, perhaps especially for those unable

110. Paap, *Nomina Sacra*, 123.

111. Roberts, *Manuscript*, 35.

112. Cf. Tuckett, "Nomina Sacra," 446-47. But he does not consider the sort of matters that I discuss here. Moreover, he relies upon Harris, *Ancient Literacy*, for his view of the likely percentage of Roman-era readers. But see the criticism of Harris's work in Mary Beard et al., *Literacy in the Roman World*, JRASup 3 (Ann Arbor: Journal of Roman Archaeology, 1991).

113. "What made Greco-Roman Egypt a literate society, in spite of the fact that the mass of the population was illiterate, was that even people who did not have direct access to writing had to reckon with it in their daily lives, and they recognized the framework of conven-

to decipher them, texts can hold a certain, almost mysterious, aura. It is entirely likely that a good many semiliterate or illiterate early Christians would have regarded with particular favor, even awe, those texts that were treated as scripture in their gatherings, and might well have welcomed a chance to view with reverence the written words. It is equally reasonable to suspect that Christian leaders seeking to promote respect for such texts would have been ready to show copies of them. I suggest that devout believers may well have asked to be shown especially the name of Jesus and the other key epithets for Jesus and God. So the visual encounter with the *nomina sacra* may have been experienced much more widely than the circle of those able to read aloud the texts in which they occur.

But even if this be rejected as too speculative, and the only Christians visually acquainted with *nomina sacra* were those who copied and read the Christian texts in which these curious abbreviations appear, they still represent an interesting and significant visual expression of early Christian piety.[114] Also, if, as most scholars think, this scribal practice is related somehow to the special treatment of the divine name by ancient Jewish scribes, the *nomina sacra* also reflect the historical connection of the early Christian movement and its Jewish religious matrix.

Although overlooked or little understood by many scholars, since the late 1990s the *nomina sacra* have come in for comparatively more attention. As this chapter shows, some lively issues are currently under debate. Over the many decades since Traube's influential study, some assumptions and theories have been rendered invalid as progressively earlier and greater bodies of manuscripts were made available for study. Whatever the validity of the particular views that we have considered here, including those that I have defended, the *nomina sacra* represent an important body of evidence for all students of early Christianity.

---

tions and expectations that governed it" (Cribiore, *Gymnastics,* 163). See, e.g., Cribiore's emphasis on the more "extemporaneous and casual" use of writing and reading in Greco-Roman Egypt, in contrast with earlier Egyptian periods and also medieval centuries in Europe (*Gymnastics,* 159, and also 177-78).

114. It is not an effective objection against this to point to the simple nature of the *nomina sacra:* abbreviations with a supralinear stroke over them. My claim is that it was enough to set off certain words visually, writing them in a distinctive manner, which made them readily recognizable even to those who could not read.

Illustration: *Nomina Sacra*

(Contractions shown here include nominative and genitive forms as illustrating how the nouns are written in the various cases. I have also written the words in majuscule characters and with the "open" *sigma*, to give more of a sense of their actual appearance in early manuscripts.)

The Four Epithets Most Frequently and Most Regularly Abbreviated

ΙΗϹΟΥϹ. Contracted forms: ΙϹ, ΙΥ, etc. Suspended: ΙΗ. Conflated forms: ΙΗϹ, ΙΗΥ, etc.

ΘΕΟϹ. Contracted forms: ΘϹ, ΘΥ, etc.

ΚΥΡΙΟϹ. Contracted forms: ΚϹ, ΚΥ, etc. Conflated forms: ΚΡϹ, ΚΡΥ, etc.

ΧΡΙϹΤΟϹ. Contracted forms: ΧϹ, ΧΥ, etc. Conflated forms: ΧΡϹ, ΧΡΥ, etc.

Other Words, Less Regularly/Consistently Abbreviated

ΠΝΕΥΜΑ. Contracted forms: ΠΝΑ, ΠΝΙ, etc.

ΑΝΘΡΩΠΟϹ. Contracted forms: ΑΝΟϹ, ΑΝΟΥ, etc.

ΥΙΟϹ. Contracted forms: ΥϹ, ΥΥ, etc., or ΥΙϹ, ΥΙΥ, etc.

ΠΑΤΗΡ. Contracted forms: ΠΗΡ (or ΠΡ), ΠΡϹ, etc.

ϹΤΑΥΡΟϹ. Contracted forms: ϹΤΡΟϹ, ϹΤΡΝ, etc., or ϹΡϹ, ϹΡΝ, etc. (and occasionally with the "staurogram" discussed in the next chapter)

ΔΑΥΕΙΔ. Contracted forms: ΔΔ or ΔΑΔ

ΜΗΤΗΡ. Contracted forms: ΜΗΡ, ΜΡΑ, ΜΡϹ, ΜΡΙ

ϹΩΤΗΡ. Contracted forms: ϹΗΡ, or ϹΩΡ, ϹΡϹ, etc.

ΙϹΡΑΗΛ. Contracted form: ΙΗΛ

ΙΕΡΟΥϹΑΛΗΜ. Contracted form: ΙΛΗΜ

ΟΥΡΑΝΟϹ. Contracted forms: ΟΥΝΟϹ, ΟΥΟΥ, etc.

CHAPTER FOUR

The Staurogram

We now turn to yet another intriguing scribal phenomenon found in a few early Christian manuscripts, the so-called staurogram (see plates 4-5, appendix 2).[1] This particular device is a monogram or "compendium" formed by superimposing the Greek letter *rho* upon the *tau*. In subsequent Christian usage, the *tau-rho* is one of several compendia used to refer to Jesus, and so they are sometimes referred to as "Christograms" (see the list of early Christograms at the end of this chapter).[2] The best known of these by far is the *chi-rho*, which is still widely employed to mark such things as clerical vestments as well as items of furniture and utensils intended for ecclesiastical usage.[3] The other compendia also include the

---

1. In this chapter I draw heavily upon my essay, "The Staurogram in Early Christian Manuscripts: The Earliest Visual Reference to the Crucified Jesus?" in *New Testament Manuscripts: Their Text and Their World*, ed. Thomas J. Kraus and Tobias Nicklas (Leiden: Brill, 2006), 207-26. The most important previous studies are by Kurt Aland, "Bemerkungen zum Alter und Entstehung des Christogramms anhand von Beobachtungen bei 𝔓66 und 𝔓75," *Studien zur Überlieferung des Neuen Testaments und seines Textes*, ANTF 2 (Berlin: de Gruyter, 1967), 173-79; Matthew Black, "The Chi-Rho Sign — Christogram and/or Staurogram?" in *Apostolic History and the Gospel: Essays Presented to F. F. Bruce*, ed. W. Ward Gasque and Ralph P. Martin (Grand Rapids: Eerdmans, 1970), 319-27; Erika Dinkler-von Schubert, "CTⲀⲨPOC: Vom 'Wort vom Kreuz' (1 Cor. 1,18) zum Kreuz-Symbol," in *Byzantine East, Latin West: Art-Historical Studies in Honor of Kurt Weitzmann*, ed. Doula Mouriki et al. (Princeton: Department of Art and Archaeology, 1995), 29-39.

2. See the discussion of "Abbreviations and Monograms" in Jack Finegan, *The Archeology of the New Testament: The Life of Jesus and the Beginning of the Early Church*, rev. ed. (Princeton: Princeton University Press, 1992), 352-55.

3. For example, Wolfgang Wischmeyer, "Christogramm und Staurogramm in den

iota-chi and the *iota-eta*. The more familiar usage of any of these devices for many centuries has been as freestanding symbols marking something as in some way Christian.[4] But two points in particular constitute the emphasis in this chapter.

First, contrary to some widely influential assumptions, the earliest of these Christograms appears to be the *tau-rho* (not the more familiar *chi-rho*). Second, and still more important for this book, the earliest extant Christian use of the *tau-rho* is not as a freestanding symbol and general reference to Christ but in manuscripts dated as early as around 175-225 CE, where it functions as part of the abbreviation of the Greek words for "cross" (σταυρός) and "crucify" (σταυρόω), written (abbreviated) as *nomina sacra*. As previous scholars have observed, therefore, in this particular use of the *tau-rho* we should probably see more precisely a staurogram, that is, a visual reference to Jesus' crucifixion. If this is correct, it has significant implications for our views of the history of early Christian piety, and also for the history of Christian iconography/art.[5]

Early Christograms

As a context for considering the *tau-rho*, however, it may be useful first to take some further note of the derivation and early Christian use of such monograms as references to Jesus. We may begin by noting that, with the

---

lateinischen Inschriften altkirchlicher Zeit," in *Theologia Crucis — Signum Crucis: Festschrift für Erich Dinkler zum 70. Geburtstag*, ed. Carl Andresen and Günter Klein (Tübingen: Mohr [Siebeck], 1979), 539-50.

4. In some later (post-Constantinian) instances, two or more of these devices are sometimes used together, as in the Christian inscription from Armant (ancient Hermonthis, Egypt), at the bottom of which there is a *tau-rho* and an *ankh* flanked on either side by a *chi-rho*. Finegan (*Archeology*, 387-88) gives a photograph and short discussion. The inscription is variously dated between the fourth and sixth century CE. As another example, both the *tau-rho* and the *chi-rho* appear on the sixth-century sarcophagus of Archbishop Teodoro in St. Apollinare in Classe, Ravenna. Photo in G. Bovini, *Ravenna: Its Mosaics and Monuments* (Ravenna: Longo, 1980), 139.

5. I develop here views that I advanced more briefly in an earlier publication: "Earliest Evidence," esp. 279-82. I elaborate observations by Erich Dinkler, *Signum Crucis* (Tübingen: Mohr [Siebeck], 1967), 177-78; and Kurt Aland, "Neue Neutestamentliche Papyri II," *NTS* 10 (1963-64): 62-79 (esp. 75-79); and idem, "Neue Neutestamentliche Papyri II," *NTS* 11 (1964-65): 1-21, esp. 1-3.

possible exception of the *iota-eta,* all of these compendia are actually pre-Christian devices appropriated by early Christians and invested with new meaning.[6]

Technically, a "monogram" is an interweaving or combination of two (or sometimes more) alphabetic characters, the component letters of the resultant device typically referring to a person's name or title. But such "compendia" (also called "ligatures") can also serve other purposes, particularly as abbreviations of common words. For instance, in pre/non-Christian Greek papyri of the Roman period, the *chi-rho* is used as an abbreviation for several words, including forms of χρονος, and in Greek inscriptions this ligature is found as an abbreviation for ἑκατονταρχια, ἑκατονταρχης, χιλιαρχης, and a few other terms.[7] As well as the more familiar form of the *chi-rho* device, in which one of the two letters is superimposed on the other, there are also instances where the one component letter is written just above the other.[8]

To cite another early non-Christian instance of the familiar form of this particular ligature, Randolph Richards drew attention to a *chi-rho* in P.Mur. 164a (line 11), a text of Greek "tachygraphic" (shorthand) writing on parchment that, along with the other manuscripts found in Wadi Murabbaʿat, is probably to be dated to the Jewish revolt of 132-135 CE.[9] A *chi-rho* also appears in the margin of a *hypomnēma* (commentary) text on Homer's *Iliad,* dated to the first century BCE, the device here serving as a sign for χρηστον (marking passages "useful" for excerpting).[10]

As well, the *tau-rho* combination, the focus of my discussion in this

6. For further evidence and discussion of the pre/non-Christian usage of these devices, see Blanchard, *Sigles;* McNamee, *Abbreviations;* Avi-Yonah, *Abbreviations in Greek Inscriptions.* Dinkler-von Schubert ("CTΑΥΡΟC," 33-34) also surveys the matter. The most wide-ranging discussion of ancient monograms known to me is Victor Garthausen, *Das alte Monogramm* (Leipzig: Hiersemann, 1924), but his handling of earliest Christian monograms (esp. 73-79) is clearly incorrect in light of subsequently discovered manuscript evidence such as that discussed in this chapter.

7. See, e.g., Don Pasquale Colella, "Les abréviations ʊ et ℟," *Revue biblique* 80 (1973): 547-58, who comments on the likely import of *chi-rho* marks on (non-Christian) amphorae.

8. Examples cited by McNamee, *Abbreviations,* 118; Blanchard, *Sigles,* 26 n. 36; and Avi-Yonah, *Abbreviations,* 112.

9. E. Randolph Richards, *The Secretary in the Letters of Paul,* WUNT 2/42 (Tübingen: Mohr [Siebeck], 1991), 40-41. The full description of the manuscript is in P. Benoit et al., *Les grottes de Murabbaʿāt,* DJD 2 (Oxford: Oxford University Press, 1961), 275-79.

10. Turner, *Greek Manuscripts,* plate 58.

chapter, appears in pre/non-Christian usage, for instance as an abbreviation for τρ(οπος), τρ(ιακας), and Τρ(οκονδας).[11] Among other noteworthy instances, there is also the use of this device on some coins of King Herod (37-4 BCE), the *tau-rho* here intended to identify these coins with the third year of his reign.[12]

The *iota-chi* combination was an archaic form of the Greek letter *psi*, and was also sometimes used on Roman-era coins (probably as a numerical symbol). Moreover, there is an obvious similarity to other six-pointed devices used for decoration ubiquitously in various cultures, and sometimes functioning as stylized stars.[13]

As for the *iota-eta* combination, however, in surveys of the data with which I am acquainted, all instances of its usage are Christian, and so it may be a Christian innovation. This device is comprised of majuscule forms of the first two letters of the name Ιησους and was intended as an obvious reference to him.[14] But there are analogous ligatures of other letters in non-Christian Greek documentary papyri, such as the combination of *mu* and *epsilon* (for μεγας, μερις, μετοχος, and other terms).[15] So the specific *iota-eta* combination may have been employed first as a monogram by Christians, but the basic technique was borrowed from wider scribal practice of the time. The Christian use of other ligatures, for example, the stylized six-pointed decorative compendium *iota-chi* to refer to Ιησους Χριστος, may have helped to suggest this particular device. In any case, the basic technique of joining various letters to form a ligature was familiar to readers of the time, especially in documentary texts and inscriptions.

As noted already, in Christian usage all of the monograms/compendia under review here served in one way or another as references to Jesus. Thus

11. McNamee, *Abbreviations,* 119; Avi-Yonah, *Abbreviations,* 105.

12. Baruch Kanael, "The Coins of King Herod of the Third Year," *JQR* 62 (1951-52): 261-64; idem, "Ancient Jewish Coins and Their Historical Importance," *BA* 26 (1963): 38-62, esp. 48. Use of devices involving a *tau-rho* ligature were also noted on items from Dura Europos, at least some instances likely craftsmen's marks. See R. N. Frye, J. F. Gillam, H. Inghold, and C. B. Welles, "Inscriptions from Dura-Europos," *Yale Classical Studies* 14 (1955): 123-213, esp. 191-94.

13. For instances and discussion see Max Sulzberger, "Le symbole de la croix et les monogrammes de Jésus chez les premiers Chrétiens," *Byzantion* 2 (1925): 394-95 (337-448), who also cites Victor Emil Gardthausen, *Das alte Monogramm, mit fünf Tafeln* (Leipzig: Hiersemann, 1924), 76-77.

14. Avi-Yonah, *Abbreviations,* 72.

15. Blanchard, *Sigles,* 4.

the Christian appropriation of them all reflects the enormous place of Jesus in early Christian devotion, and these curious devices thereby functioned as expressions of this piety.[16] The *chi-rho*, for example, uses the first two letters of Χριστός, and became one of the most familiar and widely used emblems in Christian tradition.[17] The *iota-chi* seems to have been appropriated as a combination of the initial letters of Ιησους Χριστος, and likewise served simply as another device by which to refer to him, as did the *iota-eta*.[18]

Moreover, it is important to note that all of these compendia represent *visual* phenomena. So, just as I have proposed was the case with the *nomina sacra*, these devices served as reverential references to Jesus in early Christian usage, with a certain iconographic function and significance that should be recognized. Indeed, along with the *nomina sacra*, the first uses of these devices, which take us back to the late second century and quite possibly earlier, represent the earliest extant expression of what we may term a Christian "visual culture." I shall return to this point later. But in the case of the Christian use of the *tau-rho* monogram, there are also a few interesting distinctives that now require further attention.

The Staurogram: Origin

The first matter to highlight is that, whereas all of the other Christian compendia that I have mentioned are true monograms, the component letters in each case directly referring to Jesus by name and/or christological title, the Christian use of the *tau-rho* combination does not have any such derivation or function. Its component letters neither derive from nor refer to

---

16. See now esp. Hurtado, *Lord Jesus Christ*.

17. Note, e.g., the use of the *chi-rho* in the Trisomus inscription in the Catacomb of Priscilla (Rome), a prayer to God, the last line of which reads: "σοι δοξα εν [⳩]." For full text and discussion see Finegan, *Archeology*, 380. For other instances see M. Burzachechi, "Sull' Uso Pre-Costantiniano del Monogramma Greco di Christo," *Rendiconti della Pontificia Accademia Romana di Archeologia*, series III, 28 (1955-56), 197-211.

18. For example, the *iota-chi* on a sixth-century CE sarcophagus (with lambs and laurel), St. Apollinare in Classe, Ravenna (photo in Bovini, *Ravenna*, 138). Finegan (*Archeology*, 379-80) gives a photo and discussion of a painted sign in the Catacomb of Priscilla that appears to have an *iota-eta* compendium, but in this instance the horizontal stroke extends through and beyond the letters, giving the appearance of three connected equilateral crosses.

Jesus' name or any of the familiar christological titles. Indeed, in Christian usage the two component letters in this device do not appear to refer to any words at all, and therefore the *tau-rho* is not a monogram in the proper sense. So what suggested the Christian appropriation of this particular letter compendium?[19] Furthermore, although the *tau-rho* seems to have had some *later* usage as a freestanding reverential cipher for the figure of Jesus, or perhaps simply as an emblem intended to identify something as Christian, what was the initial function and significance of this device, and when might it first have appeared in Christian usage?

Let us first address the question of the origin of the *tau-rho* in Christian usage. Our most important evidence, and certainly the earliest, comprises the instances of the device in some very early Christian manuscripts.[20] We may begin with Papyrus Bodmer II (𝔓66, #115 in appendix 1; plate 6 in appendix 2), the extant portion of a codex of the Gospel of John (chaps. 1–14 relatively well preserved, the rest of John through chap. 21 in very fragmentary condition), dated paleographically to about 200.[21] In the extant portions of this codex the noun σταυρος (three instances) and the verb σταυροω (at least seven instances) are written in abbreviated forms, and with the *tau* and *rho* of these words written as a compendium. In each case the statement in which the noun or verb appears refers to Jesus' cross/crucifixion.[22]

19. Cf. Dinkler-von Schubert, "CTΑΥΡΟC," 32, who judged the question no closer to an answer after several decades of scholarly effort. I acknowledge the difficulty involved, as the following discussion will show. But I do not think that we are entirely without clues, and I believe that we can identify a likely basic association of the device in earliest Christian use.

20. Kurt Aland has the credit for first drawing scholarly attention to this evidence in two important articles cited already, "Neue Neutestamentliche Papyri II."

21. Victor Martin, *Papyrus Bodmer II: Évangile de Jean, chap. 1–14* (Cologny-Geneva: Bibliotheca Bodmeriana, 1956); idem, *Papyrus Bodmer II, Supplément: Évangile de Jean, chap. 14–21* (Cologny-Geneva: Bibliotheca Bodmeriana, 1958); and Victor Martin and J. W. B. Barns, *Papyrus Bodmer II, Supplément: Évangile de Jean, chap. 14–21, nouvelle edition augmentée et corrigée* (Cologny-Geneva: Bibliotheca Bodmeriana, 1962).

22. Aland identified instances in 𝔓66 of σταυρος abbreviated and with the *tau-rho* in John 19:19, 25, 31, and abbreviated forms of σταυροω with this device in John 19:6 (three), 15 (two), 16, 18 ("Neue Neutestamentliche Papyri II," *NTS* 10:75), and further possible cases in 19:17, 20. Cf. instances identified by Martin and Barns in the 1962 augmented and corrected edition of chaps. 14–21 of 𝔓66: forms of σταυρος in 19:19, 25, plus another one restored as "des plus probables" in 19:18, and forms of σταυροω in 19:6 (two), 16, 18, plus a proposed restoration of another instance in 19:20. My own examination of the photos published in their 1962 edition enabled me to verify clear instances of the compendium in abbreviated forms of σταυρος at 19:19, 31, and in forms of σταυροω at 19:15, 16, and 18.

Likewise, in 𝔓75 (##108 and 114 in appendix 1), another codex dated to about the same time and comprising portions of the Gospel of Luke (P.Bodmer XIV) and the Gospel of John (P.Bodmer XV), there are further instances of the *tau-rho* compendium used in abbreviated forms of the same two Greek words (plates 4-5 in appendix 2).²³ But the scribal practice in this manuscript was not as consistent as in 𝔓66. In all three cases in 𝔓75 where σταυρος appears in the extant portions of Luke (9:23; 14:27; 23:26) the word is written in an abbreviated form, and in two of these cases (9:23; 14:27) the *tau-rho* compendium is also used.²⁴ Of the six extant occurrences of the verb σταυροω, however, the word is abbreviated twice (23:33; 24:7), and in the other four cases is written fully (23:21 [twice]; 23; 24:20). In 𝔓75 the only use of the *tau-rho* in an abbreviation of σταυροω is in Luke 24:7.²⁵

In these instances of σταυρος and σταυροω (in each case with a horizontal stroke over the abbreviation), the copyists in question were extending to these words the special, and apparently distinctively Christian, abbreviation practice now commonly referred to as *nomina sacra*. As Kurt Aland observed, however, at least on the basis of these two early, and roughly contemporary, manuscripts, it appears that the Christian practice of writing σταυρος as a *nomen sacrum* may have become somewhat more quickly and more firmly established than was the case for the verb σταυροω.²⁶

As further evidence, we should also note that in the Vienna fragment of 𝔓45 (dated ca. 200-250), at Matthew 26:2 (the sole place where either the relevant noun or verb appears in the extant portions of the manuscript) the verb form σταυρωθηναι ("to be crucified") is written in a contracted form and with the *tau-rho* compendium.²⁷ Including this instance, we

23. Victor Martin and Rodolphe Kasser, *Papyrus Bodmer XIV: Évangile de Luc, chap. 3–24* (Cologny-Geneva: Bibliotheca Bodmeriana, 1961).

24. The statements in Luke 9:23 and 14:27 have Jesus demanding that his followers "take up daily" and "bear" their own cross. But in each case there is a clearly implied reference to his crucifixion.

25. Martin and Kasser, *Papyrus Bodmer XIV*, 18; Aland, "Neue Neutestamentliche Papyri II," *NTS* 11:2. The extant portions of John in 𝔓75 (P.Bod. XV) do not include any uses of σταυρος or σταυροω.

26. Aland, "Neue Neutestamentliche Papyri II," *NTS* 11:2.

27. Hans Gerstinger, "Ein Fragment des Chester Beatty-Evangelienkodex in der Papyrussammlung der Nationalbibliothek in Wien (Pap. Graec. Vindob. 31974)," *Aegyptus* 13 (1936): 69 (67-72). The fragment (Matt. 25:41–26:39) forms part of Chester Beatty Papyrus I (VH #371), 30 leaves of a codex originally comprising the four Gospels (in "Western" order) and Acts. See esp. Skeat, "Codicological Analysis."

have three early-third-century Christian manuscripts with this curious device, in each of which it is used in the same way, as part of a *nomina sacra*
treatment of the Greek words for "cross" and "crucify."

It is unlikely that these three manuscripts happen to be the very first
Christian usages of the *tau-rho*. We must suppose that it had already been
in Christian usage for some period of time in order for it to have been used
(apparently independently) by the copyists of these three manuscripts.[28]
This obviously means that we should date the initial Christian appropriation of the *tau-rho* at least as early as the final decades of the second century, and very plausibly somewhat earlier. It is an interesting question as to
whether the earliest appropriation was made by copyists of still earlier
Christian manuscripts in references to Jesus' cross/crucifixion, or whether
there was some previous or wider Christian usage of this compendium,
that is, beyond its use in Christian manuscripts. Unfortunately, I know of
no clear evidence to settle the matter. What is clear is that 𝔓45, 𝔓66, and
𝔓75 offer us the earliest extant Christian uses of the *tau-rho* device, and in
all these cases it is used in references to Jesus' cross/crucifixion (or to his
call to disciples to take up their crosses in response to his crucifixion).

This important manuscript evidence about the Christian appropriation of the *tau-rho* device clearly means that earlier (and still echoed)
views, such as the influential analysis of early Christian Jesus monograms
by Max Sulzberger, must be judged incorrect on a couple of crucial matters, and that any history of early Christian symbols must take account of
this.[29] Most obviously, contra Sulzberger, the Christian *tau-rho* monogram
did not first emerge in the post-Constantinian period, and was not likely
derived from a prior Christian usage of the *chi-rho*.[30] Instead, in 𝔓45, 𝔓66,

28. Although these three manuscripts are dated to a roughly similar period, the differences in scribal hands and a number of other features indicate that 𝔓45, 𝔓66, and 𝔓75 must
derive from three distinguishable settings, which means that the copyists likely worked independently of one another. See esp. James R. Royse, "Scribal Habits in Early Greek New Testament Papyri" (Th.D. diss., Berkeley, Graduate Theological Union, 1981).

29. Sulzberger, "Symbole de la croix." A very similar schema of the evolutionary development of Christian monograms was set out earlier and more briefly by Lewis Spence,
"Cross," *Encyclopedia of Religion and Ethics*, ed. James Hastings (Edinburgh: T&T Clark,
1911), 4:324-30. Likewise in need of correction is the analysis by M. Alison Frantz, "The Provenance of the Open Rho in the Christian Monograms," *American Journal of Archaeology* 33
(1929): 10-26, esp. 10-11.

30. Sulzberger also made several other claims that have been influential but are shown
to be incorrect by the manuscript evidence. He claimed that the earliest Christian symbol

and 𝔓75 we have Christian use of the *tau-rho* considerably earlier than datable instances of the Christian usage of the *chi-rho*, and well before Constantine! Indeed, as Aland noted several decades ago, in light of this manuscript evidence, the earliest Jesus monogram appears to be the *tau-rho*, not the *chi-rho*.[31] Moreover, and perhaps of equal significance, the instances of the *tau-rho* device in these manuscripts, the earliest Christian uses extant, show us that the compendium functioned in this early period not simply as a general symbol for Jesus but more specifically to refer reverentially to Jesus' death.[32]

Several decades ago Jean Savignac noted that this manuscript evidence indicating the chronological priority of the *tau-rho* over the *chi-rho* rendered Sulzberger's view of the origin of the Christian use of these two ligatures invalid. But Savignac's proposal seems to me no more persuasive. On the basis of the frequently noted Christian inscription from Armant dated to the fourth century (or later), which features a *tau-rho* and the hieroglyphic *ankh* sign flanked by two *chi-rho*s, he suggested that

---

for Jesus' cross was the *chi*, not the *tau* ("Symbole de la croix," 366), that as a general rule "on ne trouve ni croix, ni monogrammes de Jésus, ni représentations de la Passion avant le quatrième siècle" (371), that possibly with rare exceptions there are no direct representations of Jesus' cross before Constantine (386), that the *iota-chi* is the earliest-attested Jesus monogram, and that neither the *chi-rho* nor the *tau-rho* can be dated prior to the fourth century (393). Granted, Sulzberger wrote before the Chester Beatty and Bodmer papyri were available to scholars, and he leaned heavily on very limited inscriptional data. Based on Christian manuscripts then available, he observed: "Il est remarquable que, dans les papyrus chrétiens, on ne trouve ni croix ni monogramme avant le Ve siècle" (446). But he cannot be excused entirely. Even on the basis of evidence available to him, he had reason to question his views. But he seems to have allowed an elegant theory to determine how to handle evidence, rather than shaping his theory to fit the evidence. To cite an important instance, in considering an early Christian inscription from Egypt that ends with a *tau-rho* flanked by an *alpha* and an *omega*, he preferred to assume that these items were added "après coup" (376-77). 𝔓45, 𝔓66, and 𝔓75 now clearly confirm, however, that this was a serious misjudgment. The influence of his weighty article is reflected in writings of many other historians of early Christian art, e.g., C. R. Morey, *Early Christian Art*, 2nd ed. (Princeton: Princeton University Press, 1953), 128.

31. I restrict attention here to the use of these ligatures, and cannot engage the wider questions about other early Christian symbols, among which fish are prominent, including the anagram ΙΧΘΥΣ (= Ιησους Χριστος Θεου Υιος Σωτηρ), which probably goes back to the early third century or even earlier. On this anagram see, e.g., Snyder, *Ante Pacem*, 24-26 (with further references), and esp. Franz J. Dölger, *ΙΧΘΥΣ. Das Fisch Symbol in frühchristlichen Zeit* (Münster: Aschendorff, 1928).

32. Aland, "Neue Neutestamentliche Papyri II," *NTS* 10:78.

the appropriation of the *tau-rho* derived from its visual similarity to the *ankh* (a symbol for "life"). He further proposed that the *ankh* had been adopted by Christians, perhaps in certain Valentinian circles, in Egypt.[33] Savignac recognized that in general early Christians, especially those whose faith remained more influenced by Jewish monotheistic concerns, may have been reluctant to adopt a pagan religious symbol such as the *ankh*. But, pointing to the appearance of an *ankh* on the final page of the copy of the *Gospel of Truth* in the Jung Codex, and taking the widely shared view that this text derives from Valentinian circles, Savignac offered this as a basis for thinking that Valentinians may have been more ready to adopt this ancient Egyptian symbol for "life," interpreting it as referring to the life given through Jesus. There are, however, major problems with Savignac's proposals.

First, his core thesis does not adequately reflect the respective dates of the evidence. In fact, the earliest verifiable Christian uses of the *ankh* symbol are considerably *later* than the uses of the *tau-rho* device in 𝔓66, 𝔓75, and 𝔓45.[34] It is simply not sound historical method, therefore, to attribute the clearly attested Christian use of the *tau-rho* to a supposedly prior Christian use of the *ankh*. It is always a better approach to develop a theory that is shaped by the evidence! If there was any *causative* relationship between the Christian appropriation of the *ankh* and the *tau-rho* (and it is not entirely clear that there was), the chronological data make it more

33. Jean de Savignac, "Les papyrus Bodmer XIV et XV," *Scriptorium* 17 (1963): 51 (50-55). Much earlier, Gardthausen (*Alte Monogramm*, 78-79) had proposed that the *chi-rho* was the earliest Christian monogram, and that a subsequent Christian use of the *tau-rho* derived from the *ankh*. Both of his proposals are now refuted by the evidence of early Christian manuscripts.

34. Aland disputed whether an *ankh* could really be read on the last page of the Jung Codex ("Neue Neutestamentliche Papyri II," *NTS* 11:2-3). But whatever the valid reading of this particular manuscript, the *ankh* symbol indisputably appears elsewhere in the Nag Hammadi texts, particularly on the leather cover of Codex 2 and at the end of the text titled "The Prayer of the Apostle Paul." Moreover, other artifacts such as the Armant inscription mentioned above rather clearly indicate Christian appropriation of the *ankh* by the fourth to sixth century. But this appropriation seems not to have been particularly connected to Valentinian circles. Although some of the Nag Hammadi *texts* may well have originated in Greek-speaking "gnostic" circles, the fourth-century Coptic *manuscripts* of the Nag Hammadi collection were likely prepared by monastic scribes who were certainly strongly ascetic, but not particularly "Valentinians." See, e.g., the discussion by James M. Robinson, "Introduction," in *The Nag Hammadi Library*, ed. Robinson, rev. ed. (Leiden: Brill, 1988), 10-22.

likely that Savignac's proposal should be stood on its head. The appropriation of the *ankh* may have resulted from its visual resemblance to the *tau-rho* device, which appears to have been appropriated first. In any case, the *sequential* relationship between the Christian appropriation of the *tau-rho* and the *ankh* is rather clearly the opposite to Savignac's theory.

There is a second problem in Savignac's proposal, and it is not confined to him. It is a mistake to presume that the Christian appropriation of the various Jesus monograms must have involved one initial monogram from which subsequent Christian appropriation of the others then developed. It seems to me that this insufficiently examined assumption contributed to the misjudgments of Sulzberger as well as Savignac, leading them to posit their respective developmental schemes, even though the evidence available at the points when each of them wrote did not actually suggest either theory.

Why should we suppose that there had to be one initial Jesus monogram from which the others somehow developed?[35] It is at least as reasonable to view the Christian uses of the various Jesus monograms as reflecting quasi-independent appropriations of some of the various pre/non-Christian compendia, each of the appropriations suggested to Christians by the perceived capability of the respective devices to express Christian faith and piety.[36] As noted above, with the possible exception of the *iota-eta*, all the devices in question here were already in pre/non-Christian use, and thus were readily available. All that was needed for the appropriation of any one of them was for some Christian to perceive it in a new light, as capable of serving as a visual reference to Jesus and Christian faith. Of course, it is in principle possible that some initial Christian appropriation of one of these devices may have helped to stimulate Christians to seize upon others as well. But this seems to me no more than a possibility. Whatever the case, even such a scenario does not amount to the various Je-

35. Is the uncritical assumption of such a schema simply indicative of how Darwinian concepts of unilinear evolution have become so much a part of Western intellectual culture that we assume that the "historical" explanation of anything must proceed along these lines?

36. By "quasi-independent," I mean that the appropriation of the various devices as Jesus monograms obviously happened among circles of Christians, who to a greater or lesser extent shared features of faith and piety. Moreover, Christians clearly made efforts to network with other Christian circles, both locally and translocally. So if any given ligature was first adopted among some Christians, they may well have known of the appropriation of one or more of the other ligatures among their own or other circles of Christians.

sus monograms all evolving out of an initial one in the ways that Sulzberger and Savignac (and others) assumed.

To sum up the import of the chronological data, the earliest extant Christian uses of the *tau-rho* are notably prior to the attested Christian usage of any of the other ligatures. This alone makes it unlikely that the Christian appropriation of the *tau-rho* was directly influenced by prior Christian use of any of these other devices. Indeed, the chronological data suggest strongly that the *tau-rho* may have been the first of the several compendia that were appropriated by early Christians to refer to Jesus. Likewise, the earliest Christian use of the *tau-rho* was almost certainly not derived from Christian use of the *ankh*, for the latter symbol is attested in Christian evidence only considerably later.

I also want to reiterate here an earlier observation. It is significant that, in distinction from the other ligatures, the Christian *tau-rho* was not functionally a monogram. That is, unlike the other ligatures in question, the *tau-rho* was not derived from, and did not refer to, the name of Jesus or any of the titles used by Christians to confess his significance. This is a further reason for doubting that the Christian appropriation of the *tau-rho* ligature was derived from a supposedly prior use of one of the other compendia, each of which is comprised of letters that do refer directly to "Jesus" or to christological titles.

In earliest Christian usage, moreover, the *tau-rho* is the only one of these compendia that appears as part of the *nomina sacra* treatment of certain words (σταυρος and σταυρoω), and this means that it simply functioned differently as an early Christian symbol. Indeed, a complete answer to the question of how the Christian use of the *tau-rho* originated is probably connected to its earliest function. So we now direct our attention to this question.

Function and Meaning

In the earliest instances of the *tau-rho,* these letters are two of those that make up the Greek words for "cross" and "crucify." But this in itself is unlikely to explain either the reason for the Christian appropriation of the ligature or its original Christian function and meaning. The earliest manuscript evidence (cited above) shows that the writing of the Greek words in question as *nomina sacra* did not consistently involve the use of the *tau-*

rho ligature. This strongly suggests that the two phenomena, the writing of "cross" and "crucify" as *nomina sacra* and the appropriation of the *tau-rho*, arose independently.

A more likely approach to the origin and earliest function of the *tau-rho* is readily available. We know that the Greek letter *tau* was invested with symbolic significance by Christians very early, specifically as a visual reference to the cross/crucifixion of Jesus. In the preceding chapter, we noted *Epistle of Barnabas* 9:7-9 (dated sometime 70-130 CE), where the author comments on the story of Abraham's rescue of Lot with a company of 318 servants (Gen. 14:14), and refers to this number as represented by the use of the Greek letters Τ Ι Η. Recall that the author interprets the two letters *iota* and *eta* (the first two letters of Ιησους) as referring to Jesus, and the letter *tau* as a reference to (and prediction of) Jesus' cross.[37]

We have other evidence confirming that the Greek letter *tau* was viewed by Christians in the second century CE as a visual symbol of the cross of Jesus. Indeed, Justin Martyr (*1 Apol.* 55) indicates that second-century Christians could see visual allusions to Jesus' cross in practically any object with even the remote shape of a T (e.g., a sailing mast with crossbeam, a plow or other tools with a crosspiece of any kind, the erect human form with arms extended, even the face with the nose extending at a right angle to the eyes).[38] In another fascinating passage (*1 Apol.* 60),

37. This rendering of the number in Gen. 14:14 is clearly instanced in, e.g., the Chester Beatty Genesis manuscript (Chester Beatty Papyrus IV, Rahlfs 961, fourth century CE), and was almost certainly used also in the early fragment of Genesis, P.Yale 1 (P.Yale inv. 419, VH #12, variously dated from early second to third century CE). Although there is a lacuna in this fragment at this spot, the space is scarcely adequate to have accommodated the number written out in words, as I was able to verify for myself in an examination of the fragment in February 2005. The likelihood that the number was written as Τ Ι Η is one of the reasons that most papyrologists take P.Yale 1 to be an early Christian copy of Genesis. On this fragment see esp. C. H. Roberts, "P.Yale 1 and the Early Christian Book," in *Essays in Honor of C. Bradford Welles*, ed. A. E. Samuel, American Studies in Papyrology 1 (New Haven: American Society of Papyrologists, 1966), 27-28; and the stimulating reflections by Erich Dinkler, "Papyrus Yalensis 1 als ältest bekannter christlicher Genesistext: Zur Frühgeschichte des Kreuz-Symbols," in *Im Zeichen des Kreuzes: Aufsätze von Erich Dinkler, mit Beiträgen von C. Andresen, E. Dinkler-v. Schubert, E. Grässer, und G. Klein*, ed. Otto Merk and Michael Wolter (Berlin: de Gruyter, 1992), 341-45. The way the number is written out in Greek, τριακοσιους δεκα και οκτω, would have suggested to early Greek-speaking Christians the use and sequence of the three Greek letters in question to represent the number.

38. Somewhat later, Minucius Felix (*Octavius* 29; ANF 4:191) echoes basically the same attitude. On the history and various types of cross symbols, see, e.g., Erich Dinkler and Erica

147

Justin cites a statement from Plato's *Timaeus*, ἐχίασεν αὐτὸν ἐν τῷ παντί ("He placed him crosswise in the universe"), which Justin appropriates as a reference to Jesus ("concerning the Son of God," 1 Apol. 60.1). The verb ἐχίασεν suggests a *chi* shape, but Justin claims (1 Apol. 60.2-5) that Plato derived the idea from a misunderstanding of the account where Moses was directed by God to erect a brass object for the healing of the Israelites who had been bitten by serpents (Num. 21:8-9). Justin claims that Plato inaccurately took the object that Moses made as *chi*-shaped, when in fact it was in the figure of a cross (σταυρος).[39] In light of his earlier comments about cross-shaped objects in 1 Apology 55, we can say that Justin almost certainly had some T-shaped object in mind here as well, in claiming that Moses' brass object was "the figure of a cross."[40]

A bit closer still to the probable date of the manuscripts in which the *tau-rho* device appears is another significant piece of evidence. In citing the passage in Ezekiel where God directs an angel to mark the foreheads of the elect, Tertullian takes the "mark" as the Greek letter *tau*, and then comments as follows: "Now the Greek letter *Tau* and our own [Latin] letter T is the very form of the cross, which He [God] predicted would be the sign on our foreheads in the true Catholic Jerusalem."[41] So it seems most reasonable to regard the Christian appropriation of the *tau-rho* ligature as connected to, and likely prompted by, this strong *visual* association of the Greek letter *tau* with Jesus' cross. This certainly also fits with the fact that the earliest known Christian uses of the *tau-rho* device are in the special *nomina sacra* writing of the words for "cross" and "crucify."

But what is the significance of the superimposed letter *rho* in the Christian use of the *tau-rho* compendium? If the *tau* by itself was an ac-

---

Dinkler-von Schubert, "Kreuz," *Lexicon der christlichen Ikonographie*, ed. Engelbert Kirschbaum, 8 vols. (Rome: Herder, 1968-76), 2:562-90.

39. Justin says of Plato's putative reading of the Numbers account, "μηδὲ νοήσας τύπον εἶναι σταυροῦ ἀλλὰ χίασμα νοήσας, τὴν μετὰ τὸν πρῶτον θεὸν δύναμιν κεχιάσθαι ἐν τῷ παντὶ εἶπε" (1 Apol. 60.5). I cite the text from E. J. Goodspeed, *Die ältesten Apologeten: Texte mit kurzen Einleitungen* (1914; repr. Göttingen: Vandenhoeck & Ruprecht, 1984), 69.

40. The LXX has Moses fashion a brass serpent and place it ἐπὶ σημείου. The Hebrew has Moses place a brass serpent on a נֵס ("pole").

41. *Contra Marcionem* 3.22. *Contra Marcionem* was written 207 CE. I cite here the translation in ANF 3:340-41. The LXX of Ezek. 9:4, however, has the angel directed to place a σημεῖον upon the foreheads of the righteous. Tertullian seems to cite the reading that is reported by Origen to have been featured in the translations of Theodotion and Aquila (Origen, *Selecta in Ezekiel*; PG 3:802), which is a more literal rendering of the Hebrew (תו).

knowledged visual symbol of Jesus' cross, what was gained symbolically by the *tau-rho?* Many years ago, F. J. Dölger cited intriguing evidence indicating that in the ancient setting the Greek letter *rho* (which = 100) could represent "good fortune" (by "isosephy," the letters in the expression ἐπ’ ἀγαθά also amounting to 100). Dölger also cited a statement by the Christian teacher and hymnist Ephraem the Syrian (ca. 306-373) that is of interest. The statement comes in Ephraem's comments on the meaning of the Christian symbol that apparently comprised a *tau-rho* with the *alpha* and *omega* placed under the left and right horizontal arms of the *tau.*[42] Ephraem says that in this device we have represented the cross of Jesus (in the *tau,* for which he says that Moses' outstretched hands are an OT "type"), and he takes the *alpha* and *omega* as signifying that Jesus ("the crucified one") is the beginning and end. He continues, "The Ρ [in the *tau-rho*] signifies βοήθια [= 'help'], the numerical value of which is 100."[43]

Dölger took Ephraem's statement to mean that he interpreted the *tau-rho* device by isosephy as signifying "salvation is in the cross" or "the cross is our help."[44] This seems to me a persuasive inference. Might this also be the original meaning and function of the *tau-rho* device? Is this perhaps how the scribes who first employed the *tau-rho* in the *nomina sacra* forms of σταυρος and σταυροω regarded the device? But Ephraem is, of course, considerably later than the time of the manuscripts that we are focusing on here. So the question is whether Ephraem's numerical interpretation represents his own fascination with such things or reflects more broadly early Christian interpretation of the *tau-rho.*

To be sure, we have evidence that at least some Christians in the first and second centuries engaged in isosephy. Most familiar is the number of "the beast" in Revelation 13:17-18, which is "the number of his name."[45]

---

42. See n. 49 below concerning examples of this combination.

43. The more familiar spelling of the word is βοήθεια. In the spelling of the word used by Ephraem, β = 2, ο = 70, η = 8, θ = 9, ι = 10, α = 1 = 100. I translate the Greek from the citation of Ephraem in Franz J. Dölger, *Sol Salutis,* 3rd ed., Liturgische Quellen und Forschungen 16-17 (1925; repr. Münster: Aschendorffsche Verlagsbuchhandlung, 1972), 74 n. 2. On Ephraem see, e.g., Kathleen McVey, "Ephraem the Syrian," *EEC,* 1:376-77 (with bibliography). McVey describes Ephraem as holding "a vision of the world as a vast system of symbols or mysteries" (376).

44. Dölger, *Sol Salutis,* 74.

45. As is well known, there is some textual variation in manuscripts of Revelation, the

We should also again recall the interpretation of the 318 servants of Abraham in *Epistle of Barnabas* (9:7-9) mentioned already. Moreover, as indicated in the preceding chapter, I have offered support for C. H. Roberts's proposal that the *nomina sacra* writing of Jesus' name as I H may have derived from an intended connection between the numerical value of these two Greek letters (18) and the same numerical value of the Hebrew word for "life," יח.[46] But even if this last particular proposal is not deemed persuasive, it is clear that some Christians from the earliest period were interested in using numerical symbolism to express their faith.[47] So it is in principle plausible that the numerically based meaning of the *rho* in the *tau-rho* device stated by Ephraem might go back much earlier, and might even have been the originating impulse for the Christian appropriation of the *tau-rho*.

But there are some reasons to hesitate in affirming the latter. Precisely because of the other evidence of a readiness among Christians in the first few centuries to employ isosephy, it is curious that we have no hint that the *tau-rho* was interpreted in this way earlier than Ephraem. Moreover, there is to my knowledge no evidence that the number 100 featured in second-century Christian isosephy or that the word βοηθια (or βοήθεια) was particularly prominent in Christian vocabulary of that period.[48] Instead, Ephraem's strong personal interest in finding mystical symbols of his faith everywhere in the world and in all spheres of nature suggests that the particular numerical interpretation of the *tau-rho* that he proposes may well be his own contribution.

Also, most significantly, Ephraem was commenting on the Christian use of a "freestanding" *tau-rho* device, that is, the *tau-rho* used on its own as a Christian symbol, such as we see in the Armant inscription cited previously.[49] But I contend that this much later freestanding use of the *tau-*

---

best supported number being 666, but some witnesses reading 616 (C and Irenaeus), and even 665 (manuscript 2344).

46. Hurtado, "Origin of the *Nomina Sacra*," esp. 665-69, and the discussion in chapter three above.

47. To cite another example, the number 8 was appropriated by early Christians as a symbol for the resurrection and eschatological hopes. See esp. Franz J. Dölger, "Die Achtzahl in der altchristlichen Symbolik," *Antike und Christentum* 4 (1934): 153-87; Staats, "Ogdoas."

48. See, e.g., the entry for βοήθεια in G. W. H. Lampe, *A Patristic Greek Lexicon* (Oxford: Clarendon, 1961), 300.

49. Finegan, *Archeology*, 387-88. The form of the *tau-rho* that Ephraem comments on

rho is significantly different from what we have in the *earliest* evidence of Christian use of the device, in which it appears *within texts and as part of a special writing of words that refer to Jesus' cross/crucifixion.*

Used as a freestanding symbol, without such a context, a device such as the *tau-rho* invites, perhaps requires, some imaginative interpretation such as Ephraem offered. But used in the way that we have the device employed in 𝔓66, 𝔓75, and 𝔓45, the *tau-rho* takes its Christian meaning and function from the words of which it is a crucial part and the sentences in which it is deployed. That is, in its earliest extant uses the *tau-rho* is a visual phenomenon that also functions as a part of words that refer to Jesus' crucifixion.

This leads to another intriguing possibility. The *tau-rho* device may have been appropriated by Christians originally, not (or not simply) on the basis of numerical symbolism, but because it could function as *a visual reference to the crucified Jesus.* In short, in its earliest Christian usage the *tau-rho* was not simply a "Christogram" but, more precisely, a "staurogram." This basic suggestion was proposed previously, notably by Aland, and then supported strongly by Dinkler.[50] According to this proposal, the *tau-rho* device was appropriated initially because it could serve as a stylized reference to (and visual representation of) Jesus on the cross. In this view the *tau* is taken in its attested Christian sense as an early symbol of the cross, and the loop of the superimposed *rho* in the *tau-rho* as perhaps intended to suggest the head of a crucified figure.

Such a visual reference to the crucifixion of Jesus fits with the simplicity and lack of decorative detail that characterize earliest Christian art. As Robin Jensen notes in her excellent introduction to early Christian art, the simple nature of the visual expressions of faith in the earliest material "suggests that communication was valued above artistic quality or refinement and that the emphasis was on the meaning behind the images more than on their presentation."[51] Commendably (and, to my knowledge, un-

---

includes the use of the *alpha* and *omega* symbols as well. One example of this is on the sarcophagus of Archbishop Teodoro (sixth century), in S. Apollinare in Classe, Ravenna. On the lid there are a *tau-rho* on the left and right, with *alpha* and *omega* under the crossbar of the *tau,* and also a *chi-rho* in the middle, with *alpha* and *omega* in the left and right spaces of the crossbars of the *chi* (photo in Bovini, *Ravenna,* 139). A freestanding *tau-rho* also appears in a sixth-century "pluto" (in framed relief with peacocks and vine in a pot) held in the same church (photo in Bovini, *Ravenna,* 119).

50. Aland, "Bemerkungen"; Dinkler, *Signum Crucis,* 177-78.
51. Jensen, *Understanding Early Christian Art,* 24.

usually among historians of early Christian art), Jensen notes the instances of the *tau-rho* device in the early papyri to which I draw attention here, characterizing the combined letters as forming "a kind of pictogram, the image of a man's head upon a cross," and she observes that the device "seems to be an actual reference to the cross of [Jesus'] crucifixion."[52]

The wider importance of this view of the *tau-rho* is considerable. As Dinkler noted in his enthusiastic endorsement of Aland's proposals, the "staurogram" is older than the *chi-rho*, even older than any other extant Christian image, preceding all the other iconography that was adapted or developed by Christians.[53] More specifically, if this proposal is correct, the *tau-rho* represents a visual reference to Jesus' crucifixion about 150 to 200 years earlier than the late-fourth- or fifth-century artifacts that are usually taken by art historians as the earliest depictions of the crucified Jesus.[54]

Significance for Scholarship

If it is correct to understand this earliest Christian usage of the *tau-rho* as a staurogram, then this compendium is a noteworthy phenomenon to be reckoned with in charting the history of earliest Christian iconography.[55] As I noted in a previous publication, however, it is unfortunate that a good many historians of early Christian art are not aware of the stauro-

---

52. Ibid., 138.

53. Dinkler, *Signum Crucis,* 178.

54. Two Christian intaglio gems usually dated to the fourth century and a fifth-century seal held in the Metropolitan Museum of Art in New York City are the frequently cited items. For a discussion of these items and other relevant evidence, see now Jensen, *Understanding Early Christian Art,* 131-41. In a seminar presentation given in Edinburgh in May 2002, however, Robin Cormack queried the conventional dating of these items, suggesting that they might just as reasonably be dated to the third century.

55. A *tau-rho* written in red ink appears at the beginning of a single papyrus page containing Ps. 1:1 (P.Taur.inv. 27; Rahlfs 2116; VH #84) dated initially (by A. Traversa) to the second century. Writing before the publication of the early manuscript data that I underscore here, and under the influence of Sulzberger's thesis, Morey (*Early Christian Art,* 128) rejected this dating because he was confident that the Christian use of the *tau-rho* did not predate Constantine. Morey was right to suspect the second-century date of the manuscript, but his reason was wrong. Cf., e.g., Roberts, "P.Yale 1," 27-28.

gram (largely because early Christian manuscripts are not usually thought of as offering data for the study of art), and so do not take account of its import.[56] But the staurogram is both particularly important and rather unusual. As I noted about the *nomina sacra,* in its earliest extant occurrences the *tau-rho* is a *scribal* device used in a *textual* setting, but entirely with a *visual* function, and so it is an *iconographic* phenomenon, a visual/material expression of early Christian faith/piety. Whether the *tau-rho* was adopted originally as a pictogram of the crucified Jesus (as I tend to think), or was initially interpreted more along the lines of Ephraem's numerical symbolism, either way it was a *visual* reference to the cross of Jesus.

Moreover, this has ramifications far beyond papyrology or the history of early Christian art. On what has been the dominant assumption that visual references to Jesus' crucifixion do not predate the fourth century, some scholars have drawn far-reaching conclusions about the nature of Christian faith/piety in the pre-Constantinian period.[57] For instance, in a valuable review of earliest archeological evidence of Christianity (but influenced by the widely assumed theory), Graydon Snyder emphatically denied that there was any evidence of a visual reference to Jesus' crucifixion prior to the fourth century.[58] On this basis he then made the further dubious claim that there was "no place in the third century [or earlier] for a crucified Christ, or a symbol of divine death."[59] But, unfortunately, Snyder showed no awareness of the staurogram (or of the artifactual significance of early Christian manu-

---

56. Hurtado, "Earliest Evidence," esp. 281-82. I cite there, as an example of otherwise valuable histories of early Christian art that omit any reference to the staurogram, Robert Milburn, *Early Christian Art and Architecture* (Berkeley: University of California Press, 1988), but this omission is typical of the genre.

57. In an essay written before he became aware of the manuscript evidence of the Christian use of the staurogram, Dinkler ("Comments on the History of the Symbol of the Cross," *Journal for Theology and Church* 1 [1965]: 124-46 [German original 1951]) once referred to the "absolute dogma that the symbol of the cross makes its first appearance in the age of Constantine" (132), and claimed an absence of archeological evidence of cross marks made by Christians from the first two centuries (134), reflecting, of course, the influential judgment by Sulzberger (cited above). To his credit, Dinkler was ready to change his views when shown the manuscript evidence discussed here.

58. Snyder, *Ante Pacem,* 26-29. Unfortunately, it appears that this matter is not rectified in the revised edition of this work, which appeared in 2003.

59. Snyder, *Ante Pacem,* 29.

scripts generally), and so his estimate of cross symbolism in the pre-Constantinian period is simply incorrect.[60]

We can also say, therefore, that his sweeping characterization of pre-Constantinian Christian piety/faith is equally questionable. In the earliest instances of Christian usage, the staurogram (again, whether taken as a pictogram or as a numerical symbol) obviously refers to the crucifixion/ cross of Jesus, and so (along with the abundant textual evidence) reflects an importance given to Jesus' crucifixion in Christian faith/piety, from at least as early as the late second century.

The staurogram is thus another important (albeit insufficiently known) feature of earliest Christian manuscripts that deserves to be more widely known among scholars concerned to grasp the character and concerns reflected in earliest Christianity. It is another illustration of the importance of approaching early Christian manuscripts as artifacts.

Early Christograms

$\mathcal{R}$ = XPICTOC

$\maltese$ = IHCOYC XPICTOC

$\maltese$ = IHCOYC

$\maltese$ = In NT manuscripts ($\mathfrak{P}$75, $\mathfrak{P}$66, $\mathfrak{P}$45), in abbreviated forms of σταυροω and σταυρος, e.g., σ$\maltese$ος

---

60. I intend no particular condemnation of Snyder, for a failure to take account of the staurogram (and of the phenomena of early Christian manuscripts generally) is, sadly, rather widely demonstrated in contemporary studies of Christian origins.

CHAPTER FIVE

Other Scribal Features

W e now turn to several further noteworthy features of early Christian manuscripts. These phenomena are even less well known beyond the circles of papyrologists and paleographers. So I want to show that they too have implications for wider historical questions about early Christianity, and consequently merit the attention of all those concerned with these questions.

Codex Size

In chapter two I briefly noted suggestions of some scholars about possible implications of the sizes of early Christian biblical manuscripts. Here I want to take up the matter again for more extended consideration. The most important point to make is that the physical dimensions of a manuscript constitute important data that may, for instance, suggest the intended usage of the manuscript and may also be relevant for our use of the manuscript as a textual witness.

All discussion of the physical dimensions of codices today remains indebted to Eric Turner's 1977 remarkable study, *The Typology of the Early Codex*.[1] One of Turner's principal concerns was whether the sizes and

---

1. In "The Dating of the Chester Beatty–Michigan Codex of the Pauline Epistles ($\mathfrak{P}$46)," in *Ancient Christianity in a Modern University*, vol. 2: *Early Christianity, Late Antiquity and Beyond*, ed. T. W. Hillard et al. (Grand Rapids: Eerdmans, 1998), 218 (216-27), S. R. Pickering referred to Turner's book as "The most extensive single published list of carefully controlled palaeographical datings of Greek and Latin papyri."

shapes of codices were related to the approximate dates in which they were constructed, certain sizes and dimensions perhaps more typical of particular times. His aim in exploring this was to see if the size/dimension of a codex (which often can be estimated from even a single leaf) might be used as a further means of dating it, thereby supplementing paleographical judgments.[2] Toward that end, Turner's book was heavily devoted to categorizing a great number of codices by their sizes and dimensions/shapes. Consequently, one of the book's features of enduring value is the lengthy "Consolidated List of Codices Consulted," which gives a checklist of information on several hundred manuscripts of all sorts of literary texts, Christian and non-Christian.[3]

This is not the place to engage comprehensively Turner's now-classic work, and I am not competent to offer an authoritative judgment about the right answers to the questions that shaped it. One should note, however, that Turner rightly portrayed his work as a pioneering one, and therefore provisional and subject to correction. Sadly, I know of no subsequent study of the matter of equivalent thoroughness. So all that we can do is gratefully use Turner's work, with some awareness of its provisional nature, supplementing his data in the light of manuscripts that have come to light subsequent to this valuable publication.[4]

In any case, my principal concern here is not the relationship of codex size/dimensions to dating. Instead, I want to explore a bit further questions about what the sizes and dimensions of early Christian codices may

---

2. Turner (*Typology*, 2-3) hoped to "reinforce the somewhat hit-and-miss datings assigned by palaeographers to books on the basis of their handwritings." An internationally recognized expert in paleography himself, Turner was candid about the difficulty of the work, referring, for instance, to "the helplessness felt by palaeographers when they have to rely on the morphological analysis of letter forms," and he gave illustrations of the varying judgments of experts about manuscripts (*Typology*, 3). Another of his heuristic concerns was to test previous views that the papyrus codex had developed directly from the parchment codex; he found these views rendered doubtful by the data (35-42).

3. Turner, *Typology*, 101-85.

4. Note particularly Peter M. Head, "Some Recently Published NT Papyri from Oxyrhynchus: An Overview and Preliminary Assessment," *TynBul* 51 (2000): 1-16, who gives data on seventeen recently published manuscripts comprising a new portion of 𝔓77 (P.Oxy. 4405), 𝔓100 (P.Oxy. 4449), 𝔓101-105 (P.Oxy. 4401-4406), 𝔓106-109 (P.Oxy. 4445-4448), and 𝔓110-115 (P.Oxy. 4494-4499). Head gives the sizes of the actual extant portions as well as estimates of the number of lines per page, but unfortunately no estimates of original page sizes.

tell us about their intended readers and uses. For this, Turner's data will be useful, even though he did not specifically focus on this question.

What, then, can we make of codex size/dimensions? Let us approach this question by returning to Epp's proposal that many of Christian biblical manuscripts were of putatively "modest" sizes "convenient for travel," and that this might indicate some derivation from, or particular association with, an early and influential itinerant use of the codex among Christians.[5] Stanton, likewise, has portrayed early codices, Christian and non-Christian, as "quite small in size and therefore much more portable than rolls."[6] This is an intriguing suggestion, but it is important to assess the dimensions of early Christian biblical manuscripts in the context of the wider body of codices of that same time.

We should note immediately that Turner's lists of codices show a number of non-Christian ones as well (both literary and subliterary texts) in the same size/dimensions categories as the Christian biblical codices. In the final chapter of his study, Turner attempted tentatively to "formulate the characteristics of the earliest form of the codex," giving special attention to manuscripts that could be assigned to the second and third centuries CE.[7] Acknowledging both the limitations in data and occasional variations in the patterns, he judged that certain dimensions were found not later than the third century CE, and that these same sizes characterize second- and third-century papyrus codices of Christian and non-Christian provenance.

Turner identified two main early types of papyrus codices: those with oblong pages (his "Group 8," with breadth about 11-15 cm., about half their height of about 20-30 cm.; and others of still narrower dimensions, height about 28-34 cm., breadth about 11-13 cm.), and also others of a more square shape ("aberrants of Group 5," with breadth about 17-18 cm. and height about 20-23 cm.).[8] Interestingly, he found that parchment codices of the

---

5. In particular see Epp, "Codex and Literacy," 19-21. The phrase quoted is from p. 19. In what follows I offer some criticisms of my esteemed teacher's views on this particular matter. I freely acknowledge, however, the stimulus of his work among the factors that helped me to see the importance of manuscripts as historical artifacts.

6. Stanton, *Jesus and Gospel*, 84.

7. Turner, *Typology*, 89.

8. Ibid., 95. Note that he regarded the more square-shaped format (the "aberrants" of Group 5) as "competing with Group 8 for the distinction of being the earliest format of the papyrus codex" (*Typology*, 25). He classified some other square-shaped codices in his "Group 9," and granted that these were another early format.

same early period tended overall to be more square shape, with their breadths noticeably closer to their heights. Also, as with early papyrus codices, most early parchment codices are comparatively smaller than later ones.[9]

I submit that the broad effect of Turner's evidence is that it is not clear that Christian biblical codices of the second and third centuries are particularly different in sizes and shapes from non-Christian codices of the same period. Granted, these early biblical papyrus codices are generally (but not uniformly) somewhat smaller than the larger, impressive codices of later centuries. Also, a number of the early papyrus codices have tall and narrow page shapes, whereas later (parchment) codices tend toward a more square shape. But there are also some comparatively large early biblical codices, particularly P.Chester Beatty VI (Numbers–Deuteronomy, about 18 × 33 cm., ##24, 30 in appendix 1) and P.Ant. 1.9 (Proverbs, estimated about 18 × 35 cm., #63 in appendix 1). In any case, broadly speaking, whether these larger ones or the somewhat smaller early biblical codices, they are not really distinguished in size and dimensions from non-Christian ones of that same time.

All of this means that the sizes of Christian manuscripts more likely reflect preferences and practices of the times in which they were prepared, rather than some distinguishing concern for portability. Although there is some early reference to the suitability of small codices for reading while traveling (Martial's oft-cited statements noted in chapter two above), there is no reason to think that in general codices were particularly linked to translocal usage. To be sure, Christians seem to have been distinctive in their heavy use of the codex, but in the earliest period Christians basically appear to have appropriated and adapted techniques and styles in codex construction and layout available at the time.

It is not helpful, therefore, and probably not relevant, to judge the dimensions of papyrus codices of the second and early third centuries against the larger format of codices of the fourth century and later. What may seem a "modest"-size codex compared to preferences of a later century was likely regarded in its own time as a "standard"-size item of its kind.

---

9. Turner (ibid., 39) gives a list of parchment codices from ca. 300 CE and earlier. Aside from the miniature ones, their page heights range from about 14 to 22 cm., with most about 15-18 cm.

Citing Turner's calculations, however, one can genuinely view some early Christian manuscripts as somewhat more compact than others.[10] Among early Gospel codices, the pages of P.Bodmer II (John, 𝔓66) measured 14.2 × 16.2 cm., those of 𝔓64 + 𝔓67 (Matthew, Mag.Coll.Gr. 18 + P.Barc.inv. 1) and 𝔓4 (Luke, Paris Supp.Gr. 1120) about 13.5 × 17 cm.[11] 𝔓77 (Matthew, P.Oxy. 2683 + 4405) had pages about 10 × 15 cm., and 𝔓103 (Matthew, P.Oxy. 4403, which may be part of the same codex as 𝔓77) is estimated to have been about 11 × 16 cm.[12] Published subsequently to Turner's 1977 book, 𝔓90 (John, P.Oxy. 3523) had pages about the same size (about 12 × 16 cm.).[13] There are also some early compact-sized codices of Old Testament texts, including P.Lond.Lit. 202 (Genesis, about 14 × 17 cm., #9 in appendix 1), and also P.Ant. 1.8 (Proverbs, #64 in appendix 1) and P.Barc.inv. 3 (2 Chronicles, #35 in appendix 1), each about 12 × 17 cm. Likewise, among copies of extrabiblical texts there are codices of similar compact size, such as P.Bod. V (*Protevangelium of James/Nativity of Mary*, third century, 14.2 × 15.5 cm., #231, appendix 1).[14]

10. I draw here upon the data in Turner's "Consolidated List of Codices Consulted," in ibid., 101-85.

11. These are the estimated dimensions from Turner (ibid., 148). But if the columns were about 16-17 cm. high, with the sort of top and bottom margins typical of Christian biblical codices, I would expect a page height closer to 19-20 cm.

12. As noted previously, 𝔓4 may be part of the same codex as 𝔓64 and 𝔓67. So Skeat, "Oldest Manuscript." But cf. now Head, "Is 𝔓4, 𝔓64 and 𝔓67 the Oldest Manuscript?" J. D. Thomas noted that P.Oxy. 4403 (𝔓103) may be part of the same codex as P.Oxy. 2683 + 4405 (𝔓77), in E. W. Handley et al., *The Oxyrhynchus Papyri, Volume LXIV* (London: Egypt Exploration Society, 1997), 6. Epp ("Codex and Literacy," 19) referred to the page sizes of 𝔓77 and 𝔓98 as not determined; but Thomas gives an estimate of about 10 × 15 cm. for 𝔓77, and 𝔓98 (P.IFAO 2.31) is an opisthograph (a reused roll), and so has no pages.

13. The editor of P.Oxy. 3523 represents the page size as "not very different from the Rylands fragment" of John's Gospel (𝔓52), whose calculated dimensions he refers to incorrectly as about 14 × 16.3 cm. Cf., however, Turner, *Typology*, 148, who estimates the page size of 𝔓52 as about 18 × 21.3 cm., just a bit narrower than the about 20 × 21 cm. calculated by C. H. Roberts, "An Unpublished Fragment of the Fourth Gospel in the John Rylands Library," *BJRL* 20 (1936): 50 (45-55). Skeat's estimate agreed with Turner's, in *Collected Biblical Writings*, ed. Elliott, 81.

14. P.Bod. V is part of a composite codex that includes a copy of Jude (P.Bomer VII, 𝔓72), *Peri Pascha* by Melito (P.Bod. XIII), apocryphal correspondence of Paul and Corinth (P.Bod. X), *Odes of Solomon* 11 (P.Bod. XI), a hymn (P.Bod. XII), the Apology of Phileas (P.Bod. XX), Psalms 33–34 (P.Bod. IX), and 1 Peter (P.Bod. VIII, 𝔓72), all of these components trimmed to the same size. For analysis see Turner, *Typology*, 79-80, engaging the views of the editor, Testuz, *Papyrus Bodmer VII-IX*. Testuz observed (9-10) that the compact size of

With due allowance for the danger of anachronism, it may neverthe-less be helpful to give some comparison of modern books. Note, for exam-ple, the sizes of widely used desk editions of the Greek New Testament and Hebrew Old Testament. The pages of the twenty-seventh edition of the Nestle-Aland *Novum Testamentum Graece* measure about 13.8 × 18.7 cm., and the pages of *editio minor* of the *Biblia Hebraica Stuttgartensia* (1984) are about 13.2 × 18.4 cm. Like these modern books of somewhat similar di-mensions, some early Christian codices were compact in comparison with other codices of their own period, and may even have been prepared with a view for portability or personal usage. But it is also important to reiterate that their compact size is by no means particularly distinctive to *Christian* codices. All those that we have noted here fit, along with non-Christian ex-amples, in page sizes that Turner classifies as frequent among the earliest codices generally.[15]

There are also considerably smaller Christian codices, genuine minia-tures, which much more likely were prepared for private usage. If, for ex-ample, we consider a Psalms codex that measures about 6.3 × 7.3 cm. (P.Lond.Lit. 204, third century, #43 in appendix 1), a copy that could easily be carried on one's person, I think that we must presume such a purpose.[16] Likewise, the miniature size and unusual dimensions of 𝔓78 (P.Oxy. 2684, Jude, third/fourth century, #172 in appendix 1, about 5.3 × 2.9 cm., consid-erably greater in width than height!), P.Ant. 1.12 (2 John, third/fourth cen-tury, parchment, about 9 × 10 cm., #170 in appendix 1), and P.Oxy. 1594 (Tobit, third/fourth century, parchment, about 8.5 × 8.5 cm., #86 in appen-dix 1) must indicate copies of texts for personal reading.[17]

---

this anthology codex (fourth century, but some portions of it copied earlier) shows that it was probably commissioned by a Christian of financial means, and was intended for his/her own private usage. Wasserman ("Papyrus 72") provides a more recent discussion focused on the texts of Jude and 1-2 Peter in this composite codex.

15. See Turner, *Typology*, 20-22, for his listing of codices in his "Group 8," "Group 9," and "Group 10," into which all the Christian examples noted here fit rather readily.

16. I cite the sizes given by Turner (*Typology*), which in some cases differ from those given by van Haelst (*Catalogue*). As Turner sought to examine as many as possible of the items that he included, either directly or by photograph, I presume that his measurements are more likely to be accurate. In some cases, Turner offered estimated page sizes, indicating these in square brackets.

17. Along with the unusual shape of 𝔓78, its eccentric readings and the careless hand indicate a very informal copy of the text with little attention to quality. P.Ant. 2.54 (#212 in appendix 1) is a third-century copy of the Lord's Prayer with a page size about 2.6 × 4 cm.,

These codices rather clearly attest both a Christian interest in having personal-size copies of certain writings for private reading, and also an economic ability among some Christians to purchase them or (more likely) to pay to have them prepared.[18] That is, these miniature manuscripts are significant artifacts that can contribute to our picture of the religious interests and social/economic spectrum of Christians in the early centuries.

It is worth noting the increase in the number of Christian miniature codices from the fourth century and later (most of these parchment codices). This fits with the view that from Constantine's recognition of Christianity onward there was likely an easier and wider appropriation of the faith among the financially better-off sectors of the society.[19] There are miniature copies of biblical texts, but other early Christian examples include *Shepherd of Hermas* (P.Oxy. 1783), the unknown Gospel-like text in P.Oxy. 840, *Acts of Paul and Thecla* (P.Ant. 1.13), *Protevangelium of James* (P.Grenfell 1.8), *Didache* (P.Oxy. 1782), and some others. Again, note that there are certainly non-Christian examples of miniature codices of the same centuries.[20] So once more the dimensions of the Christian examples are not distinctive.

But I must emphasize that most Christian biblical codices of the second and third centuries are not properly categorized as compact or "mod-

---

but this is likely an amulet, a single sheet of text, and not a full copy of Matthew. See, e.g., van Haelst's comments (VH #347).

18. Although there is some reference to booksellers preparing copies of texts for sale, it was perhaps more common to have a copy made for one's usage. This usually involved paying a professional copyist or the use of a slave trained as a copyist. See, e.g., Haines-Eitzen's discussion of the copying of early Christian texts in *Guardians of Letters*, 21-52. See Gamble, *Books and Readers*, 231-37, for discussion of the private reading of books among Christians. Gamble notes the interesting fact that most of the extant miniature codices contain Christian texts, which suggests that this format may have been particularly favored among Christians (236). He also notes that most of the Christian texts in such miniature format are apocryphal, suggesting that these texts were perhaps mainly used for private edification and enjoyment, the texts not enjoying acceptance for liturgical usage.

19. Turner (*Typology*, 29-30) lists parchment miniature codices, and notes "a very large number of parchment codices (compared with papyrus) have a breadth of less than 10 cm" (31). Dates for several are disputed, and a few Christian ones may be third century, e.g., P.Ant. 1.12 (2 John), P.Oxy. 849 *(Acts of Peter)*, P.Oxy. 1594 (Tobit).

20. Turner (*Typology*, 22) gives a list of "miniature" papyrus codices, and also (29-30) a list of parchment miniatures. Among the latter, which are mostly from the fourth century and later, Christian texts are rather clearly predominant.

est" in size, especially if we judge them against other codices of their same period. For example, 𝔓46 (P.Chester Beatty II), with page sizes 13.5-15.2 × 26.5-27 cm., and 𝔓75, with pages 13 × 26 cm., though somewhat oblong (especially the latter), have non-Christian analogues of the same period.[21] Of the remaining biblical codices in Turner's list that are dated to the second and third centuries, a few are a bit larger than the more compact ones noted above but still somewhat smaller than others. For instance, P.Ryl. 1.5 (𝔓32, Titus, #158 in appendix 1) was about 15 × 20 cm., P.Yale 1 (Genesis, #1 in appendix 1) about 14 × 20 cm., and P.Oxy. 1596 (𝔓28, John, #121 in appendix 1) about 13 × 20.5 cm. P.Chester Beatty V (Genesis, #6 in appendix 1) was about 17 × 21 cm., and the more recently published 𝔓108 (P.Oxy. 4447, John, third century, #125 in appendix 1) had pages about 14.5 × 18.5 cm.[22]

Most, however, are well over 20 cm. tall, although a number of them have noticeably narrow breadth compared to height. For example, P.Ryl. 457 (𝔓52, John) probably measured about 18+ × 21.3 cm.[23] P.Chester Beatty VI (Numbers–Deuteronomy) was about 19 × 33 cm., P.Chester Beatty VII (Isaiah) about 15.3 × 26 cm., P.Chester Beatty III (𝔓47, Revelation, #173 in appendix 1) about 14 × 24.2 cm., and P.Chester Beatty I (𝔓45, Gospels and Acts) about 20.4 × 25.4 cm.[24] Others in Turner's list have roughly similar

21. For example, in Turner's Group 8 (page breadth about one-half of the height), we have Christian biblical examples such as 𝔓46, 𝔓75, 𝔓37, 𝔓5, and 𝔓1, but also copies of the *Odyssey* and other literary works by Homer, Menander, Hesiod, and Euripides (Turner, *Typology*, 20). The page width of 𝔓46 varies because in such a large single-quire codex (52 sheets folded to form 104 leaves or 208 pages) the pages closest to the center had to be trimmed to make their outer margins flush with the other pages. Turner also observed that ancients may not have been troubled by unevenness in page sizes (*Typology*, 23).

22. The editor of P.Oxy. 4447 (W. E. H. Cockle) classified it as an aberrant of Turner's Group 9. See M. W. Haslam et al., *The Oxyrhynchus Papyri, Volume LXV* (London: Egypt Exploration Society, 1998), s.v. P.Oxy. 4447.

23. Where only portions of a page survive with one or more of the margins, and where we can identify the text with confidence (as is the case with 𝔓52), and so can estimate the amount of space likely required for the missing part(s) of the text, such calculations are somewhat more reliable. This assumes, of course, that the text of the manuscript sufficiently resembled the text that we know. Where no margin survives, estimates of page size are a bit more approximate, involving rough averages of margins in comparable codices.

24. P.Chester Beatty I (𝔓45) is noticeably less oblong than many codices of its time (falling into Turner's Group 9), but Turner lists others of similar dimensions, including a copy of the *Acts of Paul* (Hamburg Pap. bil.1, about 20 × 26 cm.), Josephus (P.Rain. 3.36, about 20 × 25 cm.), and some others as "aberrants" of this group, which are mainly classical texts, and dated by him fourth century CE and later.

dimensions.[25] Moreover, as further fragments of other biblical codices of the second and third centuries have been published, most fall into this same range.[26]

As will be obvious, nearly all of these codices have the oblong page shape previously noted, with breadth considerably less than the height, often about one-half, and sometimes even narrower. But the question is what to make of this. Are we to think of this oblong page shape as "compact" and indicative of, or aimed for, portability? Although it is difficult to make the leap back to that ancient time and setting, I fail to see that books with pages of 21+ cm. in height are particularly modest in size or compact in shape. Many Christian codices of the second and third centuries have pages of about 25 cm. or more, and several run to about 30-34 cm.[27] As noted, the miniature size of some early codices, both Christian and non-Christian, indicates unquestionably that they were prepared for personal use and, likely, for portability, and there are others that, though significantly larger, we can rightly call "compact" (i.e., those about 10-15 × 15-20 cm.). But it seems to me to blur matters unhelpfully to portray early Christian manuscripts as *typically* compact. We would not regard books of our time with pages about 14+ × 21+ cm. as particularly modest or compact in size, and, to judge from the range of codex sizes of the second and third

25. P.Chester Beatty VIII (Jeremiah), about 15.2 × 30.5 cm.; the Freer Minor Prophets codex, 14 × about 32 cm.; P.Oxy. 1008 ($\mathfrak{P}$15, 1 Corinthians), 18 × 26.5; P.Oxy. 1226 (Psalms), about 15 × 29.8 cm.; P.Oxy. 1780 ($\mathfrak{P}$39, John), about 16 × 25.6 cm.; the "Berlin Genesis" (Berlin Staats.Bib. Cod. gr. fol.66 I,II), 18 × 25 cm.; $\mathfrak{P}$5 (P.Oxy. 208 + P.Oxy. 1781, John), about 12.5 × 25 cm.; $\mathfrak{P}$37 (P.Mich.inv. 1570, Matthew), about 12+ × 25 cm.; P.Oxy. 2 ($\mathfrak{P}$1, Matthew), 12 × about 24.7 cm.; P.Oxy. 656 (Genesis), 11+ × 24.3+ cm.; P.Chester Beatty IX (Daniel, etc.), 12.8 × 34.4 cm. (!); P.Bod. XXIV (Psalms), 13 × 24 cm.

26. For example, P.Oxy. 4401 ($\mathfrak{P}$101, Matthew) has a writing area of about 9 × 22 cm., and so (with estimated margins) a page size about 12+ × 25+ cm. Estimated page sizes of P.Oxy. 4402 ($\mathfrak{P}$102, Matthew) are about 14 × 27 cm.; P.Oxy. 4404 ($\mathfrak{P}$104, Matthew) about 14 × 25 cm.; P.Oxy. 4445 ($\mathfrak{P}$106, John) about 12 × 23.5 cm.; P.Oxy. 4448 ($\mathfrak{P}$109, John) about 12 × 24 cm.; P.Oxy. 4497 ($\mathfrak{P}$113, Romans) about 14 × 21 cm.; P.Oxy. 4498 ($\mathfrak{P}$114, Hebrews) about 15 × 25 cm.; P.Oxy. 4499 ($\mathfrak{P}$115, Revelation) about 15.5 × 23.5 cm.; and P.Oxy. 4449 ($\mathfrak{P}$100, James) about 13 × 29 cm. For fuller descriptions see the relevant entries in Handley et al., *Oxyrhynchus Papyri, Volume LXIV;* Haslam, *Oxyrhynchus Papyri, Volume LXV* ; Nick Gonis et al., eds., *The Oxyrhynchus Papyri, Volume LXVI* (London: Egypt Exploration Society, 1999).

27. Among the taller ones, note again, e.g., P.Chester Beatty VI (19 × 33 cm.), P.Oxy. 1226 (15 × 29.8 cm.), P.Chester Beatty VIII (15.2 × 30.5 cm.), Freer Minor Prophets (14 × about 32 cm.), P.Chester Beatty IX-X (12.8 × 34.4 cm.), P.Oxy. 4449 (13 × 29 cm.).

centuries, I do not think that people of that time regarded codices of these dimensions as modest or compact either.

I submit that this judgment is reinforced if we again take note of the numerous non-Christian codices of roughly similar dimensions and shapes. I remind readers that Turner's tables, including the list under "Group 8" (those with more oblong pages), include many copies of classical texts and also a few "subliterary" texts (e.g., magical texts, manuals).[28] It seems to me more plausible, thus, that an oblong page shape was simply one common codex format of the time.[29]

Moreover, from meticulous analysis of the construction of numerous papyrus codices, Turner was able to offer what I regard as a likely explanation for the tendency in papyrus codices to have oblong page dimensions.[30] It has nothing to do with the social characteristics of the users, but is influenced largely by the nature of the material used to construct papyrus codices. Recall (from my discussion in chapter two) that the sheets used to form a codex were first cut from a manufactured roll of papyrus. The maximum height of a codex was thus determined by the height of the manufactured roll (which typically appears to have been about 25-35 cm., with shorter and taller instances as well) from which the sheets were cut.[31] Sheets cut from the manufactured roll were then folded to form the bifolia of a codex, each folded sheet (a bifolium) comprising two leaves, or four pages of writing surface. So, in a papyrus codex, the leaf/page width will be no more than about one-half of the width of the folded sheet. Turner calculated that in the Roman period the width of papyrus sheets pasted together to form manufactured rolls was not more than 33-34 cm., and more typically averaged about 20 cm. or less. So the maximum width of an individual leaf/page could be no more than one-half of this.

Also, although codex makers could choose to cut bifolia of any width

---

28. Turner, *Typology,* 20-21.

29. Although it is not entirely clear whether or how preferences in the sizes of papyrus rolls may have affected tastes in papyrus codices, Johnson (*Bookrolls,* 141-43) noted that before the first century CE roll heights varied considerably, with some about 29+ cm., but 25-26 cm. most common. In the Roman period, however, roll heights tended to be in the 25-33 cm. range (with some exceptions on either end).

30. I draw here heavily on his rather richly detailed discussion: Turner, *Typology,* esp. 43-53.

31. The actual height of the codex page could be less, however, by trimming the sheet cut from the papyrus roll.

from the manufactured papyrus roll, in practice it seems that they usually sought to avoid (with varying degrees of rigor) the pasted joins where sheets of papyrus had been glued together to make the roll.[32] This means that the width of the papyrus codex bifolia will typically have been about the width of the sheets that make up the manufactured roll from which the bifolia were cut, and the width of papyrus leaves/pages about one-half of that. As Turner noted, "the desire to avoid pasted joins, or at least to restrict them to not more than one to a double leaf [bifolium], may have been an important factor contributing to determine the relative narrowness already noted as a characteristic of codices made from papyrus when compared with the relatively square format favored in codices of parchment."[33]

I have dealt with the sizes and dimensions of early Christian codices at such length and in this detail to make two points here. One point has to do with method: the importance of making judgments that are adequately informed by relevant data, especially wider information about papyrus codices generally in the same period. My other point is that analysis of the sizes/dimensions of early Christian codices does permit some inferences about their intended uses, the kinds of readers/users for which the codices were prepared, and also, to some degree, the relationship between the format preferences of Christians and the tastes and practices in codex construction in the wider culture of the time. We can probably see a certain diversity of users/usages reflected in the various sizes of earliest Christian codices, and this contributes to any larger social description of early Christianity. Moreover, although Christians were distinctive in their wide appropriation of the codex, at the same time they also seem to reflect in general the procedures and tastes in codex shapes and sizes that were favored in their setting.

Columns

In addition to page size/dimensions, we may think of other noteworthy features of codices as forming the "layout" of the text on the page. One of

32. Although these joins (which Turner called *kollēseis*) could be so carefully made that a scribe could easily write across them, they were a potential point for damage, especially in a codex where leaves were turned. A *kollēsis* at the fold of a bifolium could lead to the two leaves of the bifolium separating. A *kollēsis* running down a leaf meant a weak point for potential loss of part of the leaf.

33. Turner, *Typology*, 51.

the most readily perceived features is whether the text is written as a single column running the full width of the writing area, or as two columns.[34] Overwhelmingly, early papyrus codices, non-Christian and Christian, have their texts in single-column format, and so in a codex of typical page size the lines of the text will be noticeably longer than the usual column width of a text in a roll, especially a roll prepared with an eye for elegance and sumptuous effect.[35]

It is, therefore, notable when we happen across an early papyrus codex with two columns. This layout probably reflects a scribe who may have been more acquainted with copying texts in rolls or who may have been concerned to lay out the text so that it has something of the textual aesthetics of a literary roll.[36] Given the regnant cultural status of the roll in the earliest centuries CE, especially for literary texts, it is easy to see why some scribes (and some intended readers) might have sought to give their copies of certain Christian texts a literary/cultured cachet.[37]

However, few papyrus codices, Christian or non-Christian, from the second and third centuries can be confirmed as having more than one column.[38] But these few are worth noting. To cite the Christian ones, there is

34. Later codices have increasingly more than two columns per page (e.g., Codex Vaticanus, fourth century, three columns; and Codex Sinaiticus, fourth century, four columns), but I know of no codex from the third century or earlier with more than two columns of text. For sample photos and descriptions of a number of biblical manuscripts, see Metzger, *Manuscripts*, e.g., 74-75 (Vaticanus), and 76-79 (Sinaiticus).

35. Columns of prose literary texts in rolls range from 35 mm. wide (7-14 characters per line) to about 55 mm. (12-22 characters per line). Documentary and "subliterary" texts, however, often have wider columns. See discussion and examples in Turner, *Greek Manuscripts*, 7. For description of features of "luxury" editions of rolls, see Johnson, *Bookrolls*, esp. 155-57. One of the aesthetic features was a slim column of text with ample blank space on all sides.

36. See Turner's discussion, *Typology*, esp. 36-37.

37. It is even possible that the oblong shape of some papyrus codices, with their tall and narrow column of text, was positively appreciated as giving the book something of the visual aesthetics of the literary roll, in which prose texts were typically laid out in tall and narrow columns.

38. Turner (*Typology*, 36) gives a table of twenty-one non-Christian and Christian papyrus codices with two-column layout, but he includes manuscripts as late as the seventh century. If we count only those dated to the second or third century (including those dated third/fourth century, i.e., about 300), he lists seven non-Christian and seven "Christian" codices, to which I confine the discussion here. I am also able to take account of manuscripts published subsequently to Turner's book. In contrast to the few papyrus two-column codices, Turner described this as the favored layout for parchment codices (*Typology*, 35).

the Exodus codex, P.Baden 4.56 (second century, #10 in appendix 1).[39] The Chester Beatty Numbers–Deuteronomy codex (P.Chester Beatty VI, second-third century) and the "Berlin Genesis" codex (Berlin Staats.Bib. Cod. gr. fol.66 I,II, third/fourth century, #2 in appendix 1) are further examples.[40] The Crosby-Schøyen Codex 193, a third-century Sahidic manuscript containing several texts (Jonah, Jeremiah, Lamentations, 2 Maccabees, Melito, and 1 Peter; #83 in appendix 1), is yet another.[41]

There are also a few New Testament texts in two-column format. The codex of Matthew, of which 𝔓64 and 𝔓67 are now commonly accepted to be portions, is the earliest example (late second century), along with 𝔓4, a portion of Luke that may also be part of the same codex.[42] The recently published portion of Romans (P.Oxy. 4497, 𝔓113, third century, #138 in appendix 1) is probably another example.[43]

Moreover, we have a few copies of extracanonical Christian texts in two-column codices. One of these is a third-century copy of *Shepherd of Hermas* (P.Oxy. 3527, #187 in appendix 1). Another is what may be a portion of one of Origen's commentaries (P.Lond.Christ. 2 [P.Egerton 3], third century, #204 in appendix 1). I include as of probable Christian provenance also a third-century copy of works of Philo (Paris Bib. Nat. P.Gr. 1120, #92 in appendix 1).[44]

Of these Christian two-column codices, those that appear to be the two earliest ones are perhaps most notable: P.Chester Beatty VI (Rahlfs

---

39. Van Haelst (VH 37, #33) refers to the hand of P.Baden 4.56 as "écriture cursive," but I have not been able to check this manuscript. When I have been able to check other instances, his use of this expression seems to include fully competent hands that do not, however, consistently make neat pointed majuscule characters.

40. Curiously, however, after the first eighteen pages the Berlin Genesis codex shifts to a single-column layout.

41. See Goehring, ed., *Crosby-Schøyen Codex*.

42. On the possible relation of 𝔓4, 𝔓64, and 𝔓67, see my brief discussion (with references) in chapter one.

43. See W. E. H. Cockle's reasoning in *Oxyrhynchus Papyri, Volume LXVI*, ed. Gonis et al., 7-8. Hence Stanton's statement that 𝔓64 + 𝔓67 + 𝔓4 is the only two-column Greek NT codex (*Jesus and Gospel*, 13) must probably now be corrected.

44. See van Haelst (VH, p. 251, #695) for a basic description and the various datings offered for this codex, which include fourth and sixth centuries. I accept here, however, the judgment of Turner (*Typology*, 113). Turner (*Typology*, 36) does not include this codex among his list of "Christian" two-column codices, but nothing substantial here rests on my assumption that it is probably a Christian manuscript.

963; plate #3 in appendix 2) and the Gospels codex of which $\mathfrak{P}$64 and $\mathfrak{P}$67 (+ $\mathfrak{P}$4?) are extant portions. Both codices are dated roughly late second/ early third century, and they are both copies of biblical texts.

Their two-column layout suggests that these copies were prepared with some concern for aesthetic quality and readability, and this is confirmed by other features. Frederic Kenyon characterized the hand of P.Chester Beatty VI as "a fine example of calligraphy," and he pointed to the "grace and beauty of the hand" as well as the width of the margins as indicating "a specimen of a high class of book production."[45] In its original state, this codex comprised about 216 pages (or about 54 folded sheets of papyrus), with an estimated page size of about 18 × 33 cm.[46] This codex is certainly very early, whether one prefers the second-century dating urged by Kenyon or the slightly later date of about 200 proposed by Turner.[47] Likewise, whether one prefers Kenyon's glowing description of the scribal hand or Turner's more restrained characterization of it as one of those Christian products of "practiced scribes writing an ordinary type of hand, but writing it larger than usual," it is clear that the codex was carefully prepared for readers.[48] The page size of the Chester Beatty Numbers–Deuteronomy codex (ca. 19 × 33 cm.) permitted generously sized letters, and further suggests a copy prepared for public reading.

The two-columned Gospel codex of which $\mathfrak{P}$64 and $\mathfrak{P}$67 (and possibly $\mathfrak{P}$4) are remnants also has interesting layout features. The scribe of $\mathfrak{P}$64 and $\mathfrak{P}$67 produced clear, fully separated majuscule letters (an early stage of a type of hand that is sometimes called "Biblical Uncial"). More of $\mathfrak{P}$4 survives, and one can say that it exhibits a certain calligraphic quality fully comparable with good literary texts of the late second and early third century. Thus, especially if $\mathfrak{P}$4 is rightly to be judged part of the

45. Frederic G. Kenyon, *The Chester Beatty Biblical Papyri, Fasciculus V, Numbers and Deuteronomy: Text* (London: Walker, 1935), ix. Kenyon (vii) calculated the margins as follows: top = 2.5 in. (ca. 6.3 cm.), bottom = 3 in. (ca. 7.6 cm.), outer = 1.75 in. (ca. 4.3 cm.), inner = 1 in. (ca. 2.5 cm.).

46. The extant page numbers suggest that the codex began with Numbers and probably included only this text and Deuteronomy. Kenyon was unable to determine whether it was a single-quire or multiple-quire construction.

47. Cf. Kenyon, *Fasciculus V,* ix; and Turner, *Typology,* 167. Turner's "ii/iii" = end of second or early third century, or about 200.

48. Turner, *Typology,* 86. He lists here several Christian manuscripts that he regards as fitting this description.

same codex, Skeat's description of this codex as an *édition de luxe* is not an exaggeration.[49]

Yet its somewhat compact size (about 13 × 17 cm. = about 5 × 6.75 in.) may suggest a copy more likely prepared for personal usage.[50] If so, this reflects someone able to afford such a nicely copied, personal Gospel book.[51] But, given that only a few early Christian codices have their texts laid out in two columns, this format appears to have been somewhat experimental, not really a convention widely followed in the second and third centuries. Also, perhaps the general dearth of two-columned Christian codices reflects a small number of Christians able to afford, or particularly concerned to have, texts in copies made to resemble the aesthetics of the literary roll. But it does not follow that a single-columned codex signals a lower estimate of the text copied, or necessarily a less skillful scribe or an intended user of the codex with less acquaintance with literary texts. As a comparison with the larger body of second- and third-century codices (Christian and non-Christian) shows, the single column was simply the more characteristic format.

Margins

Another interesting and readily noted feature of the layout of texts on the page of a codex is the size of the margins. In general, the margins of Christian codices are generous. For example, 𝔓66 (P.Bodmer II) has a writing area of 11 × 11 cm. on pages of 14.2 × 16.2 cm., which produced ample margins on all sides.[52] As noted already, 𝔓75 (P.Bodmer XIV-XV) has a much

---

49. Skeat, "Oldest Manuscript," 26; = *Collected Biblical Writings*, ed. Elliott, 185.

50. Also, a personal copy might more readily have been torn up and used to bind the copy of Philo in which 𝔓4 was found.

51. If 𝔓4, 𝔓64, and 𝔓67 were all from the same codex, then it contained at least Matthew and Luke. Skeat has argued, however, that it was a four-Gospel codex, in *Collected Writings*, ed. Elliott, 158-92. Stanton (*Jesus and Gospel*, 73) remarked that the narrow columns "would have assisted reading aloud in the context of worship." Quite possibly, but such columns also carried something of the cachet of the literary roll, and this aesthetic quality may be another factor, especially in such a compact-sized codex, which strikes me as suggesting more a personal copy than one prepared for liturgical usage.

52. The outer margin of the page was usually a bit wider than the inner margin, and the bottom margin often larger than the top one. The bottom margins of literary rolls were larger as well.

more oblong page shape (13 × 26 cm.), but likewise has very ample margins, the bottom margin the largest.[53] 𝔓4's two-columned layout comprised a writing area of 10 × 13.3 cm. on pages about 13.5 × 17 cm. So, if it is a portion of the same codex as 𝔓64 + 𝔓67, these proportions can be applied to the latter also. Even in cases where only part of a leaf/page survives, it is still possible to estimate the margins (particularly where portions of one or more margins survive). An example is 𝔓52 (P.Ryl. 457), which likely had a writing area about 14 × 16.3 cm. on a page about 18 × 21.3 cm.

Margins such as in these examples indicate that the scribes were not concerned to save space or writing material.[54] Such margins also probably reflect the aesthetics of literary books of the time, which favored generous amounts of blank space surrounding the columns of text. But it is also interesting to note that these margins (and those of most early Christian biblical codices) are a bit larger than those in a number of papyrus codices of the same period containing classical literary texts.[55] This confirms the view that, whereas non-Christian use of the papyrus codex before the fourth century was heavily for informal copies of texts intended mainly for personal usage, Christians used the codex as the dominant book form for their most prized texts, and formatted many of their codex copies of these texts with some of the aesthetics of the literary roll. That is, in early Christian circles we see the papyrus codex apparently being developed as a more serious, even preferred, format for Christian literary texts, including copies intended for formal and public usage. Here again we have further reason to

53. Unfortunately, the editors of P.Bod. XIV-XV, Victor Martin and Rodolphe Kasser, did not give measurements of the writing area, though they did discuss the number of lines per page: *Papyrus Bodmer XIV: Évangile de Luc, chap. 3–24,* 9-11. Turner likewise gives only the page size (*Typology,* 150), which probably means that he did not personally examine the manuscript but relied on the photos included with the Martin/Kasser edition, which are somewhat smaller than the actual manuscript, making it difficult to calculate the size of margins. But from these photos anyone can readily see that the margins are generous in comparison to the writing area.

54. The comparatively fewer number of lines per page/column in most Christian manuscripts further confirms this, a matter that I consider a bit later in this chapter.

55. Cf., e.g., the following second/third-century CE papyrus codices of classical literary texts from Turner's list (*Typology,* 102-16): nos. 21, 106, 129, 134, 150, 151, 224, 280. The codices of classical texts with wider margins from these centuries tend mainly to be parchment: e.g., nos. 44, 47, 80, 94, 184, 216, 277. But there are also a few papyrus codices: nos. 46, 171, 250. Codices of classical texts dated to the fourth century and later often have generous margins, but it would be anachronistic to make such comparisons.

ascribe a certain innovativeness and distinctiveness to early Christian book/scribal culture.

Lines per Page/Column

We consider now yet another interesting feature of the layout of codices, the number of lines of writing per page. As with other matters, this was a choice of the scribe. That is, we have no reason to assume that in copying a text a scribe tried to copy the same number of lines per page in all circumstances. A comparatively higher number of lines per page likely reflects a desire to make good use of the available writing material to accommodate a text. Codices with a higher number of lines per page also usually have more letters per line, further confirming that in these manuscripts the scribe was concerned to accommodate a large body of text in the writing material. On the other hand, a smaller number of lines per page usually involves more generous spacing between lines and somewhat larger letters, all of which we assume were probably intended to facilitate reading, perhaps particularly public reading of a text.

In this matter, once again, Turner's classic study provides crucial data for the discussion. On the basis of his examination of hundreds of codices, Turner judged that fifty or more lines per page represented the upper end of the spectrum. Noting twice as many papyrus codices with fifty lines or more per page from the second and third centuries CE in comparison with codices from later centuries, Turner proposed that "large holding capacity was a prime recommendation for a papyrus codex in its developmental [i.e., early] period."[56] Turner listed twenty-three papyrus codices from the second and third centuries with fifty or more lines per page, but found only ten such from the fourth century or later (plus three parchment codices from this later period).[57]

---

56. Turner, *Typology*, 95. He refers here to his table 14 (pp. 96-97) as listing twenty-four papyrus codices dated second to third/fourth century CE (i.e., about 300 and earlier) with at least 50 lines per page, but I count only twenty-two relevant codices in the table. Also, for some reason Turner included Chester Beatty VI (Numbers–Deuteronomy), even though it has only 31-38 lines per page (with an estimated page size about 19 × 33 cm.).

57. Of course, we also need to take account of the page size. A miniature codex might well have fewer lines per page (but not necessarily). In Turner's table 14 (*Typology*, 96-97), the second- and third-century papyrus codices listed have page heights ranging from 28 to

Given that these twenty-three codices make up a small minority of the total number of papyrus codices from the pre-300 CE period, however, I am not sure that Turner's larger inference is justified. I would hesitate to say that holding capacity was "a prime consideration" in the development of the papyrus codex as a book form.[58] But it is a reasonable inference that those codices with a large number of lines per page may reflect a pragmatic aim to make economic use of writing material, and a greater concern simply to make a copy of a text than for a copy that was particularly easy to read.

It is thus worthwhile to note the texts found in these codices. All of the early codices with large numbers of lines per page in Turner's list are copies of classical literary texts, except for one surgical treatise (P.Ryl. iii.529), and one Christian manuscript, P.Chester Beatty IX-X (Daniel, Esther, et al., ##76 and 79 in appendix 1), which has 45-57 lines per page.[59] I find it very interesting that only this one Christian manuscript appears in Turner's list. Indeed, one of the noteworthy features of most early Christian codices is the comparatively small number of lines per page, and also often markedly few characters per line. Turner commented on this, and the examples that he gave for comparison are striking.[60]

For instance, in P.Chester Beatty IX-X, the number of lines per page varies between 49 and 57 in the text of Ezekiel, and about 44 to 46 in Daniel and Esther.[61] According to Turner, the lines in this codex com-

---

about 40 cm. The number of lines per page in these ranges from about 48-50 (*MPER* i.4 and P.Gen. 2 + P.Ryl. 548) to 65 (P.Flor. ii.110).

58. For example, by my count, in Turner's composite table of codices (*Typology*, 102-85), 156 contain literary texts that he dates to the first through the third centuries CE (codices numbered 1-156 in his table, pp. 102-34). So the twenty-two codices of this period with 50 or more lines per page are hardly a major portion of these.

59. As with numerous codices, the number of lines per page varies. One reason for this can be that a scribe adjusted the number of lines per page as he approached the end of the codex, either crowding in more lines to accommodate the text he was copying, or spacing out lines to fill up the codex. In such instances, it appears that the scribe constructed the codex first and then copied the text into it.

60. See esp. Turner, *Typology*, 85-87. Of course, it is important to compare codices of approximately similar page size and containing texts of similar genre. Turner's examples achieve this.

61. I cite figures given by Frederic G. Kenyon, *The Chester Beatty Biblical Papyri, Fasciculus VII, Ezekiel, Daniel, Esther: Text* (London: Walker, 1937), vii. Turner gives somewhat different line counts at different points: 49-54 (*Typology*, 85), 45-57 (p. 97), 49-57

prise 17-23 letters per line.[62] For comparison, he cites two codices of Homer (P.Merton 3 and Harris Homer), which have, respectively, 52-54 lines per page, with 32-38 letters per line, and 48-54 lines per page, with 32-38 letters per line.[63] However, as both of these classical texts are in verse, whereas the Christian book is prose, Turner also made a comparison with a couple of non-Christian prose texts, a codex of Xenophon (P.Oxy. 697), which has 60 lines per page, 40-45 letters per line, and a codex containing a magical text (PGM I.iv), with 50 lines per page, and 31-39 letters per line.

The obvious point in the comparison with any of these codices of classical texts is that the Chester Beatty biblical codex has considerably fewer letters per line, and the reason is that it is written in much larger (and somewhat more widely separated) letters. And, as Turner cogently suggested, the larger-than-usual size of the letters in P.Chester Beatty IX-X seems to have been intended "to ease the task of [public] reading aloud."[64]

We may also note Turner's comparison of 𝔓75 (P.Bodmer XIV-XV) and the Bodmer Menander Codex, which have nearly the same page size. In 𝔓75 the scribe started off producing about 39 lines per page and about 24-25 letters per line, but as he saw that he might run out of codex before finishing his copying task, he increased the number of lines per page and the number of letters per line (e.g., on p. 98, 43 lines and 30+ letters per line). The Menander Codex has 47-54 lines per page, with 25-34 letters per line. Again, however, the latter is in verse, and in poetic texts the line lengths are usually written to reflect the poetic structure. Still, it is clear that the classical text is copied in a more compressed layout.

Numerous other examples could be cited. For instance, in 𝔓46 (P.Chester Beatty II, Pauline Epistles) the lines per page range from about 25-28 in the early parts to about 28-31 toward the end of the codex, the number of letters per line likewise increasing from about 25-35 in

---

(p. 183), and 40-57 (p. 181). As the leaves of the codex are damaged, it is necessary to estimate the total number of lines per page.

62. I have done a quick random count of several lines of the text of Daniel in this codex, and my figures are consistent with Turner's.

63. A sample plate of "the Harris Homer" (B.M. Pap. 126) appears in Turner, *Greek Manuscripts*, 40-41.

64. Turner, *Typology*, 85. The letters in P.Chester Beatty IX-X, as with many other early Christian manuscripts, are also rather clearly separated and comparatively widely spaced, which would further aid reading.

earlier pages to about 30-38 in the later ones.[65] Compare this with two codices of classical texts, both copies of roughly similar date and page size, the one a copy of Lysias (P.Oxy. 2537), which had 45+ lines per page, and the other a copy of Homer's *Iliad* (100a in Turner's composite list), with 47 lines per page. Or compare 𝔓47 (P.Chester Beatty III, Revelation, about 14 × 24.2 cm., third century), 25-30 lines per page, about 25-30 letters per line, with an astrological treatise in a codex of similar size and date (*PSI* ii.158, 14 × 21 cm.), which has 40+ lines per page and about 40-45 letters per line.[66]

Surely, however, 𝔓52 (P.Ryl. 457) is a still more remarkable example of a codex whose layout signals an intended ease of reading and a lack of concern about making maximum use of writing material. If, as is usually assumed, the text it contained was essentially the Gospel of John as we know it, the pages (about 18 × 21.3 cm.) would have contained about 18 lines each, the lines consisting of about 28-35 characters.[67] Compare this Christian codex with a third-century codex of Homer (P.Oxy. 763, *Iliad*), with 33 lines per page. Granted, 𝔓52 is rather clearly an extreme example, as can be seen by comparison even with other Christian codices. For instance, the Chester Beatty Genesis codex (P.Chester Beatty V, third/fourth century CE, #6 in appendix 1) is roughly similar in page size (about 17 × 21 cm.) and has 17-20 lines per page. But this is still considerably closer to the layout of 𝔓52 than that of most codices of classical texts of the time. Clearly, the layout of many Christian codices, especially those containing texts that were regarded as scripture (or coming to be so regarded), shows a concern for ease of reading, probably public reading.

On the other hand, we may rightly wonder how to regard the intended usage of the famous Chester Beatty Gospels-Acts codex (𝔓45, P.Chester Beatty I). Its pages (about 20.4 × 25.4 cm.) averaged 39 lines each, with

65. Once again, it seems that the text was copied into a previously constructed codex. So when the scribe began to fear that he would run out of codex, he increased lines per page and letters per line.

66. For a description of 𝔓47, see Frederic G. Kenyon, *The Chester Beatty Biblical Papyri, Fasciculus III, Pauline Epistles and Revelation: Text* (London: Walker, 1934), xi. Turner (*Typology*, xi) gives a plate of *PSI* 158.

67. Roberts, "Unpublished Fragment," 50. The lines averaged slightly more characters on the recto sides of its pages. This codex was probably constructed first, and then copied. So the scribe, working from left to right, could not get as many letters onto the left-hand pages, as the central fold of the codex got in the way.

about 45-55 letters per line.[68] In comparison with the other Christian codices noted here, the scribe of 𝔓45 was clearly aiming to make fuller use of writing material to accommodate a sizable body of text. A further consequence of this is the somewhat smaller size of the letters in comparison with some other Christian biblical codices.[69] This compressed layout, and the somewhat less-than-calligraphic nature of the scribal hand, have led a few scholars to suggest that 𝔓45 was prepared not for liturgical reading but for private usage.[70]

This is not the place to engage this question fully, but it may be useful to explore matters a bit further, with a view to illustrating the relevance of the physical features of Christian manuscripts. I want to caution that the notion that 𝔓45 was not prepared for public/liturgical reading is dubious, or at least debatable. The manuscript does not have the marginal markings or notations that often characterize copies of literary texts used in private study.[71] The scribal hand, though perhaps not as calligraphic as that of

68. Frederic G. Kenyon, *The Chester Beatty Biblical Papyri, Fasciculus II, The Gospels and Acts: Text* (London: Walker, 1933), esp. v-vi; Skeat, "Codicological Analysis." Unfortunately, however, neither Kenyon nor Skeat gave a count of letters per line. I made my own quick count of the shortest and longest lines on one or two sample pages that survive relatively intact (e.g., folio 13). Subsequently, however, I found that my results compared well with the more detailed analysis by Günther Zuntz, "Reconstruction of One Leaf of the Chester Beatty Papyrus of the Gospels and Acts (𝔓45)," *Chronique d'Égypte* 26 (1951): 191-211, who sampled four pages, with lines ranging between 46 and 57 letters (p. 194).

69. It is regrettable that earlier scholars often did not include precise measurements of the sizes of letters in their descriptions of manuscripts, and were often content to use terms such as "small" or "medium-size." Increasingly (one hopes!), however, nowadays editors of manuscripts are beginning to provide measurements of letters (usually in the more precise terms of millimeters). In my own limited efforts to take such measurements, the sizes of letters in Christian codices (other than miniature codices) commonly range from about 2 mm. (very small) to 3-4 mm. height (and more typically tending toward the larger size). Obviously, some characters (e.g., *phi* or *tau*) will be a bit larger than others in the same hand. For comparison, in modern books printed characters have a somewhat similar range in sizes (excluding footnotes!).

70. See particularly Stanton, *Jesus and Gospel,* 198 and 73 n. 38, referring to correspondence from T. C. Skeat. In Skeat's detailed study of 𝔓45, which appeared a few years earlier, however, he referred to "the expense incurred by the Christian community (if such it was) which commissioned the project," estimating the amount to have been about 43-45 drachmae (Skeat, "Codicological Analysis," 43 = *Collected Biblical Writings,* ed. Elliott, 157).

71. Granted, however, a second hand added diacritical marks (heavy dots or slanting strokes) to mark the ends of clauses at certain points. These may well have been added by some early reader(s). See Kenyon, *Fasciculus II,* ix. Skeat ("Codicological Analysis," 31 = *Col-*

some roughly contemporary manuscripts, indicates a fully competent scribe, the letters confidently written, clear and easy to read. There are scarcely any ligatures, and, though the letters are somewhat smaller than in some other examples of early Christian biblical codices, the scribe spaced them carefully, which further aids legibility. Overall, the scribal hand is certainly not appreciably inferior to the great majority of other early Christian biblical codices of the second and third centuries.[72]

The main difference between 𝔓45 and some other Christian biblical codices is that the text is written in somewhat smaller-sized letters. But, obviously, this was the unavoidable corollary of the decision to include all four Gospels and Acts as well in one codex. Indeed, 𝔓45 probably represents the roughly maximum size of a codex of its time. Moreover, as I have noted already, the scribe sought to compensate for the effects of having to write somewhat smaller letters by carefully writing and spacing them for ease of reading.

We must realize that 𝔓45 represents an ambitious and very significant artifact of early Christian use of these particular texts. Even with the somewhat more compressed layout, 𝔓45 originally comprised 224 pages (or 56 bifolia), with pages about 20 × 25 cm., a codex about 5-6 cm. thick (excluding any binding).[73] This was thus a substantial production, containing texts that amount to nearly 60% of the New Testament.[74] 𝔓45 may well not

---

lected Biblical Writings, ed. Elliott, 146) observed that these marks appear in "*all* the fragments of Mark and in *all* the fragments of Acts, but nowhere else in the codex [emphasis his]." Skeat pointed to this and other indications that in this codex Mark stood last among the four Gospels (the so-called Western order of the Gospels, found also in Codex W), and that Acts followed Mark (pp. 31-32 = *Collected Biblical Writings*, ed. Elliott, 146-47). For a survey of various ordering of the Gospels, see Bruce M. Metzger, *The Canon of the New Testament: Its Origin, Development, and Significance* (Oxford: Clarendon, 1987), 295-300. As a contrasting example of a Christian biblical codex with earmarks of having been copied for private usage, there is 𝔓72 (Jude and 1-2 Peter, P.Bod. VII-VIII, ##166 and 168 in appendix 1). On this manuscript see now Wasserman, "Papyrus 72," esp. 148-54.

72. For a detailed analysis of the scribal proclivities in 𝔓45, see Royse, "Scribal Habits," 88-181. There are "few nonsense readings, few corrections, few obvious errors," which reflects a competent scribe concerned primarily "to produce a readable text" (156).

73. I cite calculations by Skeat, "Codicological Analysis," 41 (= *Collected Biblical Writings*, ed. Elliott, 156).

74. Granted, 𝔓46 is an equally substantial codex of roughly similar date, a single-gathering manuscript originally comprising 52 sheets of papyrus (208 pages). But, in comparison with the Gospels and Acts, the much smaller body of text copied in 𝔓46 (Pauline Epistles) allowed the scribe to use larger letters, and thus and fewer lines per page (25-32) and fewer letters per line.

have been the first, but it remains the earliest extant indisputable instance of a codex comprising this sizable collection of texts.[75]

In sum, although it is in principle fully possible that 𝔓45 was prepared primarily for personal reading/study, I see no sufficient reason to prefer this view over the assumption that it was commissioned by an early Christian community and intended primarily for liturgical reading. If, nevertheless, we suppose private usage, then we certainly must posit someone with sufficient interest and economic resources to afford the copying of such a large body of text.[76] All things considered, however, I think that it is more likely that this codex was made for the use of some early Christian church.

But it is not crucial to settle the matter here. My main concern in this discussion is to urge that, in questions about the purposes for which 𝔓45 or any other manuscript was copied, the layout of the text (including numbers of lines per page and letters per line) has to be considered, along with its other scribal features.

"Readers' Aids"

There are also a few other characteristics of early Christian manuscripts that we can regard collectively as "readers' aids." Whereas in the wider aesthetic preferences of the time the uncluttered and unbroken line of text was an ideal *(scripta continuo)*, with no spaces between words and little or no punctuation, particularly in formal copies of Greek literary texts, by contrast, many early Christian manuscripts, especially copies of biblical texts, have a variety of scribal devices that reflect a concern to guide and facilitate reading of the texts. These range from the simple addition of a diaeresis (a double dot) over an initial *iota* or *upsilon* (to help readers avoid taking the vowel as part of the preceding word), or breathing marks over aspirated initial vowels, on through punctuation (to mark off a sense unit roughly equivalent to our sentence or clause), and other devices to mark

---

75. Even if we follow Stanton (*Jesus and Gospel*, 71-75) in accepting Skeat's argument that 𝔓64 + 𝔓67 + 𝔓4 constituted a somewhat earlier fourfold Gospel manuscript, and that 𝔓75 may have been another, the further inclusion of Acts still makes 𝔓45 unique among early codices.

76. Skeat ("Codicological Analysis," 43 = *Collected Biblical Writings*, ed. Elliott, 157) calculated the cost as about 43-44 drachmae (a drachma perhaps equivalent to a day laborer's wage, at least in the first and second centuries CE).

larger sense-unit divisions (paragraphs or sections). Of course, the identification of smaller and larger sense units in particular reflects and promotes a certain construing or interpretation of the text, and so is one important clue to Christian exegesis in these early centuries.[77]

In modern texts we take for granted word spacing, punctuation, and paragraph divisions, along with a variety of other features that signal how the text should be read (e.g., use of italics, boldface, and headings). But readers of ancient Greek literary texts usually had to construe the largely uninterrupted lines of letters so as to perceive the individual words and the syntactical units that we think of as clauses, sentences, and larger divisions of text such as paragraphs. In the words of Colin Roberts, "As a rule Greek manuscripts make very few concessions to the reader."[78] So, at the initial stages of learning to read, a lot of effort was required in acquiring the ability to deal with unbroken blocks of text.

In chapter three I referred briefly to the various ways that copies of texts used in elementary levels of schooling were laid out and marked up to cue those learning to read.[79] But the Christian manuscripts in question were not generally school texts, and the scribal devices in them were not those used to teach reading (e.g., syllable markers). Instead, we are apparently dealing with particular efforts to facilitate the public/liturgical usage of texts, especially, of course, those texts treated as scriptures.[80] In the

77. There is a European-based project focused on analysis of such sense units in early biblical manuscripts, and a new series of publications arising from the project: Pericope: Scripture as Written and Read in Antiquity. The initial/introductory volume is Marjo C. A. Korpel and Josef M. Oesch, eds., *Delimitation Criticism* (Assen: Van Gorcum, 2000). The most recent volume includes studies of text-unit divisions in several NT manuscripts: S. E. Porter, "Pericope Markers in Some Early Greek New Testament Manuscripts," and D. Trobisch, "Structural Markers in New Testament Manuscripts with Special Attention to Observations in Codex Boernerianus (G012) and Papyrus 46 of the Letters of Paul," in *Layout Markers in Biblical Manuscripts and Ugaritic Tablets*, ed. Marjo Korpel and Josef Oesch (Assen: Van Gorcum, 2005), 161-76 and 177-90, respectively.

78. Roberts, "Two Biblical Papyri," 227. For further discussion of how Greek literary texts characteristically lack the sorts of readers' aids that we expect in books today (e.g., word division, sense-unit division, punctuation), see esp. Turner, *Greek Manuscripts*, 7-12.

79. I refer here again to Cribiore's discussion of these matters in *Gymnastics of the Mind*, esp. 132-43.

80. Especially in the early centuries, when the idea of a canon and the boundaries thereof were still under consideration, the widespread public reading of a text in the worship setting is probably the best indication that the text was functioning as scripture, at least in a given circle.

course of time, the basic sorts of devices exhibited in early Christian manuscripts came to be taken for granted as standard features of correct writing and publishing, and today are familiar features in printed works. But in their time the earliest Christian manuscripts represented the leading edge of such developments in book practices.

I first emphasize that the scribal devices that we consider here appear in our earliest Christian manuscript artifacts. For example, in the famous Rylands fragment of the Gospel of John (𝔓52, second century) mentioned earlier, although only a few incomplete lines remain, we can see two clear instances of a diaeresis over an initial *iota* (recto, line 2, and verso, line 2).[81] There is no punctuation observable in this fragment, but the slightly wider spaces between words at certain points raise the intriguing possibility that they may be intended to mark off clauses and to signal the reader to make a slight pause, similarly to the way a comma functions in printed texts today.[82]

In the Madgalen papyrus fragments of Matthew, 𝔓64 (Mag.Col.Gr. 18), there is a clear instance of another device called "ekthesis." This involves the projection of the first letter of the first full line of a new paragraph/section out into the left margin.[83] Roberts noted that the point

81. In both cases the diaeresis is placed over the initial letter of the word ινα. On the verso the diaeresis is not strictly needed, however, as the preceding word, κοσμον, ends with a consonant. I have offered some further analysis of the scribal features of this fragment in "𝔓52," which I draw upon here. Images of the Rylands fragment are readily available on the Internet: www.rylibweb.man.ac.uk/data1/dg/text/recto.htm (recto), http://rylibweb.man.ac.uk/data1/dg/text/frag3.htm (verso).

82. In 𝔓52 there is such a slightly wider space between ουδενα and ινα (recto, line 2), between [ει]πεν and σημαινων (recto, line 3), and between [κοσ]μον and ινα (verso, line 2). Interestingly, these spaces occur at points where modern printed editions of the text often place punctuation. For example, Nestle-Aland27 places a high stop after ουδενα at the end of John 18:31, and a comma after κοσμον in 18:37. See also Roberts, "Two Biblical Papyri," esp. 226-27, who noted the use of such spaces to mark sense units in P.Ryl. 458 (Deuteronomy, second century BCE), and pointed to something similar in P.Egerton 2 and 𝔓52 (though he thought that in the last two it was perhaps used only to mark the end of clauses).

83. The new paragraph actually begins with τοτε λεγει, which in 𝔓64 is written in the preceding line of text. So in this case the scribe indicates the new paragraph by ekthesis in what is the first *full* line of the new paragraph. Another tactic taken by some scribes, however, was to start the first line of a new paragraph with its first word, and leave the remainder of the preceding line blank or use filler marks (such as ">>>>"). Roberts discusses the device (*Manuscript*, 16-18), emphasizing a likely derivation from Greek scribal practices, whence Jewish and Christian scribes adopted it. Note also the Greek biblical manuscripts from Judea in which the device is used, listed in Tov, *Scribal Practices*, 161.

where this occurs in the extant fragments (the αυτοις in Matt. 26:31) corresponds to the place where a new section/paragraph of the text of Matthew is marked in later manuscripts (e.g., Codex Bezae and Codex Alexandrinus), and he judged that a system of text division reflected in these later codices "can now be carried back a couple of centuries if our dating of the papyrus [late second century CE] is correct."[84]

This is an intriguing suggestion that resonates with observations by other scholars. Several decades previously, having noted the punctuation and deliberate use of enlarged spaces at certain points in the text in Codex W (Washington/Freer Gospels Codex) and similarities to phenomena in some other early textual witnesses, Henry Sanders had suggested that "we have to do with an ancient system of phrasing, used in reading the Scriptures in church service," and he proposed that the origin of this system "must have been as early as the second century."[85]

Sanders's hunch was thus echoed later by Roberts, and was basically confirmed by other scholars as well who noted the instances of devices to mark sense units, both sentences/clauses and paragraph-size units, in the early biblical papyri published subsequently to Sanders's study of Codex W. To cite an important example, in his edition of P.Bodmer II (𝔓66), Victor Martin compared the sense-unit divisions in this papyrus of the Gospel of John dated about 200 with the divisions in the text of John in Codex W, and found sufficient correspondence to conclude that the same basic system of text division was evident, although more thoroughly developed in Codex W.[86]

Not long thereafter, when they came to edit 𝔓75 (P.Bodmer XIV-XV), Martin and Kasser noted that in this codex, as well, new paragraphs/sections were marked, often with a punctuation point at the end of the preceding section, a blank space, and the first full line of the new section extending out into the left margin, though sometimes the scribe used only one or two of these devices.[87] They compared unit divisions in 𝔓75 with

84. Colin H. Roberts, "An Early Papyrus of the First Gospel," *HTR* 46 (1953): 234 (233-37).

85. Henry A. Sanders, *The New Testament Manuscripts in the Freer Collection, Part I: The Washington Manuscript of the Four Gospels* (New York: Macmillan, 1912), 14. Sanders noted similarities to the use of spacing and punctuation in Codex Bezae (Codex D), Δ, and the Curetonian Syriac.

86. Martin, *Papyrus Bodmer II: Évangile de Jean, chap. 1–14,* 18-20, esp. 19-20.

87. Martin and Kasser, *Papyrus Bodmer XIV: Évangile de Luc,* 14-16 (on subdivision of

those in 𝔓66, noting frequent agreement, and also a number of cases where they differ in the specific ways that the divisions are marked. They suggested that in the early period when these two copies of the Gospels were made (ca. 175-225), although there was not yet a fully fixed system of text divisions, the Christian scribal practice of marking such sense units in biblical texts was already emergent and developing.[88]

Martin and Kasser were right, however, in cautioning that this scribal convention was not yet fixed, or uniform in the precise ways that scribes indicated sense units or in what units they chose to mark. In illustration of this, note that 𝔓45 (ca. 250) and 𝔓46 do not seem to exhibit any system of larger text divisions, and punctuation by the original scribes was used only occasionally.[89] Thus, indicating text divisions, though practiced somewhat more consistently by some early scribes (albeit using varying devices to mark the divisions), was not a uniform practice among all copyists of Christian biblical manuscripts of the early third century.

On the other hand, it is certainly clear, and notable, that by about 200 some Christian scribes were registering sense-unit divisions in biblical texts by various scribal devices. To repeat a point for emphasis, this means that the early manuscripts in which these devices were deployed are artifacts of early Christian exegesis of these texts, and probably also reflect something of how these texts were read liturgically, by about 200. Moreover, it is unlikely that our earliest evidence of these devices represents the first instances of them in Christian scribal tradition. So we have to project the use of these devices at least somewhat earlier than the extant manuscripts, which makes their import all the greater for historical purposes. Studies of the early Christian reception of these texts, the canonization process, early liturgical practices, and related matters should all take due notice of this evidence.

In further demonstration that the readers' aids in view here appear

---

the text), and 16-17 (on the use of punctuation). I note here simply one instance of ekthesis among many in 𝔓75, at Luke 11:1, where the first full line of the new section begins with εν τω ειναι αυτον and extends noticeably into the left margin (easily visible on plate 25, included in the Martin and Kasser edition).

88. Ibid., 15.

89. See Kenyon's description of scribal devices of 𝔓45 in *Fasciculus II,* ix; and for 𝔓46 see Kenyon, *Fasciculus III,* xiii-xiv. Kenyon noted, however, that in 𝔓46 "pauses in sense" were occasionally indicated by "slight space-intervals," suggesting "some perception by the scribe of the sense of what he was writing" (xiv).

early and frequently in Christian codices, I add data from Peter Head's helpful survey of some features of more recently published New Testament fragments from Oxyrhynchus.[90] Restricting ourselves to those fragments of New Testament codices dated to the second and third centuries, we have further clear evidence of diaeresis (𝔓100, also 𝔓66, 𝔓45), breathing marks (𝔓77, 𝔓104, 𝔓107, 𝔓113, also 𝔓45), punctuation marks (𝔓77, 𝔓102, 𝔓103, 𝔓113, 𝔓115, and, e.g., 𝔓45, 𝔓66, 𝔓75),[91] paragraph division (𝔓77, in addition to codices cited already), and also page numbering (𝔓106, also 𝔓66).

I emphasize that I intend here merely adequate illustration of the phenomena in question, not an exhaustive listing of early biblical codices in which these features appear. I trust, however, that the early evidence cited here will suffice to make the point. Although the codices that Head cites happen to be copies of New Testament texts, similar scribal devices appear in early Christian manuscripts of other literary texts as well, such as Old Testament writings.[92]

In addition to reflecting a particular scribal concern for legibility and probable Christian use of certain texts in public reading, these scribal devices may also suggest a historical relationship of Christian to Jewish scribal practices. Many years ago Colin Roberts noted the curious spaces used to mark the ends of a sentences or clauses in fragments of a second-century BCE Greek copy of Deuteronomy (P.Ryl. 458, #28 in appendix 1), and he commented that he knew of no Greek literary papyrus with a similar system. He did, however, also note something roughly similar in a couple of then recently published Christian papyri of very early date, P.Egerton 2 (an unknown Gospel-like text) and P.Ryl. 457 (𝔓52), and he mooted the possibility of some sort of influence from Jewish to early Christian scribal practice.[93]

90. Head, "Some Recently Published NT Papyri," esp. the table on p. 5.

91. These dots mark clauses and sentences, and are placed variously in relation to the line of text. The precise force of the placement of the dots varies somewhat in early manuscripts from one to another. Users of modern printed editions, such as Nestle-Aland27, will note the use of the "low" stop/point (to signal the end of a sentence) and the "high" stop/ point (e.g., to mark a shift to direct speech).

92. For example, P.Chester Beatty VI (Numbers–Deuteronomy, late second century CE) has occasionally paragraph division, a diaeresis over initial *iota* and *upsilon,* an apostrophe following proper names of non-Greek derivation, all these supplied by the original scribe. See Kenyon, *Fasciculus V,* ix-x.

93. Roberts, "Two Biblical Papyri," esp. 226-28. Roberts contrasted the use of such spaces in these manuscripts with the typical layout in copies of classical literary texts: "As a

At the time when he published P.Ryl. 458, however, Roberts had very little other evidence of Jewish scribal practice of equivalent dating with which to compare it. But thanks to the painstaking labors of Emanuel Tov, it is now possible to say a good deal more about the scribal practices reflected in early Jewish Hebrew, Aramaic, and Greek manuscripts.[94] Note, for example, his results with reference to the use of spaces to mark sense/reading units (sentences, verses, or larger units). Tov shows that the practice goes back to the copying of Hebrew texts (both biblical and nonbiblical literary texts, but not documentary texts), and was then carried over by Jewish scribes in copying Greek biblical texts also.[95] To be sure, once again, we are dealing here with a scribal tradition that involved a certain amount of variation, and perhaps scribal judgment, in actual practice. But the basic idea of identifying sense units by one or another scribal device is rather widely demonstrated already in the earliest Jewish manuscripts of biblical texts.

Moreover, Tov cogently posits continuities (albeit with some variation and further developments in specifics) between Jewish scribal traditions and subsequent Christian practice, which can be perceived most directly by comparing Greek biblical manuscripts of clearly Jewish and Christian provenances.[96] The use of spaces to mark larger sense units is a good example of this. Among Greek biblical manuscripts from Jewish scribes, we

---

rule Greek manuscripts make very few concessions to the reader" (227). There also are a plate of P.Ryl. 458 and brief description in Ernst Würthwein, *The Text of the Old Testament*, trans. Erroll F. Rhodes, rev. ed. (Grand Rapids: Eerdmans, 1979), 176-77. The elegant hand, very wide top margin, and good quality of the papyrus combine to suggest that this "unusually handsome manuscript" (Roberts, "Two Biblical Papyri," 226) was likely prepared for public reading.

94. Tov's analyses in several earlier publications have now been brought together helpfully in *Scribal Practices*.

95. Ibid., 131-63. Tov posits three stages of development in the ways that Jewish scribes indicated section divisions in Greek biblical manuscripts (159-62). His appendix 5, "Scribal Features of Early Witnesses of Greek Scripture" (pp. 303-15), gives detailed tables of scribal features of manuscripts down through the fifth century CE. Tov also notes that techniques for indicating sections of texts seem to be in use earlier than any of our extant biblical manuscripts, as evidenced a variety of ancient Near Eastern materials. Consequently, he judges that "the earliest Scripture rolls already indicated section division" (p. 155).

96. Ibid., 160-61, and the table of manuscripts with discussion of features in pp. 303-15. Tov's evidence concerning Christian scribal practice is limited to copies of OT texts. But the same influence is evident also in the ways that Christian scribes indicated section/paragraph units in copies of NT texts.

have already noted P.Ryl. 458, with its use of sense-unit spaces and punctuation (the use of a high dot/stop). Tov also cites other Greek biblical manuscripts of Jewish provenance that exhibit related features. These include P.Fouad 266a-c (Genesis–Deuteronomy, first century BCE, section divisions with *paragraphos* sign, ##5, 26, and 27 in appendix 1),[97] 4QpapLXXLeva&b (Leviticus, first century BCE, section divisions and *paragraphos* sign, #19 and 20 in appendix 1), 8HevXIIgr (Minor Prophets, Nahal Hever, first century BCE, section divisions, *paragraphos* signs, ekthesis, #81 in appendix 1), P.Oxy. 4443 (Esther, late first or early second century CE, sections, *paragraphos*, ekthesis, #36 in appendix 1).[98]

Early biblical manuscripts of Christian provenance show similar features, particularly the identification of sections/paragraphs by the original scribe, for example, P.Chester Beatty VI (Numbers–Deuteronomy), P.Chester Beatty IX + P.Scheide (Ezekiel, #76 in appendix 1), P.Oxy. 4442 (Exodus, #12 in appendix 1), P.Chester Beatty X (Daniel, #79 in appendix 1), and a number of others.[99] In general, however, the possible continuity between Jewish and Christian practice is reflected more at the level of section/paragraph-unit divisions, not at sentence or verse level. Moreover, as noted numerous times previously, we are dealing with a scribal tradition that was not legislated or enforced by any authority in these early centuries. That is, we can probably assume influence of some scribal features

97. The *paragraphos* sign is usually a horizontal (or slightly curved) mark that served to designate the end of a preceding section. The device appears often in copies of Greek classical texts, and also in Jewish and Christian manuscripts. In classical texts such marks can be from the original copyist or, more commonly, were inserted subsequently by a user of the manuscript. For further background see Turner, *Greek Manuscripts,* 8-9; and on its use (and use of other scribal marks) in ancient Jewish manuscripts in particular, see Tov, *Scribal Practices,* 178-87. Tov notes that in the Greek Jewish manuscripts the mark is usually placed between the last line of one section and the first line of the new section, as typical in copies of classical texts, whereas in Hebrew and Aramaic manuscripts such a mark appears mainly in the margin (183). He gives a list of Greek biblical (OT) manuscripts with the *paragraphos* sign (184). As he elsewhere notes (161), both the *paragraphos* sign and the use of ekthesis probably derive from Greek practices, and were adopted in Jewish and then Christian scribal circles.

98. See Tov's list, *Scribal Practices,* 311.

99. Tov (ibid., 160-61) also lists P.Oxy. 1007 (Genesis, the provenance of which is less certain), P.Berl. 17213 (Genesis), P.Rendel Harris 166 (which could be Jewish, and might also be an excerpt text rather than a continuous text of Genesis), Washington Freer V (Minor Prophets), P.Berl. 11778 (Job 33–34 on verso of another text, perhaps a magical text), P.Chester Beatty V (Genesis), P.Alex. 203 (Isaiah, a roll, perhaps Jewish), P.Chester Beatty IV (Genesis, fourth century CE), and P.Genève Gr. 252 (Jeremiah, fourth century CE).

found in Jewish biblical manuscripts upon early Christian copying practices, such as the practice of signaling at least major sense units of the texts. But we should not expect uniformity in practice on the one hand, or, on the other hand, fail to recognize the continuity amid variation.

As Tov points out, the identification of units of a text, and also whether to identify major and minor units, required the judgment of a copyist, and so we find variations among the extant manuscripts, especially among the early ones.[100] But this means that any division of a text into units (from sentences or verses on through larger units such as paragraphs or "sections") reflects exegesis of the text in question, giving us further reason to pay attention to these features of the physical/visual layout of the text in ancient manuscripts. Any significant variations and changes in the identification of sense units in a given text probably indicate differences or developments in the way that text was understood and used.

Corrections

In this final section of this chapter, I want to draw attention briefly to the phenomenon of scribal corrections in early Christian papyri. New Testament textual critics are well aware of the phenomenon in copies of New Testament writings, and the textual apparatus of a good critical edition of the Greek New Testament will often indicate whether a given variant reading is original to a particular manuscript or a correction in it. There have been more detailed studies of corrections in a few important textual witnesses, the invaluable analysis of Codex Sinaiticus by Milne and Skeat perhaps the enduring model for such work.[101] As for early New Testament papyri, the doctoral dissertation by James Royse is essential.[102] My aim here is not so much to discuss specifics of particular corrections, or to focus on

---

100. See ibid., 149, for discussion of unit divisions in Hebrew biblical manuscripts. Tov judges that, to some degree, "scribes must have felt free to change the section divisions of their *Vorlage* and to add new ones in accord with their understanding of the context," and "must have made their decisions *ad hoc*, guided mainly by their general understanding of the content" (150). This makes such unit divisions in ancient manuscripts all the more important testimony to the ways ancients understood the texts in question.

101. H. J. M. Milne and T. C. Skeat, *Scribes and Correctors of the Codex Sinaiticus* (London: British Museum, 1938).

102. Royse, "Scribal Habits."

the particular kinds of variants involved (the sorts of matters more typically treated in text-critical discussion). Instead, I want to point more generally at what we can discern from the presence of corrections in early manuscripts about ancient Christian scribes and their attitudes toward the texts that they copied.

We may begin by noting that it is important to distinguish between corrections made by the original scribe, corrections made by another scribe but in a contemporary hand, and corrections that appear to be from a later hand. The last sort of corrections may offer important indications of how readers later than the time of the original scribe read a given text, and what sorts of readings they preferred.[103] Corrections in the hand of the original scribe, however, tell us more about the attitude of that scribe toward the task of copying, and how concerned the scribe was to produce a satisfactory copy. These corrections in most cases reflect the scribe going back over the copied text, comparing it with the exemplar, and catching mistakes (e.g., accidental omissions or repetitions, misspellings, or other confusions). Corrections by a contemporary hand, but distinguishable from the copyist, may suggest something else, likely a setting in which the copyist's work was regularly checked and corrected by another copyist or perhaps by a person in a supervisory role aiming for some quality control.

In the corrections made by the original scribe and those made by a contemporary, we have historically important evidence suggesting a concern for a satisfactory, "accurate" copy of a text, this concern datable to the time of the manuscript. Of course, the changes in question ("corrections") were meant to produce a copy "satisfactory" to the person(s) who made them. What modern editors think of the changes in relation to the question of any "original" wording of the text is another matter.[104] The point to underscore, however, is that corrections reflect a mentality toward the text in which its wording is invested with some significance and concern. In our efforts to probe questions about what early Christian attitudes were toward the writings that later became part of the closed canon, what early Christian "textuality" might have been, and what dynamics might have affected the transmission of these writings, the corrections in our earliest

---

103. For example, Royse (ibid., 238-40) judged that later (third century) corrections in 𝔓46 reflected a tendency toward the "Alexandrian" text of the Pauline Epistles.

104. For recently perceived problems with the notion of an "original" text, see Epp, "Multivalence."

manuscripts constitute crucial evidence. Granted, other evidence indicates an interesting fluidity and diversity in the text of these writings in the second century in at least some Christian circles and situations.[105] I submit, however, that these corrections offer counterindications that all was not simply fluidity, and that, at least among some Christian scribes and in some circumstances, there was a somewhat greater care in copying.

To register another related matter on which, in particular, corrections by a hand contemporary with that of the original scribe of a manuscript are important, there is the question of when Christian scriptoria first appeared.[106] Some have assumed that there cannot have been Christian scriptoria before the third century or even later, but such corrections in early manuscripts may point to another conclusion.[107] In part, of course, the answer depends on what we mean by a "scriptorium." If the term designates solely a dedicated physical structure, with multiple copies of texts produced in programmatic fashion, then it will be difficult to prove such an operation in the second century. On the other hand, as Gamble rightly noted, if the term refers somewhat more broadly to a setting in which the copying of texts involved more than a single scribe, "any of the larger Christian communities, such as Antioch or Rome, may have already had scriptoria in the early second century."[108]

The particular importance of manuscript corrections by a hand con-

---

105. Emphasized, e.g., by David C. Parker, *The Living Text of the Gospels* (Cambridge: Cambridge University Press, 1997); and Helmut Koester, "The Text of the Synoptic Gospels in the Second Century," in *Gospel Traditions in the Second Century: Origins, Recension, Text, and Transmission,* ed. William L. Petersen (Notre Dame: University of Notre Dame Press, 1989), 19-37. I have hesitations, however, on some points, such as the claim that 𝔓75 represents "the first attempt to establish a controlled text" of the Gospels in the late second century (Parker, *Living Text,* 200). I rather suspect that the textual transmission of the Gospels in the second century was more complex than the picture presented by Parker (and, admittedly, assumed by many other scholars as well), and that a concern for careful copying (along with much freer attitudes) may go back much earlier than our earliest manuscripts. I have expressed disagreement with Koester previously: Hurtado, "Beyond the Interlude?" 40-43, and see also Hurtado, "The New Testament in the Second Century: Text, Collections and Canon," in *Transmission and Reception: New Testament Text-Critical and Exegetical Studies,* ed. J. W. Childers and D. C. Parker (Piscataway, NJ: Gorgias Press, 2006), 3-17.

106. Gamble (*Books and Readers,* 121-26) gives a generally excellent discussion, but does not invoke the possible significance of corrections.

107. For example, Kurt Aland and Barbara Aland, *The Text of the New Testament,* trans. E. F. Rhodes, rev. ed. (Grand Rapids: Eerdmans, 1989), 70.

108. Gamble, *Books and Readers,* 121.

temporary with the original copyist is that they point to a setting in which the work of a copyist was reviewed and supervised by someone else, someone with the authority to correct the copyist's work. Such a copy setting, I contend, amounts to a scriptorium, at least in the attitude toward the texts copied and the concern for the copying process and product. If so, then it is important to take note of such corrections, how early we can trace them, and what particular tendencies they may reflect.

As indicated in Peter Head's survey of recently published New Testament papyri fragments, we can detect corrections even among some of the earliest of these, including P.Oxy. 4405 (a further portion of 𝔓77, second/third century) and P.Oxy. 4403 (𝔓103, second/third century). In the latter case, the editor explicitly attributes corrections to a hand other than (though contemporary with) the original copyist.[109]

But the more substantially preserved New Testament papyri obviously provide a greater opportunity to do any serious analysis, and for this Royse's study is the fullest known to me.[110] For each of six major papyri, 𝔓45 (Gospels and Acts), 𝔓46 (Pauline Epistles), 𝔓47 (Revelation), 𝔓66 (John), 𝔓72 (Jude, 1-2 Peter), and 𝔓75 (Luke and John), Royse gives detailed analysis of their various scribal features, including corrections.[111]

It is neither practical nor necessary to rehearse the details here. I restrict myself to pointing out that Royse notes repeatedly that the corrections in these papyri give us important data on attitudes toward copying and toward the texts copied. The copyists' skills reflected in these papyri are of various levels, and the types and number of corrections vary among them too. For instance, the scribe of 𝔓45 seems to have been a skilled worker who copied with conscious attention to the sense of the text, and so made remarkably few errors in comparison with some of the others that Royse analyzed. On the other hand, even less skillful scribes, such as the copyist of 𝔓66 (a few hundred corrections noted), showed by their zealousness in correcting their mistakes that they too felt "the obligation to make an exact copy."[112]

In short, we can get impressions of the varying abilities of the scribes

---

109. J. D. Thomas, in *The Oxyrhynchus Papyri, Volume LXIV*, ed. E. W. Handley et al. (London: Egypt Exploration Society, 1997), 6.

110. Royse, "Scribal Habits." This important study is forthcoming in SD.

111. Ibid., 122-24 (𝔓45), 235-40 (𝔓46), 344-46 (𝔓47), 391-97 (𝔓66), 476-77 (𝔓72), 538-40 (𝔓75), with an extended discussion of 𝔓75 on "Accuracy and Copying Technique."

112. Ibid., 541.

(which, in turn, suggests something of the varying economic and cultural levels of those for whom texts were copied). We can sense the more precise ways that these scribes worked, some copying rather woodenly (and often not very skillfully) syllable by syllable or even letter by letter, and others copying with clear attention to the sense units and reflecting more of an engagement with the text. Even the mistakes of scribes give us hard data for estimating attitudes toward the texts copied, their own efforts and those of unknown others reflecting a concern for the wording of these texts and for careful transmission of them.

Summary

My main concern in the foregoing pages has been to illustrate the larger historical significance of several particular features of early manuscripts. For example, as other scholars have suggested, the sizes/dimensions of codices likely do reflect the uses for which they were prepared. But I hope to have shown that our discussions of the matter must be adequately informed by evidence of the wider tastes and conventions affecting construction of codices in the periods in which the earliest Christian ones were copied. We can say easily, however, that the varying sizes of early Christian codices reflect both private and public/liturgical uses of them.

Likewise, the layout of the text is important, a two-column layout, for example, likely reflecting an effort to give the codex page a somewhat more sophisticated appearance in terms of the textual aesthetics of the second and third centuries CE. Even the size of margins, the number of lines per page, and the number of letters per line are all worth noting, and may well illumine the specific nature of the manuscript as an artifact of early Christian usage and religious life.

I also noted how a number of early Christian codices have features that are rather clearly intended to facilitate the reading of them, perhaps especially public reading in the setting of the gathered church. Moreover, even scribal mistakes and efforts to correct them provide us with often overlooked but richly suggestive data bearing on central questions about the place of particular texts in early Christian circles.

Concluding Remarks

A s I indicated in the introduction, this book is not a recruiting call for scholars in New Testament and Christian origins to leave their field and become paleographers and papyrologists. I have sought only to emphasize that the work produced by scholars in these specialties yields valuable data with which all of us interested in historical questions about early Christianity should reckon. I hope, therefore, that this book will interest and encourage other scholars to take more account of these early Christian artifacts, and of their implications for description and analysis of Christianity in the earliest centuries.

I hope also (indeed, particularly) that the current generation of students, especially those contemplating or engaged in doctoral research, will be stimulated to acquaint themselves with these important testimonies to early Christian texts, and the processes of transmission and usage of them. In early Christian manuscripts we come as close as we can to actual copying, reading, and study of biblical and extrabiblical texts in Christian circles as far back as the second century. No one concerned with the origins of Christianity can rightly ignore this material.

As with anything worthwhile, some effort is certainly required to become familiar with the specific features of early manuscripts. Granted, the voluminous flow of scholarly publication and the diversity of approaches employed in the study of Christian origins make it increasingly difficult to feel that one can aim for much more than a restricted focus on some particular text or approach. One cannot be an expert in everything, of course, and the scholarly task is properly cooperative and collegial, scholars learning from one another and making their own particular contributions. But

I repeat the hope that some newer and aspiring scholars in the field will find their interests drawn to the study of early manuscripts, and that many others of those aiming to pursue historical investigations of the New Testament and early Christianity will be encouraged to develop at least a sufficient acquaintance with these artifacts to benefit from the data that they afford.

At a point when we now have a significant body of early Christian papyri (and we may hope for still further material to be published), it is unfortunate for the study of Christian origins that these intriguing remnants of early Christianity continue to be overlooked or underappreciated. The particular proposals that I have advanced in this book about the implications of these earliest Christian artifacts are not proffered as the last word, and my views on specific issues may well be subject to correction. Instead, my aim is to stimulate further research and reflection on these matters by others, and I look forward to the results.

Suggestions for Further Reading

For those ready to take up my appeal, I append a few suggestions for initial, further reading. These will help one to gear up for further exploration of what early manuscripts provide us. For a brief, readable, and very engaging introduction to papyrology, see Eric G. Turner, *Greek Papyri: An Introduction* (Oxford: Clarendon, 1980). Bruce M. Metzger, *Manuscripts of the Greek Bible: An Introduction to Palaeography* (New York: Oxford University Press, 1981), is a concise entrée to biblical manuscripts and their scribal features. Harry Y. Gamble, *Books and Readers in the Early Church: A History of Early Christian Texts* (New Haven: Yale University Press, 1995), gives a fascinating discussion of how early Christians produced, circulated, and used texts, and should be required reading of all Ph.D. students in the fields of New Testament and Christian origins.

Aland, Barbara, et al., eds. *Novum Testamentum Graece.* 27th ed. Stuttgart: Deutsche Bibelgesellschaft, 1993.

Aland, Kurt. "Bemerkungen zum Alter und Entstehung des Christogramms anhand von Beobachtungen bei 𝔓66 und 𝔓75." In Aland, *Studien zur Überlieferung des Neuen Testaments und seines Textes.* Berlin: de Gruyter, 1967. Pp. 173-79.

Aland, Kurt. *Kurzgefasste Liste der griechischen Handschriften des Neuen Testaments.* 2nd revised and enlarged edition. Berlin: de Gruyter, 1994.

Aland, Kurt. "Neue Neutestamentliche Papyri II." *New Testament Studies* 10 (1963-64): 62-79.

Aland, Kurt. "Neue Neutestamentliche Papyri II." *New Testament Studies* 11 (1964-65): 1-21.

Aland, Kurt. *Repertorium der griechischen christlichen Papyri, I: Biblische Papyri, Altes Testament, Neues Testament, Varia, Apokryphen.* Patristische Texte und Studien 18. Berlin: de Gruyter, 1976.

Aland, Kurt. *Repertorium der griechischen christlichen Papyri, II: Kirchenväter — Papyri, Teil 1: Beschreibungen.* Berlin: de Gruyter, 1995.

Aland, Kurt. *Studien zur Überlieferung des Neuen Testaments und seines Textes.* Arbeiten zur neutestamentlichen Textforschung. Berlin: de Gruyter, 1967.

Aland, Kurt, and Barbara Aland. *The Text of the New Testament.* Trans. E. F. Rhodes. Grand Rapids: Eerdmans, 1987.

Attridge, Harold W. "Appendix: The Greek Fragments." In *Nag Hammadi Codex II, 2-7, together with XIII, 2*, Brit.Lib.Or. 4926(1), and P.Oxy. 1, 654, 655,* vol. 1: *Gospel according to Thomas, Gospel according to Philip, Hypostasis of the Archons, and Indexes,* ed. Bentley Layton. Leiden: Brill, 1989. Pp. 95-128.

Avi-Yonah, Michael. *Abbreviations in Greek Inscriptions (The Near East, 200 B.C.–A.D. 1100).* London: Humphrey Milford, 1940. Reprinted in *Abbreviations in*

Greek Inscriptions, Paypri Manuscripts and Early Printed Books, ed. Al. N. Oikonomides. Chicago: Ares, 1974. Pp. 1-125.

Bagnall, Roger. *Reading Papyri, Writing Ancient History*. London: Routledge, 1995.

Bauckham, Richard. *The Climax of Prophecy: Studies on the Book of Revelation*. Edinburgh: T&T Clark, 1993.

Bauckham, Richard. "For Whom Were the Gospels Written?" *The Gospels for All Christians: Rethinking the Gospel Audiences*, ed. Richard Bauckham. Grand Rapids: Eerdmans, 1998. Pp. 9-48.

Beard, Mary, et al. *Literacy in the Roman World*. Journal of Roman Archaeology Supplement Series 3. Ann Arbor: Journal of Roman Archaeology, 1991.

Becker, Adam H., and Annette Yoshiko Reed, eds. *The Ways That Never Parted: Jews and Christians in Late Antiquity and the Early Middle Ages*. Tübingen: Mohr Siebeck, 2003.

Bedodi, Flavio. "I 'nomina sacra' nei papyri greci veterotestamentari prechristiani." *Studia Papyrologica* 13 (1974): 89-103.

Bell, H. Idris. *Jews and Christians in Egypt: The Jewish Troubles in Alexandria and the Athanasian Controversy*. London: British Museum, 1924.

Bell, H. Idris, and T. C. Skeat. *Fragments of an Unknown Gospel and Other Early Christian Papyri*. London: Trustees of British Museum, 1935.

Benoit, Pierre, et al. *Les grottes de Murabba'āt*. Discoveries in the Judaean Desert 2. Oxford: Oxford University Press, 1961.

Black, C. Clifton. *Mark: Images of an Apostolic Interpreter*. Columbia, SC: University of South Carolina Press, 1994.

Black, Matthew. "The Chi-Rho Sign — Christogram and/or Staurogram?" In *Apostolic History and the Gospel: Essays Presented to F. F. Bruce*, ed. W. Ward Gasque and Ralph P. Martin. Grand Rapids: Eerdmans, 1970. Pp. 319-27.

Blanchard, Alain, ed. *Les débuts du codex: Actes de la journée d'étude organisée à Paris les 3 et 4 juillet 1985 par l'Institut de papyrologie de la Sorbonne et l'Institut de recherche et d'histoire des texts*. Turnhout: Brepols, 1989.

Blanchard, Alain. *Sigles et abbréviations dans les papyrus documentaires grecs: Recherches de paléographie*. Bulletin of the Institute for Classical Studies Supplement 30. London: Institute of Classical Studies, 1974.

Böcher, Otto. *Christus Exorcista: Dämonismus und Taufe im Neuen Testament*. Stuttgart: Kohlhammer, 1972.

Bovini, G. *Ravenna: Its Mosaics and Monuments*. Ravenna: Longo, 1980.

Bovon, François. "Names and Numbers in Early Christianity." *New Testament Studies* 47 (2001): 267-88.

Brown, Schuyler. "Concerning the Origin of the *Nomina Sacra*." *Studia Papyrologica* 9 (1970): 7-19.

Bureth, P. *Les titulatures imperiales dans les papyrus, les ostraca et les inscriptions d'Egypte*. Brussels: Fondation égyptologique reine Elisabeth, 1964.

Burzachechi, M. "Sull' Uso Pre-Costantiniano del Monogramma Greco di Christo." *Rendiconti della Pontificia Accademia Romana di Archeologia, Series III* 28 (1955-56): 197-211.

Casson, Lionel. *Travel in the Ancient World.* London: Allen & Unwin, 1974.

Cavallo, Guglielmo. *Libri, Editori e Pubblico nel mondo antico: Guida storica e critica.* Rome: Laterza, 1975.

Cohen, Abraham. *Parting of the Ways: Judaism and Christianity.* London: Lincolns, 1954.

Colella, Don Pasquale. "Les abréviations ⩖ et ⳨," *Revue biblique* 80 (1973): 547-58.

Comfort, Philip. *Encountering the Manuscripts: An Introduction to New Testament Paleography and Textual Criticism.* Nashville: Broadman & Holman Publishers, 2005.

Comfort, Philip W. "Exploring the Common Identification of Three New Testament Manuscripts: 𝔓4, 𝔓64 and 𝔓67." *Tyndale Bulletin* 46 (1995): 43-54.

Comfort, Philip W. "New Reconstructions and Identifications of New Testament Papyri." *Novum Testamentum* 41 (1999): 214-30.

Cribiore, Raffaella. *Gymnastics of the Mind: Greek Education in Hellenistic and Roman Egypt.* Princeton: Princeton University Press, 2001.

Cribiore, Raffaella. *Writing, Teachers, and Students in Graeco-Roman Egypt.* Atlanta: Scholars Press, 1996.

Dagenais, John. *The Ethics of Reading in Manuscript Culture.* Princeton: Princeton University Press, 1994.

Daniels, Jon. "The Egerton Gospel: Its Place in Early Christianity." Ph.D. dissertation, Claremont Graduate School, 1989.

Dassmann, Ernst. *Der Stachel im Fleisch: Paulus in der frühchristlichen Literatur bis Irenaeus.* Münster: Aschendorff, 1979.

Davis, C. J. *The Name and Way of the Lord.* Journal for the Study of the New Testament Supplement 129. Sheffield: JSOT Press, 1996.

de Savignac, Jean. "Les papyrus Bodmer XIV et XV." *Scriptorium* 17 (1963): 50-55.

Deissmann, Adolf. *Bible Studies.* Trans. Alexander Grieve. Edinburgh: T&T Clark, 1901 (German original 1895).

Delcor, M. "Des diverses manières d'écrire le tétragramme sacré dans les anciens documents hébraïques." *Revue de l'histoire des religions* 147 (1955): 145-73.

Dinkler, Erich. "Älteste christliche Denkmäler: Bestand und Chronologie." In *Signum Crucis.* Tübingen: Mohr (Siebeck), 1967. Pp. 134-78, reprinted in *Art, Archaeology, and Architecture of Early Christianity,* ed. Paul Corby Finney. New York: Garland, 1993. Pp. 22-66.

Dinkler, Erich. "Comments on the History of the Symbol of the Cross." *Journal for Theology and Church* 1 (1965): 124-46 (German original 1951).

Dinkler, Erich. "Papyrus Yalensis 1 als ältest bekannter christlicher Genesistext: Zur Frühgeschichte des Kreuz-Symbols." In *Im Zeichen des Kreuzes: Aufsätze von Erich Dinkler, mit Beiträgen von C. Andresen, E. Dinkler-v.Schubert, E. Grässer, und G. Klein,* ed. Otto Merk and Michael Wolter. Berlin/New York: de Gruyter, 1992. Pp. 341-45.

Dinkler, Erich. *Signum Crucis.* Tübingen: Mohr (Siebeck), 1967.

Dinkler, Erich, and Erica Dinkler-von Schubert. "Kreuz." *Lexicon der christlichen Ikonographie,* ed. Engelbert Kirschbaum. 8 vols. Rome: Herder, 1968-76. 2:562-90.

Dinkler-von Schubert, Erika. "ΣΤΑΥΡΟΣ: Vom 'Wort vom Kreuz' (1 Cor. 1,18) zum Kreuz-Symbol." In *Byzantine East, Latin West: Art-Historical Studies in Honor of Kurt Weitzmann,* ed. Doula Mouriki et al. Princeton: Department of Art and Archaeology, 1995. Pp. 29-39.

Dölger, Franz J. "Die Achtzahl in der altchristlichen Symbolik." *Antike und Christentum* 4 (1934): 153-87.

Dölger, Franz J. *IΧΘΥΣ. Das Fisch Symbol in frühchristlichen Zeit.* Münster: Aschendorff, 1928.

Dölger, Franz J. *Sol Salutis: Gebet und Gesang im christlichen Altertum mit besonderer Rücksicht auf die Ostung in Gebet und Liturgie.* 3rd ed. Liturgische Quellen und Forschungen 16-17. 1925. Reprint Münster: Aschendorffsche Verlagsbuchhandlung, 1972.

Dunn, J. D. G. *The Partings of the Ways: Between Judaism and Christianity and Their Significance for the Character of Christianity.* Philadelphia: Trinity Press International, 1991.

Elliott, J. K., ed. *The Apocryphal New Testament.* Oxford: Clarendon, 1993.

Epp, Eldon J. "The Codex and Literacy in Early Christianity and at Oxyrhynchus: Issues Raised by Harry Y. Gamble's *Books and Readers in the Early Church.*" *Critical Review of Books in Religion 1997,* ed. Charles Prebish. Atlanta: American Academy of Religion and Society of Biblical Literature. Pp. 15-37.

Epp, Eldon J. "The Multivalence of the Term 'Original Text' in New Testament Textual Criticism." *Harvard Theological Review* 92 (1999): 245-81.

Epp, Eldon J. "The New Testament Papyri at Oxyrhynchus in Their Social and Intellectual Context." In *The Sayings of Jesus: Canonical and Non-canonical: Essays in Honour of Tjitze Baarda,* ed. William L. Petersen, Johan S. Vos, and Henk J. de Jonge. Leiden: Brill, 1997. Pp. 47-68.

Epp, Eldon J. "New Testament Papyrus Manuscripts and Letter Carrying in Greco-Roman Times." In *The Future of Early Christianity: Essays in Honor of Helmut Koester,* ed. Birger A. Pearson. Minneapolis: Fortress Press, 1991. Pp. 35-56.

Epp, Eldon J. "New Testament Textual Criticism in America: Requiem for a Discipline." *Journal of Biblical Literature* 98 (1979): 94-98.

Epp, Eldon J. "The Oxyrhynchus New Testament Papyri: 'Not Without Honor Except in Their Hometown'?" *Journal of Biblical Literature* 123 (2004): 5-55.

Epp, Eldon J. "The Significance of the Papyri for Determining the Nature of the

New Testament Text in the Second Century: A Dynamic View of Textual Transmission." In *Gospel Traditions in the Second Century: Origins, Recensions, Text, and Transmission*, ed. William L. Petersen. Notre Dame: University of Notre Dame Press, 1989. Pp. 71-103.

Falcetta, Alessandro. "A Testimony Collection in Manchester: Papyrus Rylands Greek 460." *Bulletin of the John Rylands Library* 83 (2002): 3-19.

Farrar, F. W. *History of Interpretation, Bampton Lectures 1885*. 1886. Reprint, Grand Rapids: Baker, 1961.

Ferguson, Everett, ed. *Encyclopedia of Early Christianity*. 2nd ed. 2 vols. New York: Garland, 1997.

Finegan, Jack. *The Archeology of the New Testament: The Life of Jesus and the Beginning of the Early Church*. Rev. ed. Princeton: Princeton University Press, 1992.

Finney, Paul Corby. *The Invisible God: The Earliest Christians on Art*. Oxford: Oxford University Press, 1994.

Fitzmyer, Joseph A. "'4QTestimonia' and the New Testament." In *Essays on the Semitic Background of the New Testament*. Missoula, MT: Scholars Press, 1974. Pp. 59-89.

Fitzmyer, Joseph A. "The Oxyrhynchus Logoi of Jesus and the Coptic Gospel according to Thomas." In *Essays on the Semitic Background of the New Testament*. Missoula: Scholars Press, 1974. Pp. 355-433.

Foster, Paul. "Are There Any Early Fragments of the So-called *Gospel of Peter?*" *New Testament Studies* 52 (2006): 1-28.

Frantz, M. Alison. "The Provenance of the Open Rho in the Christian Monograms." *American Journal of Archaeology* 33 (1929): 10-26.

Frösèn, Jaakko, ed. *The Petra Papyri, Volume 1*. American Center of Oriental Research Publications 4. Amman: American Center of Oriental Research, 2002.

Frye, R. H., J. F. Gillam, H. Inghold, and C. B. Welles. "Inscriptions from Dura-Europos." *Yale Classical Studies* 14 (1955): 123-213.

Gallo, Italo. *Greek and Latin Papyrology*. London: Institute of Classical Studies, 1986.

Gamble, Harry Y. *Books and Readers in the Early Church: A History of Early Christian Texts*. New Haven: Yale University Press, 1995.

Gardthausen, Victor Emil. *Das alte Monogramm, mit fünf Tafeln*. Leipzig: Hiersemann, 1924.

Gascou, Jean. "Les codices documentaires Egyptiens." In *Les débuts du codex*, ed. Alain Blanchard. Turnhout: Brepols, 1989. Pp. 71-101.

Gerstinger, Hans. "Ein Fragment des Chester Beatty-Evangelienkodex in der Papyrussammlung der Nationalbibliothek in Wien (Pap. Graec. Vindob. 31974)." *Aegyptus* 13 (1936): 67-72.

Ginzberg, Louis. *Legends of the Jews*. 7 vols. New York: Jewish Publication Society, 1909-38.

Goehring, James E., ed. *The Crosby-Schøyen Codex: MS 193 in the Schøyen Collection.* Leuven: Peeters, 1990.

Gonis, Nick, et al. *The Oxyrhynchus Papyri, Volume LXVI.* London: Egypt Exploration Society, 1999.

Gonis, Nick, et al. *The Oxyrhynchus Papyri, Volume LXIX.* London: Egypt Exploration Society, 2005.

Goodspeed, E. J. *Die ältesten Apologeten: Texte mit kurzen Einleitungen.* 1914. Reprint, Göttingen: Vandenhoeck & Ruprecht, 1984.

Grenfell, Bernard P., and Arthur S. Hunt. *ΛΟΓΙΑ ΙΗΣΟΥ: Sayings of Our Lord from an Early Greek Papyrus.* London: Egypt Exploration Fund, 1897.

Grenfell, Bernard P., and Arthur S. Hunt. *The Oxyrhynchus Papyri. Part I.* London: Egypt Exploration Fund, 1898.

Grenfell, Bernard P., and Arthur S. Hunt. *The Oxyrhynchus Papyri, Part IV.* London: Egypt Exploration Fund, 1904.

Gronewald, Michael. "Unbekanntes Evangelium oder Evangelienharmonie (Fragment aus dem 'Evangelium Egerton')." *Kölner Papyri (P.Köln), Vol. VI.* Cologne: Rheinisch-Westfälischen Akademischer Wissenschaften unter Universität Köln, 1987. Pp. 136-45.

Guarducci, Margherita. *The Tomb of St. Peter.* Trans. J. McLellan. London: Harrap, 1960.

Hagedorn, Dieter. "P.IFAO II 31: Johannesapokalypse 1,13-20." *Zeitschrift für Papyrologie und Epigraphik* 92 (1992): 243-47.

Haines-Eitzen, Kim. *Guardians of Letters: Literacy, Power, and the Transmitters of Early Christian Literature.* New York: Oxford University Press, 2000.

Handley, E. W., et al. *The Oxyrhynchus Papyri, Volume LXIV.* London: Egypt Exploration Society, 1997.

Harris, William V. *Ancient Literacy.* Cambridge: Harvard University Press, 1989.

Hartman, Lars. *"Into the Name of the Lord Jesus": Baptism in the Early Church.* Edinburgh: T&T Clark, 1997.

Haslam, M. W., et al. *The Oxyrhynchus Papyri, Volume LXV.* London: Egypt Exploration Society, 1998.

Hay, David M. *Glory at the Right Hand: Psalm 110 in Early Christianity.* Society of Biblical Literature Monograph Series 18. Nashville: Abingdon, 1973.

Head, Peter M. "Is 𝔓4, 𝔓64 and 𝔓67 the Oldest Manuscript of the Four Gospels? A Response to T. C. Skeat." *New Testament Studies* 51 (2005): 450-57.

Head, Peter M. "Some Recently Published NT Papyri from Oxyrhynchus: An Overview and Preliminary Assessment." *Tyndale Bulletin* 51 (2000): 1-16.

Herbert, Kevin. *Roman Imperial Coins: Augustus to Hadrian and Antonine Selections, 31 BC–AD 180.* John Max Wulfing Collection in Washington University, no. 3. Wauconda, IL: Bolchasy-Carducci, 1996.

Hill, Charles E. "Did the Scribe of 𝔓52 Use the *Nomina Sacra?* Another Look." *New Testament Studies* 48 (2002): 587-92.

Hill, Charles E. *The Johannine Corpus in the Early Church.* Oxford: Oxford University Press, 2004.

Horsley, G. H. R. "Classical Manuscripts in Australia and New Zealand and the Early History of the Codex." *Antichthon: Journal of the Australian Society for Classical Studies* 27 (1995): 60-85.

Horsley, G. H. R. *New Documents Illustrating Early Christianity, Volume 2.* Sydney: Ancient History Documentary Centre, Macquarie University, 1982.

Howard, George. "The Tetragram and the New Testament." *Journal of Biblical Literature* 96 (1977): 63-68.

Howard, George. "Tetragrammaton in the New Testament." *Anchor Bible Dictionary,* ed. D. N. Freedman. 6 vols. New York: Doubleday, 1992. 6:392-93.

Hurtado, Larry W. *At the Origins of Christian Worship.* Carlisle: Paternoster, 1999; Grand Rapids: Eerdmans, 2000.

Hurtado, Larry W. "Beyond the Interlude? Developments and Directions in New Testament Textual Criticism." In *Studies in the Early Text of the Gospels and Acts,* ed. D. G. K. Taylor. Birmingham: University of Birmingham Press; Atlanta: Society of Biblical Literature, 1999. Pp. 26-48.

Hurtado, Larry W. "The Binitarian Shape of Early Christian Worship." In *The Jewish Roots of Christological Monotheism: Papers from the St. Andrews Conference on the Historical Origins of the Worship of Jesus,* ed. Carey C. Newman, James R. Davilia, and Gladys S. Lewis. Leiden: Brill, 1999. Pp. 187-213.

Hurtado, Larry W. "The Earliest Evidence of an Emerging Christian Material and Visual Culture: The Codex, the *Nomina Sacra* and the Staurogram." In *Text and Artifact in the Religions of Mediterranean Antiquity: Essays in Honour of Peter Richardson,* ed. Stephen G. Wilson and Michel Desjardins. Waterloo, Ont.: Wilfrid Laurier University Press, 2000. Pp. 271-88.

Hurtado, Larry W. *Lord Jesus Christ: Devotion to Jesus in Earliest Christianity.* Grand Rapids: Eerdmans, 2003.

Hurtado, Larry W. "The New Testament in the Second Century: Texts, Collections and Canon." In *Transmission and Reception: New Testament Text-Critical and Exegetical Studies,* ed. J. W. Childers and D. C. Parker. Piscataway, NJ: Gorgias Press, 2006. Pp. 3-17.

Hurtado, Larry W. "The Origin of the *Nomina Sacra:* A Proposal." *Journal of Biblical Literature* 117 (1998): 655-73.

Hurtado, Larry W. "𝔓52 (P.Rylands Gk. 457) and the Nomina Sacra: Method and Probability." *Tyndale Bulletin* 54 (2003): 1-14.

Hurtado, Larry W. "The Staurogram in Early Christian Manuscripts: The Earliest Visual Reference to the Crucified Jesus?" In *New Testament Manuscripts: Their*

Text and Their World, ed. Thomas J. Kraus and Tobias Nicklas. Leiden: Brill, 2006. Pp. 207-26.

Hurtado, Larry W. *Text-Critical Methodology and the Pre-Caesarean Text: Codex W in the Gospel of Mark.* Studies and Documents 43. Grand Rapids: Eerdmans, 1981.

Jensen, Robin Margaret. *Understanding Early Christian Art.* London: Routledge, 2000.

Johnson, Gary J. *Early Christian Epitaphs from Anatolia.* Atlanta: Scholars Press, 1995.

Johnson, William A. *Bookrolls and Scribes in Oxyrhynchus.* Toronto: University of Toronto Press, 2004.

Johnson, William A. "The Function of the Paragraphus in Greek Literary Prose Texts." *Zeitschrift für Papyrologie und Epigraphik* 100 (1994): 65-68.

Joosten, Jan. "The Dura Parchment and the Diatessaron." *Vigiliae Christianae* 57 (2003): 159-75.

Judge, Edwin A. "Papyri." *Encyclopedia of Early Christianity,* ed. Everett Ferguson. 2nd ed. 2 vols. New York: Garland, 1997. 2:867-72.

Judge, Edwin A. *The Social Pattern of Christian Groups in the First Century.* London: Tyndale, 1960.

Judge, Edwin A., and S. R. Pickering. "Biblical Papyri Prior to Constantine: Some Cultural Implications of Their Physical Form." *Prudentia* 10 (1978): 1-13.

Judge, Edwin A., and S. R. Pickering. "Papyrus Documentation of Church and Community in Egypt to the Mid-Fourth Century." *Jahrbuch für Antike und Christentum* 20 (1977): 47-71.

Kanael, Baruch. "Ancient Jewish Coins and Their Historical Importance." *Biblical Archaeologist* 26 (1963): 38-62.

Kanael, Baruch. "The Coins of King Herod of the Third Year." *Jewish Quarterly Review* 62 (1951-52): 261-64.

Kearsley, R. A. "The Epitaph of Aberkios: The Earliest Christian Inscription?" *New Documents Illustrating Early Christianity, Volume 6,* ed. S. R. Llewelyn. North Ryde, NSW: Ancient History Documents Research Centre, Macquarie University, 1992. Pp. 177-81.

Kenyon, Frederic G. *The Chester Beatty Biblical Papyri.* London: Walker, 1933-58.

Kenyon, Frederic G. "Nomina Sacra in the Chester Beatty Papyri." *Aegyptus* 13 (1933): 5-10.

Keppie, Lawrence. *Understanding Roman Inscriptions.* London: Batsford, 1991.

Koester, Helmut. "The Text of the Synoptic Gospels in the Second Century." In *Gospel Traditions in the Second Century: Origins, Recension, Text and Transmission,* ed. William L. Petersen. Notre Dame: University of Notre Dame Press, 1989. Pp. 19-37.

Korpel, Marjo, and Josef M. Oesch, eds. *Delimitation Criticism.* Assen: Van Gorcum, 2000.

Korpel, Marjo, and Josef M. Oesch, eds. *Layout Markers in Biblical Manuscripts and Ugaritic Tablets.* Assen: Van Gorcum, 2005.

Kraft, Robert A. "The 'Textual Mechanics' of Early Jewish LXX/OG Papyri and Fragments." In *The Bible as Book: The Transmission of the Greek Text,* ed. Scot McKendrick and Orlaith O'Sullivan. London: British Library, 2003. Pp. 51-72.

Kraft, Robert A. "An Unnoticed Fragment of Barnabas." *Vigiliae Christianae* 21 (1967): 150-63.

Kraus, Thomas J., and Tobias Nicklas, eds. *Das Petrusevangelium und die Petrusapokalypse: Die griechischen Fragmente mit deutscher und englischer Übersetzung.* Die griechische christliche Schriftsteller der ersten [drei] Jahrhunderte 11. Berlin: de Gruyter, 2004.

Kraus, Thomas J., and Tobias Nicklas, eds. *New Testament Manuscripts: Their Texts and Their World.* Texts and Editions for New Testament Study, 2. Leiden: Brill, 2006.

Kreitzer, Larry J. *Striking New Images: Studies on Roman Imperial Coinage and the New Testament World.* Sheffield: Sheffield Academic Press, 1996.

Lauterbach, Jacob Z. "Substitutes for the Tetragrammaton." *Proceedings of the American Academy for Jewish Research* 2 (1930-1931): 39-67.

Layton, Bentley. *The Gnostic Scriptures: A New Translation with Annotations and Introductions.* New York: Doubleday, 1987.

Lehmann, O. H. "Number-Symbolism as a Vehicle of Religious Experience in the Gospels, Contemporary Rabbinic Literature and the Dead Sea Scrolls." In *Studia Patristica, Vol. IV,* ed. F. L. Cross. Theologische Untersuchungen 79. Berlin: Akademie-Verlag, 1961. Pp. 125-35.

Lieu, Judith M. *Neither Jew Nor Greek? Constructing Early Christianity.* London: T&T Clark, 2002.

Lindemann, Andreas. "Der Apostel Paulus im 2. Jahrhundert." In *The New Testament in Early Christianity: La Réception des écrits Néotestamentaires dans le Christianisme primitif,* ed. Jean-Marie Sevrin. Leuven: Peeters, 1989. Pp. 39-67.

Lindemann, Andreas. *Paulus im ältesten Christentum: Das Bild des Apostels und die Rezeption der paulinischen Theologie in der frühchristlichen Literatur bis Marcion.* Tübingen: Mohr (Siebeck), 1978.

Llewelyn, Stephen R., ed. *New Documents Illustrating Early Christianity, Volume 7.* North Ryde, NSW: Ancient History Documentary Centre, Macquarie University, 1994.

Lührmann, Dieter. *Die apokryph gewordenen Evangelien: Studien zu neuen Texten und zu neuen Fragen.* Novum Testamentum Supplement 112. Leiden: Brill, 2004.

Lührmann, Dieter. "POx 2949: EvPt 3-5 in einer Handschrift des 2./3.

Jahrhunderts." *Zeitschrift für die neutestamentliche Wissenschaft* 72 (1981): 216-26.

Lührmann, Dieter. "POx 4009: Ein neues Fragment des Petrusevangeliums?" *Novum Testamentum* 35 (1993): 390-410.

Malherbe, Abraham J. *Social Aspects of Early Christanity.* Baton Rouge: Louisiana State University Press, 1977.

Martin, Victor. *Papyrus Bodmer II: Évangile de Jean, chap. 1–14.* Cologny-Geneva: Bibliotheca Bodmeriana, 1956.

Martin, Victor. *Papyrus Bodmer II, Supplément: Évangile de Jean, chap. 14–21.* Cologny-Geneva: Bibliotheca Bodmeriana, 1958.

Martin, Victor, and J. W. B. Barns. *Papyrus Bodmer II, Supplément: Évangile de Jean, chap. 14–21, nouvelle edition augmentée et corrigée.* Cologny-Geneva: Bibliotheca Bodmeriana, 1962.

Martin, Victor, and Rodolphe Kasser. *Papyrus Bodmer XIV: Évangile de Luc, chap. 3–24.* Cologny-Geneva: Bibliotheca Bodmeriana, 1961.

McCormick, Michael. "The Birth of the Codex and the Apostolic Life-Style." *Scriptorium* 39 (1985): 150-58.

McDonald, Lee M., and James A. Sanders, eds. *The Canon Debate.* Peabody, MA: Hendrickson, 2002.

McNamee, Kathleen. *Abbreviations in Greek Literary Papyri and Ostraca.* Bulletin of the American Society of Papyrologists Supplement 3. Chico, CA: Scholars Press, 1981.

Meeks, Wayne A. *The First Urban Christians: The Social World of the Apostle Paul.* New Haven: Yale University Press, 1983.

Metzger, Bruce M. *The Canon of the New Testament: Its Origin, Development, and Significance.* Oxford: Clarendon, 1987.

Metzger, Bruce M. *Manuscripts of the Greek Bible: An Introduction to Palaeography.* New York: Oxford University Press, 1981.

Milburn, Robert. *Early Christian Art and Architecture.* Berkeley: University of California Press, 1988.

Millard, Alan. *Reading and Writing in the Time of Jesus.* Biblical Seminar 69. Sheffield: Sheffield Academic Press, 2000.

Milne, H. J. M., and T. C. Skeat. *Scribes and Correctors of the Codex Sinaiticus.* London: British Museum, 1938.

Morey, C. R. *Early Christian Art.* 2nd ed. Princeton: Princeton University Press, 1953.

Moyise, Steve, and J. J. Maarten, eds. *The Psalms in the New Testament.* London: T&T Clark International, 2004.

Nachmanson, Ernst. "Die schriftliche Kontraktion auf den griechischen Inschriften." *Eranos* 10 (1910): 100-141.

New, Silva. "The Name, Baptism, and the Laying on of Hands." In *The Beginnings of Christianity*, ed. F. J. Foakes Jackson and Kirsopp Lake. 1933. Reprint, Grand Rapids: Baker, 1966. 5:121-40.

Nunn, H. V. P. *Christian Inscriptions.* Eton: Saville, 1951.

O'Callaghan, José. "Lista de los papiros de los LXX." *Biblica* 56 (1975): 74-93.

O'Callaghan, José. *"Nomina Sacra" in Papyris Graecis Saeculi III Neotestamentariis.* Analecta biblica 46. Rome: Biblical Institute Press, 1970.

O'Connor, D. W. "Peter in Rome: A Review and Position." *Christianity, Judaism and Other Greco-Roman Cults: Studies for Morton Smith at Sixty*, ed. Jacob Neusner. 4 vols. Studies in Judaism in Late Antiquity 12. Leiden: Brill, 1975. 2:146-60.

Old, Hughes Oliphant. "The Psalms of Praise in the Worship of the New Testament Church." *Interpretation* 39 (1985): 20-33.

Osiek, Carolyn. *The Shepherd of Hermas.* Hermeneia. Minneapolis: Fortress Press, 1999.

Paap, A. H. R. E. *Nomina Sacra in the Greek Papyri of the First Five Centuries A.D.: The Sources and Some Deductions.* Papyrologica Lugduno-Batava 8. Leiden: Brill, 1959.

Pack, Roger Ambrose. *The Greek and Latin Literary Texts from Greco-Roman Egypt.* 2nd revised and enlarged edition. Ann Arbor: University of Michigan Press, 1965.

Painter, John. *Just James: The Brother of Jesus in History and Tradition.* Columbia, SC: University of South Carolina Press, 1997.

Parker, David C. *Codex Bezae: An Early Christian Manuscript and Its Text.* Cambridge: Cambridge University Press, 1992.

Parker, David C. *The Living Text of the Gospels.* Cambridge: Cambridge University Press, 1997.

Parker, D. C., D. G. K. Taylor, and M. S. Goodacre. "The Dura-Europos Gospel Harmony." In *Studies in the Early Text of the Gospels and Acts*, ed. D. G. K. Taylor. Birmingham: University of Birmingham Press, 1999. Pp. 192-228.

Parkinson, William Q. "'In the Name of Jesus': The Ritual Use and Christological Significance of the Name of Jesus in Early Christianity." Ph.D. dissertation, University of Edinburgh, 2003.

Pearson, B. A. "Pre-Alexandrian Gnosticism in Alexandria." In *The Future of Early Christianity: Essays in Honor of Helmut Koester*, ed. B. A. Pearson. Minneapolis: Fortress Press, 1991. Pp. 455-66.

Pickering, Stuart R. "The Dating of the Chester Beatty–Michigan Codex of the Pauline Epistles (𝔓46)." In *Ancient Christianity in a Modern University*, vol. 2: *Early Christianity, Late Antiquity and Beyond*, ed. T. W. Hillard et al. Grand Rapids: Eerdmans, 1998. Pp. 216-27.

Pickering, Stuart R. *Recently Published New Testament Papyri: 𝔓89–𝔓95.* Sydney: Ancient History Documentary Research Centre, Macquarie University, 1991.

Rahlfs, Alfred, and Detlef Fraenkel. *Verzeichnis der griechischen Handschriften des Alten Testaments.* Göttingen: Vandenhoeck & Ruprecht, 2004.

Richards, E. Randolph. *The Secretary in the Letters of Paul.* Wissenschaftliche Untersuchungen zum Neuen Testament 2/42. Tübingen: Mohr (Siebeck), 1991.

Roberts, C. H. "The Christian Book and the Greek Papyri." *Journal of Theological Studies* 50 (1949): 155-68.

Roberts, C. H. "The Codex." *Proceedings of the British Academy* 40 (1954): 187-89.

Roberts, C. H. "An Early Papyrus of the First Gospel." *Harvard Theological Review* 46 (1953): 233-37.

Roberts, C. H. *Greek Literary Hands, 350 B.C.–A.D. 400.* Oxford: Clarendon, 1955.

Roberts, Colin H. *Manuscript, Society and Belief in Early Christian Egypt.* Schweich Lectures 1977. London: Oxford University Press for the British Academy, 1979.

Roberts, C. H. "P.Yale 1 and the Early Christian Book." In *Essays in Honor of C. Bradford Welles,* ed. A. E. Samuel. New Haven: American Society of Papyrologists, 1966. Pp. 27-28.

Roberts, C. H. "Two Biblical Papyri in the John Rylands Library, Manchester." *Bulletin of the John Rylands Library* 20 (1936): 241-44.

Roberts, C. H. "An Unpublished Fragment of the Fourth Gospel in the John Rylands Library." *Bulletin of the John Rylands Library* 20 (1936): 45-55.

Roberts, Colin H., and T. C. Skeat. *The Birth of the Codex.* London: Oxford University Press, 1983.

Roberts, C. H., et al. *The Antinoopolis Papyri.* London: Egypt Exploration Society, 1950-67.

Robinson, James M., ed. *The Nag Hammadi Library in English.* Rev. ed. Leiden: Brill, 1988.

Roetzel, Calvin J. "Paul in the Second Century." In *The Cambridge Companion to St. Paul,* ed. J. D. G. Dunn. Cambridge: Cambridge University Press, 2003. Pp. 227-41.

Royse, James R. "Scribal Habits in Early Greek New Testament Papyri." Th.D. dissertation, Graduate Theological Union, Berkeley, 1981.

Ruck-Schröder, Adelheid. *Der Name Gottes und der Name Jesu: Eine neutestamentliche Studie.* Wissenschaftliche Monographien zum Alten und Neuen Testament 80. Neukirchen-Vluyn: Neukirchener Verlag, 1999.

Rudberg, Gunnar. *Neutestamentlicher Text und Nomina Sacra.* Uppsala: Humanistika Vetenskapssa fundet Skrifter, 1915 (1917).

Rudberg, Gunnar. "Zur paläographischen Kontraktion." *Eranos* 10 (1910): 71-100.

Sanders, Henry A. *The New Testament Manuscripts in the Freer Collection,* part I: *The Washington Manuscript of the Four Gospels.* New York: Macmillan, 1912.

Sanders, Henry A. "A Third Century Papyrus of Matthew and Acts." In

Quantulacumque: Studies Presented to Kirsopp Lake, ed. Robert P. Casey, Silva Lake, and Agnes K. Lake. London: Christophers, 1937. Pp. 151-61.

Sawyer, John F. A. *The Fifth Gospel: Isaiah in the History of Christianity.* Cambridge: Cambridge University Press, 1996.

Sawyer, John F. A. *Sacred Languages and Sacred Texts.* London: Routledge, 1999.

Shaw, Frank. "The Earliest Non-Mystical Jewish Use of IAΩ." Ph.D. dissertation, University of Cincinnati, 2002.

Sirat, Colette. "Le codex de bois." In *Les débuts du codex,* ed. Alain Blanchard. Turnhout: Brepols, 1989. Pp. 37-40.

Sirat, Colette. "Le livre Hébreu dans les premiers siècles de notre ère: Le témoignage des texts." In *Les débuts du codex,* ed. Alain Blanchard. Turnhout: Brepols, 1989. Pp. 115-24.

Skeat, T. C. "A Codicological Analysis of the Chester Beatty Papyrus Codex of the Gospels and Acts (𝔓45)." *Hermathena* 155 (1993) 27-43 (= *Collected Biblical Writings,* ed. Elliott, 141-57).

Skeat, T. C. *The Collected Biblical Writings of T. C. Skeat,* ed. J. K. Elliott. Novum Testamentum Supplement 113. Leiden: Brill, 2004.

Skeat, T. C. "'Especially the Parchments': A Note on 2 Timothy 4:13." *Journal of Theological Studies* 30 (1979): 173-77 (= *Collected Biblical Writings,* ed. Elliott, 262-66).

Skeat, T. C. "The Length of the Standard Papyrus Roll and the Cost-Advantage of the Codex." *Zeitschrift für Papyrologie und Epigraphik* 45 (1982): 169-76 (= *Collected Biblical Writings,* ed. Elliott, 65-70).

Skeat, T. C. "The Oldest Manuscript of the Four Gospels?" *New Testament Studies* 43 (1997): 1-34 (= *Collected Biblical Writings,* ed. Elliott, 158-92).

Skeat, T. C. "The Origin of the Christian Codex." *Zeitschrift für Papyrologie und Epigraphik* 102 (1994): 263-68 (= *Collected Biblical Writings,* ed. Elliott, 79-87).

Skeat, T. C. "Roll versus Codex — A New Approach?" *Zeitschrift für Papyrologie und Epigraphik* 84 (1990): 297-98 (= *Collected Biblical Writings,* ed. Elliott, 71-72).

Skehan, Patrick W. "The Divine Name at Qumran, in the Masada Scroll, and in the Septuagint." *Bulletin of the International Organization for Septuagint and Cognate Studies* 13 (1980): 14-44.

Snyder, Graydon F. *Ante Pacem: Archaeological Evidence of Church Life Before Constantine.* Macon, GA: Mercer University Press, 1985.

Snyder, H. Gregory. *Teachers and Texts in the Ancient World.* London: Routledge, 2000.

Spence, Lewis. "Cross." *Encyclopedia of Religion and Ethics,* ed. James Hastings. Edinburgh: T&T Clark, 1911. 4:324-30.

Staats, Reinhart. "Ogdoas als ein Symbol für die Auferstehung." *Vigiliae Christianae* 26 (1972): 29-52.

Stanton, Graham N. *Jesus and Gospel*. Cambridge: Cambridge University Press, 2004.

Stegemann, Hartmut. "Religionsgeschichtliche Erwägungen zu den Gottesbezeichnungen in den Qumrantexten." In *Qumrân: Sa piété, sa théologie et son milieu*, ed. M. Delcor. Bibliotheca ephemeridum theologicarum lovaniensium 46. Leuven: Leuven University Press, 1978. Pp. 195-217.

Sulzberger, Max. "Le symbole de la croix et les monogrammes de Jésus chez les premiers Chrétiens." *Byzantion* 2 (1925): 337-448.

Tabbernee, W. "Christian Inscriptions from Phrygia." *New Documents Illustrating Early Christianity, Volume 3*, ed. G. H. R. Horsley. North Ryde, NSW: Ancient History Documents Research Centre, Macquarie University, 1983. Pp. 128-39.

Testuz, Michel. *Papyrus Bodmer VII-IX*. Cologny-Genève: Bibliotheca Bodmeriana, 1959.

Tov, Emanuel. "The Greek Biblical Texts from the Judean Desert." In *The Bible as Book: The Transmission of the Greek Text*, ed. Scot McKendrick and Orlaith A. O'Sullivan. London: British Library, 2003. Pp. 97-122.

Tov, Emanuel. "Scribal Features of Early Witnesses of Greek Scripture." In *The Old Greek Psalter: Studies in Honour of Albert Pietersma*, ed. Robert J. V. Hiebert, Claude E. Cox, and Peter J. Gentry. Journal for the Study of the Old Testament Supplement 332. Sheffield: Sheffield Academic Press, 2001. Pp. 125-48.

Tov, Emanuel. *Scribal Practices and Approaches Reflected in the Texts Found in the Judean Desert*. Studies on the Texts of the Desert of Judah 54. Leiden: Brill, 2004.

Trachtenberg, Joshua. *Jewish Magic and Superstition*. New York: Atheneum, 1982.

Traube, Ludwig. *Nomina Sacra: Versuch einer Geschichte der christlichen Kürzung*. Munich: Beck, 1907.

Treu, Kurt. "Die Bedeutung des Griechischen für die Juden im römischen Reich." *Kairos* 15 (1973): 123-44.

Trobisch, David. *Die Endredaktion des Neuen Testaments*. Göttingen: Vandenhoeck & Ruprecht, 1996. English translation: *The First Edition of the New Testament*. Oxford: Oxford University Press, 2000.

Tuckett, C. M. "'Nomina Sacra': Yes and No?" In *The Biblical Canons*, ed. J.-M. Auwers and H. J. de Jonge. Bibliotheca ephemeridum theologicarum lovaniensium 98. Leuven: Peeters, 2003. Pp. 431-58.

Turner, C. H. "The *Nomina Sacra* in Early Latin Christian MSS." In *Miscellanea Francesco Ehrle: Scritti di Storia e Paleografia*, vol. IV: *Paleografia e Diplomatica*, 62-74. Rome: Biblioteca Apostolica Vaticana, 1924.

Turner, Eric G. *Greek Manuscripts of the Ancient World*, ed. P. J. Parsons. 2nd rev. ed. London: Institute of Classical Studies, 1987.

Turner, Eric G. *Greek Papyri: An Introduction*. Oxford: Clarendon, 1980.

Turner, Eric G. *The Typology of the Early Codex*. Philadelphia: University of Pennsylvania Press, 1977.

van Haelst, Joseph. *Catalogue des papyrus littéraires juifs et chrétiens*. Paris: Publications de la Sorbonne, 1976.

van Haelst, Joseph. "Les origines du codex." In *Les débuts du codex,* ed. Alain Blanchard. Turnhout: Brepols, 1989. Pp. 13-36.

Wasserman, Tommy. "Papyrus 72 and the *Bodmer Miscellaneous Codex.*" *New Testament Studies* 51 (2005): 137-54.

Wessely, Charles. "Les plus anciens monuments du Christianisme écrits sur papyrus." *Patrologia Orientalis. Tomus Quartus*. Paris: Librairie de Paris, 1908. Pp. 135-38.

Williams, Michael A. *Rethinking "Gnosticism": An Argument for Dismantling a Dubious Category*. Princeton: Princeton University Press, 1996.

Wischmeyer, W. K. "Die Aberkiosinschrift als Grabepigramm." *Studia Patristica,* ed. E. A. Livingstone. Oxford: Pergamon, 1982. Pp. 777-81.

Wischmeyer, Wolfgang. "Christogramm und Staurogramm in den lateinischen Inschriften altkirchlicher Zeit." In *Theologia Crucis — Signum Crucis: Festschrift für Erich Dinkler zum 70. Geburtstag,* ed. Carl Andresen and Günter Klein. Tübingen: Mohr (Siebeck), 1979. Pp. 539-50.

Würthwein, Ernst. *The Text of the Old Testament*. Trans. Erroll F. Rhodes. Rev. ed. Grand Rapids: Eerdmans, 1979.

Zuntz, Günther. "Reconstruction of One Leaf of the Chester Beatty Papyrus of the Gospels and Acts ($\mathfrak{P}$45)." *Chronique d'Égypte* 26 (1951): 191-211.

Zuntz, Günther. *The Text of the Epistles: A Disquisition upon the Corpus Paulinum*. Schweich Lectures 1946. London: Oxford University Press for the British Academy, 1953.

Selected Online Resources

- Advanced Papyrological Information System (APIS): http://www.columbia.edu/cu/lweb/projects/digital/apis/
- Catalogue of New Testament Papyri and Codices 2nd-10th Centuries: http://www.kchanson.com/papyri.html#NTP
- Catalogue of Paraliterary Papyri: http://perswww.kuleuven.ac.be/%7Eu0013314/paralit.htm http://promethee.philo.ulg.ac.be/cedopal/index.htm
- Interpreting Ancient Manuscripts (Earlham College): http://www.earlham.edu/~seidti/iam/home.html
- Leuven Database of Ancient Books, Leuven University (LDAB): http://ldab.arts.kuleuven.ac.be

- Mertens-Pack Supplement to R. Pack, *The Greek and Latin Literary Texts from Greco-Roman Egypt:* www.ulg.ac.be/facphl/services/cedopal/indexanglais.htm
- Oxyrhynchus Papyri Online: http://www.papyrology.ox.ac.uk/
- Papyri from the Rise of Christianity in Egypt project (Macquarie University): http://www.anchist.mq.edu.au/doccentre/PCEhomepage.htm

Christian Literary Texts in Manuscripts of the Second and Third Centuries

The arrangement is by text, under broad headings, for example, "Old Testament." Manuscripts that contain more than one text (except for manuscripts of the Minor Prophets) are cited for each text, with cross-references to the numbers of the other texts on this list. In the "Identification" column, each manuscript is identified using a standard papyrological reference, with other identifiers as appropriate. Items marked with an asterisk (*) are Jewish manuscripts listed for interest/comparison; and double asterisks (**) are items with some question about their dating, genre, or other matter, including some that are difficult to identify as to whether Christian or Jewish. Information in the "Comments" box is not systematically supplied for each manuscript, but reflects only my own information and choices of what seemed relevant here. Likewise, I have supplied estimated page sizes of some manuscripts (under "Form"), but have not been able to do so systematically for all items listed. In addition to the usual abbreviations, the following are used: col(s). = column(s); Copt. = Coptic; corr. = correction(s); doc. = documentary; est. = estimate; frg(s). = fragment(s); Gk. = Greek; Heb. = Hebrew; ms. = manuscript; *nom.sac.* = *nomina sacra;* opis. = opisthograph; pag. = pagination; pap. = papyrus; par. = paragraph marker(s); parch. = parchment; punct. = punctuation; r. = recto; theol. = theological; v. = verso.

Old Testament

Text	Identification	Date	Material	Form	Comments
1. Genesis (14:5-8,12-15)	P.Yale 1; LDAB 3081; VH 12; Rahlfs 814	CE2-3	pap.	codex (ca. 14×20cm.)	318 as τιη (Gen. 14:14)
2. Genesis (1–35)	Berlin Staats.Bib. Cod. gr. fol.66 I,II; VH 4; LDAB 3103; Rahlfs 911	CE3end	pap.	codex (18×28cm.)	κς, 30 leaves, 2 cols. (then 1 col.), pag., cursive hand, numerous corr.
3. **Genesis (2:7-9,16-18; 2:23–3:1,6-7)	P.Oxy. 1007; VH 5; LDAB 3113; Rahlfs 907	CE3late	parch.	codex	Tetragrammaton as double yod, χς; (Christian or Jewish?)
4. **Genesis (frgs. of 14,15,19,20,24,27)	P.Oxy. 656; LDAB 3094; Rahlfs 905; VH 13	CE2-3	pap.	codex, single quire of ca. 50 leaves	uncontracted θεος & κυριος, pag. & corr. by 2nd hand, Jewish? (Roberts)
5. *Genesis (3:10-12; 4:5-7,23; 7:17-20; 37:34–38:1; 38:10-12)	P.Fouad 266a; VH 56; LDAB 3450; Rahlfs 942 (cf. LDAB 3451, 3453)	BCE1	pap.	roll (Jewish)	θεος uncontracted, no Tetragrammaton
6. Genesis (8–9,24–25,30–35,39–46 passim)	P.Chest.Beatty V; LDAB 3109; Rahlfs 962; VH 7	CE2	pap.	codex (17×21cm.)	κς, some pars.
7. **Genesis (16:8-12)	P.Oxy. 1166; VH 14; LDAB 3114; Rahlfs 944	CE3	pap.	roll	early "biblical majuscule" hand; κς & χς? (Jewish?)
8. Genesis (19:11-13,17-19)	P.Berl. 17213; VH 15; LDAB 3101; Rahlfs 995	CE3early	pap.	codex	
9. Genesis (46–47)	P.Lit.Lond. 202; Rahlfs 953; VH 30	CE3-4	pap.	codex (14×17cm.)	
10. Exodus (8:5-9,12-20) [+ Deut.]	P.Baden 4.56; VH 33; LDAB 3086; Rahlfs 970	CE2	pap.	codex	semi-cursive, but 2 cols. See #29
11. Exodus (4:2-6,14-17)	P.Deissmann (= P.Horsley); LDAB 3095; Rahlfs 865	CE2-3	pap.	codex (ca. 10×12-15cm.)	20-22 lines/p.; χς, κς
12. Exodus (20:10-22)	P.Oxy. 4442; LDAB 3118; Rahlfs 993	CE3early	pap.	codex (ca. 12+×22cm.)	χς, single col.; LXX text
13. **Exodus (22–23)	P.Harris 2.166; LDAB 3104; Rahlfs 896	CE3	pap.	roll (Jewish?)	reading marks, excerpt text?

Text	Identification	Date	Material	Form	Comments
14. *Exodus (28:4-6,7)	7QLXXExd (7Q1); VH 38; LDAB 3456; Rahlfs 805	BCE2-1	pap.	roll (Jewish)	"highly decorated formal" hand
15. Exodus (31:13-14; 32:7-8)	P.Oxy. 1074; VH 40; LDAB 3096; Rahlfs 908	CE3	pap.	codex	
16. Exodus (34:35–35:8)	P.Berl. 14039; VH 42; LDAB 3129	CE3-4	parch.	codex	κς
17. Exodus (40:5-14,19-25)	P.Rein. 2.59; VH 43; LDAB 3121; Rahlfs 1000	CE3	pap.	codex	pag.
18. **Exodus (40:26-32) (v. = Rev. 1:4-7)	P.Oxy. 1075; LDAB 3477 (cf. LDAB 2786); Rahlfs 909; VH 44 (cf. VH 559)	CE3	pap.	roll (Jewish? Christian?)	κς; v. = Rev. in later hand
19. *Leviticus (2:3-5,7; 3:4,9-13; 4:6-8,10-11,18-20,26-29; 5:8-10,18-24)	4QpapLXXLevb (4Q120); VH 46; Rahlfs 802; LDAB 3452	BCE1	pap.	roll (Jewish)	Qumran, high decorated hand, ιαω = Tetragrammaton
20. *Leviticus (26:2-16)	4QpapLXXLeva(4Q119); VH 49; LDAB 33454; Rahlfs 801	BCE1-CE1	leather	roll (Jewish)	Qumran, par.
21. Leviticus (27:12,15-16,19-20,24)	P.Oxy. 1351; VH 50; LDAB 3133; Rahlfs 954	CE3	parch.	codex	
22. Leviticus (parts of 10,11,12,23,25)	Schøyen 2649; LDAB 8120; Rahlfs 0830	CE2-3 (ca. 200)	pap.	codex (ca. 10×20cm.)	(same scribe as Schøyen 2648?)
23. Leviticus (19:16-19,31-33)	P.Heid. 4.290; LDAB 3112; Rahlfs 858	CE3	pap.	codex	χς
24. Numbers [+ Deut.]	P.Chest.Beatty VI (+P.Mich.inv. 5554); LDAB 3091; Rahlfs 963; VH 52	CE2-3	pap.	codex (ca. 19×33cm.)	2 cols.; *nom.sac.*; 50 pp. of original 108. See #30
25. *Numbers (3:30–4:14)	4QLXXNum (4Q121); VH 51; LDAB 3455; Rahlfs 803	BCE1-CE1	leather	roll (Jewish)	highly decorated hand, no Tetragrammaton
26. *Deuteronomy (17:14–33:29)	P.Fouad 266b; VH 56; LDAB 3451; Rahlfs 848 (cf. Rahlfs 942 & 847; LDAB 3450, 3453)	BCE1	pap.	roll (Jewish)	יהוה by 2nd hand, pars., spacing

Text	Identification	Date	Material	Form	Comments
27. *Deuteronomy (10,17–33)	P.Fouad 266c; VH 56; LDAB 3453; Rahlfs 847	BCE1	pap.	roll	uncontracted θεος
28. *Deuteronomy (23:24–24:3; 25:1-3; 26:12,17-19; 28:31-33)	P.Ryl. 458; VH 57; Rahlfs 957; LDAB 3459	BCE2	pap.	roll (Jewish, col. 28+cm.)	"hieratic elegance," small & larger spacing
29. Deuteronomy (29:18-19,23-24) [+ Exod.]	P.Baden 4.56; VH 33; LDAB 3086; Rahlfs 970	CE2	pap.	codex	See #10
30. Deuteronomy [+ Num.]	P.Chest.Beatty VI (+P.Mich.inv. 5554); LDAB 3091; Rahlfs 803	CE2-3	pap.	codex	See #24
31. *Deuteronomy (11)	4QLXX Deut (4Q122); Rahlfs 819	BCE2-1	leather	roll	Qumran
32. Joshua (9:27–11:3)	Schøyen 2648; LDAB 8119; Rahlfs 816	CE2-3 (ca. 200)	pap.	codex (ca. 11×20cm.)	nom.sac., oldest Gr. ms. of Joshua (same scribe as Schøyen 2649?)
33. Judges (1:10-19)	Flor.Bib.Laur. PSI 127; Rahlfs 968	CE3early	pap.	codex (ca. 11.5× 16.2cm.)	nom.sac., pars.
34. 2 Chronicles (24:17-27)	P.Lond.Christ. 3; VH 75; Rahlfs 971; LDAB 3093	CE3	pap.	codex	κς, same codex as P.Barc.inv. 3?
35. 2 Chronicles (29:32-35; 30:2-6)	P.Barc.inv. 3; LDAB 3089; VH 76; Rahlfs 983	CE2-3	pap.	codex (ca. 12×17cm.)	same codex as P.Lond.Christ. 3?
36. *Esther (8–9)	P.Oxy. 4443; LDAB 3080; Rahlfs 996	CE1-2	pap.	roll (Jewish?)	"luxurious," 30.2cm. height, semi-doc. hand, pars., no Tetragrammaton, θεος uncontracted
37. Esther [+ Ezek., Dan., Sus.]	P.Chest.Beatty IX (et al.); Rahlfs 967	CE2-3	pap.	codex (12.8× 34.4cm.)	See ##76, 79
38. Esther (4:4-5, 8-11)	P.Palau Rib.Inv. 163; Rahlfs 869	CE3/4	pap.	codex	κς (no stroke)

Text	Identification	Date	Material	Form	Comments
39. *Job (42:11-12)	P.Oxy. 3522; LDAB 3079; Rahlfs 857	CE1	pap.	roll (14cm. height, Jewish)	Paleo-Heb. Tetragrammaton, spacing, LXX text
40. Job (9:2, 12-13)	P.Chest.Beatty XVIII; LDAB 3107; Rahlfs 854	CE3	pap.	codex	
41. Psalms (1:2-3)	*PSI* inv. 1989; LDAB 3085; Rahlfs 2122	CE2	pap.	roll or sheet?	v. blank, sense-unit markings
42. Psalms (1:4-6)	P.Oxy. 1779; VH 90; LDAB 3106; Rahlfs 2073	CE3 (CE4, Rahlfs)	pap.	codex	
43. Psalms (2:3-12)	P.Lit.Lond. 204; VH 92; Rahlfs 2051; LDAB 3115	CE3	pap.	codex (miniature, 6.3×7.3cm.)	κς
44. Psalms (7–8)	P.Oxy. 1226; VH 99; Rahlfs 2025	CE3-4 (CE3early, Turner)	pap.	codex (ca. 15×29.8cm.)	κς, χς; 35 lines/p.
45. Psalms (8:3-9; 9:7-17)	P.Mich. 3.133; VH 101; Rahlfs 2067; LDAB 3143; michigan.apis 1588	CE3-4	pap.	codex	book hand; pars.; κς
46. **Psalms (11:7–14:4)	P.Lit.Lond. 207; VH 109; LDAB 3473; Rahlfs 2019	CE3-4	pap.	roll? sheet? (Isocrates on v.); school text?	syllables (musical?) notation, κς, etc., but θεος
47. *Psalms (14:3-5)	P.Barc.inv. 2 (Montserrat II/2); LDAB 3082; Rahlfs 2160	CE2early	parch.	roll (Jewish?)	sense-unit spaces (cf. P.Colon.Inv. 525 [Rahlfs 2140], CE5, Treu)
48. Psalms (17–53,55–118)	P.Bod. 24; LDAB 3098; Rahlfs 2110; VH 118	CE2-3	pap.	codex	pars.; κς
49. **Psalms (19:7-8)	P.Ryl.Gk. Add.Box 3.1,N; VH 121; LDAB 3142; Rahlfs 2142	CE3-4	pap.	sheet? amulet? liturgical?	sense lines; illegible text on v.
50. Psalms (21,22,23)	*PUG* 1; VH 125; Rahlfs 2157	CE3-4	pap.	codex	pars., κς
51. Psalms (32:11-8; 33:9-13)	P.Mich.inv. 5475.c	CE3	pap.	codex	bookhand ("biblical majuscule"); LXX text

Text	Identification	Date	Material	Form	Comments
52. **Psalms (43:20-33)	P.Harris 31; Rahlfs 2108; VH 148; LDAB 3198	CE3-4	pap.	roll (Jewish?)	CE4 (VH), CE3-4 (Roberts); hand of "hieratic elegance" (Roberts); θεος
53. Psalms (48:20-21; 49:1-3,17-21)	Bodl.Ms.Gr.bibl.g.5; LDAB 3083; Rahlfs 2082; VH 151	CE1-2? (CE2-3 Turner)	pap.	codex	sense lines; earliest Christian Pss. ms.?
54. **Psalms (77)	PSI 8.921v (= P.Alex. 240); LDAB 3088; Rahlfs 2054; VH 174	CE2-3	pap.	opis. (2 cols., nom.sac.)	document on r.
55. Psalms (67:35–68:4, 8-4)	MPER ns 4.12 (= P.Vindob.G. 26035B); VH 165; LDAB 3125; Rahlfs 2094	CE3	pap.	codex	χς
56. **Psalms (68:13-14,31-32; 80:11-14)	Stud.Pal. 11.114 (P.Vindob.G. 39777); VH 167; LDAB 3492	CE3-4	parch.	roll (Jewish?), imported? (Judge/ Pickering)	Tetragrammaton archaic Heb., uncontracted θεος, Symmachus text, elegant hand
57. Psalms (81:1-4; 82:4-9,16-17)	P.Ant. 1.7; LDAB 3087; VH 179; Rahlfs 2077	CE2	pap.	codex (miniature, 14×12cm.)	κς
58. Psalms (88:4-8,15-18)	P.Duke Inv. 740; Rahlfs 2198	CE3/4	pap.	codex	
59. Psalms (118:27-64)	P.Leip.inv. 170; VH 224; LDAB 3092; Rahlfs 2014	CE2-3	pap.	codex	sense lines
60. **Psalms (119:7)	P.Monts.				
61. Psalms (143–148)	PSI 8.980; VH 238; Rahlfs 2055	CE3-4	pap.	codex	κς
62. Psalms (144:1-10; 145:4)	BKT 9.169 (= P.Berl.inv. 21265); LDAB 3102; Rahlfs 2117	CE3	pap.	codex	
63. Proverbs (2:9-15; 3:13-17)	P.Ant. 1.9; VH 252; LDAB 3119; Rahlfs 987	CE3?	pap.	codex (ca. 18×35cm.?)	sense lines
64. Proverbs (frgs. of 5–9,19–20) [+Wis. 11–12; Sir. 45]	P.Ant. 1.8+3.210; VH 254; Rahlfs 928; LDAB 3120	CE3	pap.	codex (16×24cm.)	κς, χς, ανος, πρα, sense lines; hand like P.Chest.Beatty II. See ##88, 90

Text	Identification	Date	Material	Form	Comments
65. Ecclesiastes (complete)	Hamb. Staats/Univ. Bibliothek pap. bil. 1; VH 263; Rahlfs 998; LDAB 3138	CE3	pap.	codex	χϲ, composite ms.,+*Acts Paul* (VH 605)+Cant. and Lam. (Copt.)
66. Ecclesiastes (3:17-18,21-22; 6:3-5,8-11)	P.Med. 1.13+P.Mich. 3.135; VH 264+265; Rahlfs 818; LDAB 3144	CE3-4	pap.	codex	sense lines
67. Isaiah (8–60)	P.Chest.Beatty VII (= P.Merton 2); LDAB 3108; Rahlfs 965; VH 293	CE3	pap.	codex (15×26cm.)	25-26 lines/p.; pag.; Gk., + Copt. glosses; κϲ
68. Isaiah (23:4-7,10-13)	Wash.Lib.Cong.inv. 4082B; VH 295; LDAB 3122; Rahlfs 844	CE3-4	pap.	codex (12.4× 16.2cm.)	κϲ
69. Isaiah (23:9-10,14-15)	Princ.inv. Garrett Dep. 1924; Bell II 2G	CE2-3	pap.	codex	Unpublished frg. 5×5.7cm.
70. Isaiah (33:7-8,17-19; 40:13-14,24-26)	P.Vindob.G. 23164+17417; Rahlfs 881	CE3	pap.	codex (ca. 15×30cm.)	similar to P.Vindob.G. 2320
71. Isaiah (38:3-5,13-16)	Stud.Pal. 9.1 (P.Vindob.G. 2320); VH 298; LDAB 3126; Rahlfs 948	CE3	pap.	codex	
72. **Isaiah (48:6-8,11-14, 17-18)	P.Alex.inv. 203; VH 300; LDB 3127; Rahlfs 850	CE3-4	pap.	roll (Jewish?)	κϲ?, v. blank
73. Jeremiah (2:2-3,8-9,16-19,24-26,30-32; 2:37–3:1,6-7,12-13,18,24-25)	P.Berl.inv. 17212; VH 303; Rahlfs 837; LDAB 3100	CE3	pap.	codex	κϲ; pars.
74. Jeremiah (4:30-35; 5:9-14,23-24)	P.Chest.Beatty VIII; VH 304; Rahlfs 966; LDAB 3084	CE2-3 (CE4 Turner)	pap.	codex (ca. 14.5× 30.5cm.)	ca. 48 lines/p.
75. Ezekiel (5:12–6:3)	P.Bod. Gr.bibl. d.4; Rahlfs 922	CE3/4	pap.	codex	κϲ, ανοϲ

Text	Identification	Date	Material	Form	Comments
76. Ezekiel (11–36,38–39,37,40–48)	P.Chest.Beatty IX-X (+P.Princeton Scheide Ms 97; P.Cologne inv. theol.22-28, 29:1-6; P.Matr.bibl.1; P.Barc.inv. 42/43); LDAB 3090; Rahlfs 967; VH 315	CE2-3	pap.	codex (12.8× 34.4cm.)	109 of 118 original leaves. (+Dan. & Bel, Sus.; Est). See ##37, 79
77. Daniel (1:2-10)	P.Coll.Priv; VH 318; LDAB 3123; Rahlfs 875	CE3	pap.	codex	
78. **Daniel (1:17-18)	P.Lit.Lond. 211; VH319; LDAB 3493; Rahlfs 925	CE4	parch.	roll (Jewish?)	uncontracted θεοσ; "elegant script" (Roberts)
79. Daniel (1:1–12:3)	P.Chest.Beatty X (et al.)	CE3	pap.	codex (12.8× 34.4cm.)	+ Bel & Dragon, Sus. See ##37, 76
80. Minor Prophets (Hos. 1:10 — Mal. 4:6)	Wash.Freer 5; VH 284; Rahlfs W; LDAB 3124	CE3-4	pap.	codex	+Copt. glosses & unknown text (VH 636); pars.; κς
81. *Minor Prophets (frgs. of Hos.-Zech.)	8HevXIIgr (Nahal Hever Minor Prophets); VH 285; Rahlfs 943; LDAB 3457	BCE2-1	parch.	roll (Jewish)	Paleo-Heb. Tetragrammaton; oldest Gk. Minor Prophets ms.
82. Hosea & Amos	MPER 18.257 (Brit.Lib.inv. 10825); VH 286; LDAB 3141; Rahlfs 829	CE3-4	pap.	opis.	doc. text on r.; v. = word list Gk./Copt.
83. **Jonah	Crosby-Schøyen Codex 193	CE3	pap.	codex	Sahidic, 2 cols., + Melito, 1 Pet., Jer., Lam., et al. See also ##87, 167
84. *Baruch (6; Ep. Jer.)	7Q2 (7QLXXEpJer); VH 312; LDAB 3460; Rahlfs 804	BCE2-1	pap.	roll (Qumran)	
85. Tobit (12:6-7,8-11)	PSI inv.Cap. 46; Rahlfs 878	CE3	pap.	codex	θν, θυ
86. Tobit (12:14-19)	P.Oxy. 1594; VH 82; LDAB 3131; Rahlfs 990	CE3/4	parch.	codex (miniature, 8.5×8.5cm.)	
87. **2 Maccabees	Crosby-Schøyen Codex 193	CE3	pap.	codex	**Sahidic, 2 cols. + Melito, 1 Pet., Jonah. See also ##83, 166

Text	Identification	Date	Material	Form	Comments
88. Wisdom (11–12) [+Prov. 5–9; Sir. 45]	P.Ant. 1.8+3.210; VH 254; Rahlfs 928; LDAB 3120	CE3	pap.	codex (16×24cm.)	See ##64, 90
89. Sirach (29:15-18, 25-27)	Flor. Istituto Papirologico inv. 531; VH 281; LDAB 3135; Rahlfs 828	CE3-4	pap.	codex (ca. 15×27cm.)	sense lines; χς
90. Sirach (45:14,19,20-22) [+Prov. & Wis.]	P.Ant. 1.8+3.210; VH 254; LDAB 3120; Rahlfs 928	CE3	pap.	codex	See ##64, 88
91. Philo (*Ebr.* et al.)	P.Oxy. 1173+1356+2158+*PSI* 11.1207 & P.Haun. 1.8; LDAB 3540; VH 696; Pack 1344	CE3	pap.	codex (15×17.5 cm.; Jewish or Christian?)	3 different hands; 289+ pp.
92. Philo (*Her.; Sacr.*)	Paris Bib. Nat. P.Gr. 1120; VH 695	CE3?	pap.	codex (16.5× 17.8cm.)	2 cols. Cf. dates CE4-6 in VH.

New Testament

Text	Identification	Date	Material	Form	Comments
93. Matthew (21:34-37,43,45)	P.Oxy. 4404; LDAB 2935; 𝔓104	CE2late	pap.	codex (ca. 14×25cm.; Group 8)	"carefully written," serifs
94. Matthew (3:9,15; 5:20-22,25-28; 26:7-8,10,14-15,22-23,31-33; & Luke)	Mag.Coll.Gr. 18+P.Barc.inv. 1; (+Paris Supp.Gr. 1120?); LDAB 2936; 𝔓64+𝔓67(+𝔓4?); VH 336(+403)	CE2-3	pap.	codex (13.3+×17+ cm.; same codex as 𝔓4?)	*nom.sac.;* early "biblical uncial," 2 cols., ekthesis, punct.
95. Matthew (23:30-39)	P.Oxy. 2683+4405; LDAB 2937; 𝔓77; VH 372	CE2-3	pap.	codex (ca. 10×15cm.)	= P.Oxy. 4403?
96. Matthew (13:55-57)	P.Oxy. 4403; LDAB 2938; 𝔓103	CE2-3	pap.	codex (ca. 11×16cm.)	(= P.Oxy. 2683+4405?); hand "quite elegant"
97. Matthew (3)	𝔓101; P.Oxy. 4401; LDAB 2939	CE3	pap.	codex (Group 8)	πνι, πνς, υς, "plain & competent, rather than elegant"

Text	Identification	Date	Material	Form	Comments
98. Matthew (1:1-20)	P.Oxy. 2; LDAB 2940; 𝔓1; VH 332	CE3	pap.	codex	
99. Matthew (26:19-52)	P.Mich.inv. 1570; LDAB 2941; 𝔓37; VH 378; Michigan.apis 1469	CE3-4	pap.	codex	
100. Matthew (2:13-16; 2:22–3:1; 11:26-27; 12:4-5; 24:3-6,12-15)	P.Oxy. 2384; LDAB 2942; VH 360; 𝔓70	CE3-4	pap.	codex	
101. Matthew (4:11-12,22-23)	P.Oxy. 4402; LDAB 2943; 𝔓102	CE3-4	pap.	codex (Group 8, ca. 14× 27cm.)	hand "quite distinctive"
102. Matthew (26:29-40) [+Acts 9:34-38; 9:40–10:1]	P.Mich.inv.6652; 𝔓53; LDAB 2981; VH 380	CE3	pap.	codex	4 Gospels+Acts? See #133
103. Matthew (10:17-23,25,32) [+Luke]	P.Berl.inv. 11863+P.SI 1.2+2.124; Aland 0171; LDAB 2982; VH 356	CE3-4	vellum	codex	2 cols. See #113
104. **Matthew (10:10-15,25-27)	P.Oxy. 4494; 𝔓110; LDAB 7156	**CE4?	pap.	codex (ca. 12×22 cm.; Group 8)	ca. 40-43 lines/p.; breathings, punct.; κς
105. Matthew (20:24-32; 21:13-19; 25:41–26:39)	P.Chest.Beatty I; 𝔓45; LDAB 2980; VH 371	CE3	pap.	codex (single-sheet quires, 20.4× 25.4cm.)	+John, Luke, Mark, Acts. See ##106, 109, 129, 130
106. Mark (4–8,11–12) [+Matt., Luke, John, Acts]	P.Chest.Beatty I; 𝔓45	CE3	pap.	codex	See ##105, 109, 129, 130
107. Luke (1:58-59,62; 2:6-7; 3:8–4:2,29-32,34-35; 5:3-8; 5:30–6:16	𝔓4 (𝔓64+𝔓67?); Paris Supp.Gr. 1120 (+P.Barc.inv. 1+Mag.Gr. 18?); LDAB 2936; VH403 (+VH336)	CE2-3 (CE4 Kenyon, Merell)	pap.	codex (13.3+× 17+cm.)	2 cols.; early "biblical uncial," punct.
108. Luke (3–8,22–24) [+John 1–15]	P.Bod. XIV-XV; LDAB 2895; VH 406; 𝔓75	CE2-3 (CE3 Turner)	pap.	codex	See #114

Text	Identification	Date	Material	Form	Comments
109. Luke (6–10) [+Matt., John, Mark, Acts]	P.Chest.Beatty I; 𝔓45; VH 371	CE3	pap.	codex	See ##105, 106, 129, 130
110. Luke (14:7-14)	𝔓97; LDAB 2850; P.Chest.Beatty XVII	CE3	pap.	codex	
111. Luke (22:41,45-48,58-61)	P.Oxy. 2383; 𝔓69; LDAB 2852; VH 422	CE3	pap.	codex	
112. Luke (17:11-13,22-23)	P.Oxy. 4495; 𝔓111; LDAB 7157	CE3	pap.	codex (no est. of page size given)	ca. 21-22 lines/p.; semi-doc. hand; ιην
113. Luke (22:54-56,61,64) [+Matt.]	P.Berl.inv. 11863+PSI 1.2+2.124; Aland 0171; LDAB 2982; VH 356	CE3-4	pap.	codex	See #103
114. John (1–15) [+Luke 3–8,22–24]	P.Bod. XIV-XV; 𝔓75	CE2-3	pap.	codex	See #108
115. John (1:1-6,11; 6:35–14:26,29-30; 15:3-26; 16:2-4,6-7,11-20,22; 20:25–21:9)	P.Bod. II; LDAB 2777; 𝔓66; VH 426	CE2-3	pap.	codex (ca. 14.2× 16.2cm.)	
116. John (1,16,20)	P.Oxy. 208 (+P.Oxy. 1781); LDAB 2780; VH 428; 𝔓5	CE2-3	pap.	codex	
117. John (1:29-35,40-46)	P.Oxy. 4445; LDAB 2781; 𝔓106	CE3	pap.	codex (ca. 12×23.5 cm.; Group 8)	page numbers, *nom.sac.;* ca. 36 lines/p.
118. John (2:11-22)	P.Oxy. 847; Aland 0162; LDAB 2787; VH 436	CE3-4	parch.	codex	
119. John (3:34+biblical oracles)	𝔓80; P.Barc. 83; VH 441 (cf. VH 429)	CE3-4	pap.	codex	*tau-rho* end of line 7 v. & on r.
120. John (5:26-29,36-38)	P.Laur.inv.II/31; 𝔓95; LDAB 2801	CE3	pap.	codex	
121. John (6:8-12,17-22)	P.Oxy. 1596; 𝔓28; VH 444	CE3/4	pap.	codex (13×20.5cm.)	(CE4 VH; CE3 Turner, Aland)
122. John (8:14-22)	P.Oxy. 1780; 𝔓39; LDAB 2788; VH 448	CE3-4	pap.	codex	large elegant hand
123. John (15,16)	P.Oxy. 1228; LDAB 2779; 𝔓22; VH 459	CE3	pap.	opis.?	2 cols. extant on v., r. blank

Text	Identification	Date	Material	Form	Comments
124. John (17:1-2,11)	P.Oxy. 4446; LDAB 2782; 𝔓107	CE3	pap.	codex (no size est. given)	ca. 33 lines/p.
125. John (17:23-24; 18:1-5)	P.Oxy. 4447; LDAB 2783; 𝔓108	CE3	pap.	codex (ca. 14.5×18.5cm.; Group 9 "aberrant")	ca. 23 lines/p.; "practised" "handsome" hand
126. John (18)	P.Ryl. 457; LDAB 2774; 𝔓52; VH 462	CE2	pap.	codex (ca. 18×21cm.)	
127. John (18)	P.Oxy. 3523; LDAB 2775; 𝔓90	CE2	pap.	codex (ca. 12×16cm., Group 9)	ekthesis
128. John (21:18-20,23-25)	P.Oxy. 4448; LDAB 2784; 𝔓109	CE3	pap.	codex (ca. 12×24cm.; Group 8)	ca. 26 lines/p.; hand "inept one of literary pretensions"
129. John (10–11) [+Matt., Mark, Luke, Acts]	P.Chest.Beatty I; 𝔓45	CE3	pap.	codex	See ##105, 106, 109, 130
130. Acts (4–11,13,15,17) [+Matt., Mark, Luke, John]	P.Chest.Beatty I; 𝔓45; VH 371	CE3	pap.	codex	See ##105, 106, 109, 129
131. Acts (2:30-37; 2:46–3:2)	𝔓91; P.Mil.Vogl.inv. 1224+P.Macq.inv. 360; LDAB 2851	CE3	pap.	codex	earliest copy of these verses
132. Acts (5:3-21)	P.Berl.inv. 11765; LDAB 2848; Aland 0189; VH 479	CE2-3	parch.	codex	
133. Acts (9:34-38; 9:40–10:1)	P.Mich.inv. 6652; 𝔓53; LDAB 2981; VH 380	CE3	pap.	codex	See #102
134. Acts (18:27–19:16)	P.Mich. 3.138; 𝔓38; LDAB 2855; VH 485	CE3	pap.	codex	
135. Acts (23:11-17,24-29)	PSI 10.1165; 𝔓48; LDAB 2854; VH 486	CE3-4	pap.	codex (ca. 16×25cm.)	42-47 lines/p.
136. Acts (26:7-8,20)	P.Oxy. 1597; 𝔓29; LDAB 2853; VH 488	CE3-4	pap.	codex (ca. 17×27cm.)	38-41 lines/p.
137. Rom (5,8–10,14–16) [+Heb., 1-2 Cor., Eph., Gal., Phil., Col., 1 Thess.]	P.Chest.Beatty II+P.Mich 222; LDAB 3011; 𝔓46; VH 497	CE2-3	pap.	codex (single quire; 16×28cm.)	25-31 lines/p. See ##142, 144, 145, 148, 149, 151, 153, 159

Text	Identification	Date	Material	Form	Comments
138. Romans (2:12-13, 29)	P.Oxy. 4497; 𝔓113; LDAB 7159	CE3	pap.	codex (ca. 14-15×21cm.; Group 7)	ca. 35 lines/p.; 2 cols? punct.; line filler; breathings
139. Romans (4:23–5:3,8-13)	Schøyen 113; Aland 0220; LDAB 2995; VH 495	CE3-4	vellum	codex (ca. 13×15cm.)	2nd oldest vellum NT ms.
140. Romans (8:12-22,24-27; 8:33–9:3,5-9)	P.Oxy. 1355; 𝔓27; VH 498	CE3	pap.	codex	
141. **Romans (frgs. of 1,3,6,9)	P.Heid.inv. 45 (P.Baden 4.57); 𝔓40; VH 492	CE5-6? (ed.)	pap.	codex (19×30cm.)	35 lines/p.; **CE3 (Aland)
142. 1 Corinthians (2:3–3:5) [+Rom., Heb., 2 Cor., Eph., Gal., Phil., Col., 1 Thess.]	P.Chest.Beatty II+P.Mich. 222; 𝔓46	CE2-3	pap.	codex	See ##137, 144, 145, 148, 149, 151, 153, 159
143. 1 Corinthians (7:18–8:4)	𝔓15; P.Oxy. 1008; VH 505; LDAB 3016	CE3-4	pap.	codex	= 𝔓16 (POxy. 1009)? (Pauline codex?)
144. 2 Corinthians (9:7–13:13) [+Rom., 1 Cor., Heb., Gal., Phil., Col., 1 Thess.]	P.Chest.Beatty II+P.Mich. 222; 𝔓46	CE2-3	pap.	codex	See ##137, 142, 145, 148, 149, 151, 153, 159
145. Galatians (1:1–6:10) [+Rom., 1-2 Cor., Heb., Eph., Phil., Col., 1 Thess.]	P.Chest.Beatty II+P.Mich 222; 𝔓46	CE2-3	pap.	codex	See ##137, 142, 144, 148, 149, 151, 153, 159
146. Ephesians (4:16-29; 4:31–5:13)	𝔓49; P.Yale 1.2+2.86; VH 522; LDAB 3014; yale.apis.0004150000	CE3	pap.	codex	= 𝔓65? (Pauline codex? Comfort)
147. Ephesians (1:11-13,19-21) [+2 Thess.]	P.Medinet Madi (P.Narmuthis) 69.39a+69.229a; 𝔓92; LDAB 3008	CE3-4	pap.	codex	single-gathering Pauline codex? See #155
148. Ephesians [+Rom., Heb., 1-2 Cor., Gal., Phil., Col., 1 Thess.]	P.Chest.Beatty II+P.Mich 222; 𝔓46	CE2-3	pap.	codex	See ##137, 142, 144, 145, 149, 151, 153, 159

Text	Identification	Date	Material	Form	Comments
149. Philippians [+Rom., Heb., 1-2 Cor., Gal., Eph., Col., 1 Thess.]	P.Chest.Beatty II+P.Mich 222; 𝔓46	CE2-3	pap.	codex	See ##137, 142, 144, 145, 148, 151, 153, 158
150. Philippians (3:9-17; 4:2-8)	P.Oxy. 1009; 𝔓16; VH524; LDAB 3016	CE3-4	pap.	codex	=𝔓15 (P.Oxy. 1008)? (Pauline codex?)
151. Colossians	P.Chest.Beatty II+P.Mich. 222; 𝔓46	CE2-3	pap.	codex	See ##137, 142, 144, 145, 148, 149, 153, 158
152. 1 Thessalonians (4–5) [+2 Thess.]	P.Oxy. 1598; 𝔓30; VH 528	CE3-4	pap.	codex	pag. (207-8); may = Pauline codex. See #155
153. 1 Thessalonians (1:1–2:3; 5:5-9,23-28) [+Rom., Heb., 1-2 Cor., Gal., Phil., Col.]	P.Chest.Beatty II+P.Mich. 222; 𝔓46	CE2-3	pap.	codex	See ##137, 142, 144, 145, 148, 149, 151, 158
154. 1 Thess. (1:3–2:1; 2:6-13)	PSI14.1373; 𝔓65; VH526	CE3	pap.	codex	= P49 (P.Yale 2)?; 29 lines/p.
155. 2 Thessalonians (1:4-5,11-12) [+Eph.]	P.Medinet Madi (P.Narmuthis) 69.39a+69.229a; 𝔓92	CE3-4	pap.	codex	See #147
156. 2 Thessalonians (1:1-2 [+1 Thess. 4–5]	P.Oxy. 1598; 𝔓30	CE3-4	pap.	codex	See #152
157. Philemon (13-15,24-25)	P.Köln 4.170; 𝔓87; LDAB 3013	CE3	pap.	codex	CE2? (Skeat)
158. Titus (1–2)	P.Ryl. 1.5; LDAB 3009; VH 534; 𝔓32	CE2-3	pap.	codex (15×20cm.)	
159. Hebrews (1:1–8:8; 9:10-26) [+Rom., 1-2 Cor., Gal., Eph., Phil., 1 Thess.]	P.Chest.Beatty II+P.Mich. 222; 𝔓46	CE2-3	pap.	codex	See ##137, 142, 144, 145, 148, 149, 151, 153
160. Hebrews (1:1)	P.Amherst 1.3; 𝔓12; VH 536	CE3-4	pap.	letter, with biblical texts by other hands	Heb. 1:1 in 2nd hand; Gen. 1:1-5 on v.

Text	Identification	Date	Material	Form	Comment
161. Hebrews (1:7-12)	P.Oxy. 4498; 𝔓114; LDAB 7160	CE3	pap.	codex? (ca. 15×25cm.; Group 7)	χϛ; blank v. (title page?); 27 lines/p.
162. Hebrews (2:14–5:5; 10; 11)	P.Oxy. 657+*PSI* 12.1292; 𝔓13; VH 537; LDAB 3018	CE3-4	pap.	opis.	may have included Romans too; Epitome of Livy on r.
163. James (2–3)	P.Oxy. 1171; 𝔓20; VH 547; Princeton.apis.p.1	CE3	pap.	codex	
164. James (1:10-12,15-18)	P.Oxy. 1229; 𝔓23; VH 543	CE3-4	pap.	codex	CE2/3? (Comfort-Barrett, Aland)
165. James (3:13–4:4; 4:9–5:1)	P.Oxy. 4449; 𝔓100; LDAB 2769	CE3-4	pap.	codex (ca. 13×29cm.; Group 8)	κσ, pag., sense-unit spacing
166. 1 Peter	P.Bod. VIII; 𝔓72; VH 548	CE3	pap.	codex (ca. 14.2×16cm.)	same copyist as P.Bod. VII. See also ##168, 171
167. **1 Peter	Crosby-Schøyen Codex 193	CE3	pap.	codex	Sahidic, earliest complete text + Melito, Jonah, et al. See also ##83, 87
168. 2 Peter	P.Bod. VIII; 𝔓72	CE3	pap.	codex	composite codex. See ##165, 170
169. 1 John (4:11-12,14-17)	P.Oxy. 402; 𝔓9; LDAB 2789; VH 554	CE3-5	pap.	codex	
170. 2 John (1-5,6-9)	P.Ant. 1.12; Aland 0232; LDAB 2805; VH 555	CE3?	parch.	codex (miniature, 9×10cm.)	page numbers = perhaps included GJohn, Rev., Epistles?
171. Jude	P.Bod. VII; 𝔓72; VH 557	CE3	pap.	codex (ca. 14.5×16cm.)	same copyist as P.Bod. VIII. See ##166, 168
172. Jude (4-5,7-8)	𝔓78; P.Oxy. 2684; VH 558	CE3-4	pap.	codex (miniature, amulet? 5.3×2.9cm.)	NB: greater width than height!
173. Revelation (9–17)	P.Chest.Beatty III; LDAB 2778; 𝔓47; VH 565	CE3	pap.	codex (14× 24.2cm.)	
174. **Revelation (1:4-7)	P.Oxy. 1079; 𝔓18; LDAB 2786; VH 559	CE3-4	pap.	opis.	Exod. on r. = VH 44. Part of same roll as P.IFAO 2.31? ιη, χρ

Text	Identification	Date	Material	Form	Comment
175. **Revelation (1:13-20)	P.IFAO 2.31; LDAB 2776; 𝔓98	CE2-3	pap.	opis. (unknown text on r.)	Part of same roll as P.Oxy. 1079 (see #173)?
176. Revelation (26 frgs. of 2–3,5,6,8–15)	P.Oxy. 4499; 𝔓115; LDAB 7161	CE3-4	pap.	codex (15.5+× 23.5+cm.)	corrections (1&2 hand), nom.sac.; 33-36 lines/p.; earliest witness to 616 as number of beast
177. Revelation (11:15-18)	P.Oxy. 4500; Aland 0308; LDAB 7162	CE3-4	parch.	codex (miniature)	

Other Christian Texts

Text	Identification	Date	Material	Form	Comments
178. Hermas (Vis. I.1:8-9)	P.Oxy. 4705	CE3	pap.	opisthograph (recto = lit. text)	θς, punct.
179. Hermas (frags. of Vis. III-IV; Mand. II, v-x)	P.Oxy. 4706	CE2-3	pap.	roll	θεοφ, κψριος, diaeresis, titles for Vis. IV & Mand. III
180. Hermas (sim. VI.3–VII.2)	P.Oxy. 4707	CE3	pap.	codex	θψακε, paragraphus, diaeresis, ca. 55 lines/p.
181. Hermas (Mand. 11–12)	P.Iand. 1.4; LDAB 1094; Pack 2846; Aland, Repertorium, II, KV36	CE2-3	pap.	codex	
182. Hermas (Mand. 2.6–3.1)	P.Mich. 130 (= P.Mich. 44); VH 657; LDAB 1096	CE2-3	pap.	opis. (r. = land register)	θεω
183. Hermas (Sim.)	P.Oxy. 3528; LDAB 1095	CE2-3	pap.	codex	pag. = Sim. separate from Vis. & Mand.
184. Hermas (Sim. 2.7-10; 4.2-5)	BKT 6.2.1 (P.Berl. 5513); VH 662; LDAB 1100	CE3	pap.	roll	2 cols. extant
185. Hermas (Sim. 6.1.1-12)	P.Oxy. 1828; VH 665; LDAB 1099	CE3-4	parch.	codex	maybe = P.Oxy. 1783 (VH 659, dated CE4!)

Text	Identification	Date	Material	Form	Comment
186. Hermas (*Sim.* 2–9)	P.Mich. 129 (inv. 917); Michigan.apis 3155; VH 660; LDAB 1097	CE3latter	pap.	codex	
187. Hermas (*Sim.* 8)	P.Oxy. 3527; LDAB 1098	CE3early	pap.	codex (ca. 21×30cm.)	2 cols.; 33 lines/col.; book hand
188. Hermas (*Sim.* 10.3.2-4)	P.Oxy. 404; VH 668; LDAB 1101	CE3-4	pap.	codex	earliest witness to passage
189. Irenaeus (*Adv.Haer.*)	P.Oxy. 405; LDAB 2459; VH 671	CE2-3	pap.	roll	
190. Irenaeus (*Adv.Haer.*)	P.Jena inv. 18+21; VH 672; LDAB 2460	CE3-4	pap.	roll	*Adv.Haer.* on r. & continues on v. + mythological text (LDAB 5522)
191. Melito (*Paschal Homily*)	P.Bod. 13; LDAB 2565; VH 678	CE3-4	pap.	codex	same copyist as for VH 599. Composite codex (+*PseudEzek* & *1 En.*)
192. Melito (*Paschal Hymn?*)	P.Bod. 12; LDAB 2565; VH 681	CE3-4	pap.	codex	palimpsest
193. Melito (*On Prophecy?*)	P.Oxy. 5; VH 682; LDAB 2607	CE3-4	pap.	codex	
194. Gospel Harmony (Tatian?)	P.Dura 10; LDAB 3071; VH 699; Aland 0212	CE3	parch.	roll	Fragment of *Diatessaron?* ΧΥ, ΙΗ
195. *Odes of Solomon* (1–24)	P.Bod. 11; LDAB 2565; VH 569	CE3-4	pap.	codex	composite (+Paul/Corinth correspondence, Jude, Melito, *Paschal Hom.*)
196. Theol. text and/or homily	P.Gen.inv. 253 (= P.Gen. 3.125); VH 1130; LDAB 5033	CE2-3	pap.	opis.? (or single leaf of codex)?	3 hands/texts, words of Jesus & theodicy-type discussion. *Nom.sac.*
197. Theol. text	P.Iand. 5.70; VH 1139; LDAB 3111	CE3	pap.	roll or sheet (v. blank)	comments on Exod. 17:3; Num. 20:5-6
198. Theol. text	P.Oxy. 210; VH 1151	CE3	pap.	codex	Allusion to Matt. 7 & Luke 6. Homily?
199. Theol. text	P.Oxy. 406; VH 1152; LDAB 3500	CE3	pap.	codex	cites Isa. 6:10; Origen?

Text	Identification	Date	Material	Form	Comment
200. Eschatological discourse	*PSI* 11.1200; LDAB 4669	CE2	pap.	roll	
201. Hymn	P.Oxy. 1786; VH 962; LDAB 5403	CE3late	pap.	sheet (v. of account of wheat)	earliest Christian hymn with musical notation
202. Julius Africanus, *Cesti*	P.Oxy. 412 (P.Lit.Lond. 174); VH 674; LDAB 2550	CE3	pap.	roll	doc. text on v. (dated 275-276 CE)
203. Origen (*Hom. on Luke/ Matt.*)	P.Bon. 1.1; VH 688; LDAB 3499	CE3	pap.	codex	
204. Origen (*Comm.?*)	P.Lond.Christ. 2 (P.Egerton 3); VH 691; LDAB 3502	CE3early	pap.	codex	2 cols. = Firenze inv. 2101 [LDAB 3501]?
205. Origen (*Comm.?*)	Firenze inv. 2101; LDAB 3501	CE3	pap.	codex	= P.Lond.Christ. 2?
206. Origen (*Princ.* 3.16+7; 3.18)	P.Amst. 1.25; LDAB 3504	CE3-4	pap.	codex	
207. Theonas? (*Ep. Against Manichaeans*)	P.Ryl. 3.469; VH 700; LDAB 4016	CE3-4	pap.	roll	oldest anti-Manichaean text
208. Liturgical Prayers	*BKT* 6.6.1 (P.Berl. 9794); VH 722; LDAB 5201	CE3	pap.	roll	5 (?) prayers
209. **Exorcistic text	VH 850; LDAB 4902	CE2	gold	single sheet rolled up inside gold cover	amulet
210. **Exorcistic text	P.Fouad 203; VH 911; LDAB 4436	CE1-2	pap.	roll (sheet?)	blank v.; Jewish?
211. **Magical text/amulet	P.Harris 55; LDAB 4599; VH 1076	CE2	pap.	single sheet/ leaf	blank v.; allusions to Isa. 66:1, perhaps also Matt. 5:34. Jewish or Christian?
212. **Magical text	P.Ant. 2.54; VH 347	CE3?	pap.	sheet (amulet?)	invocation + trisagion & partial Lord's Prayer
213. **Magical text	P.Lond. 1.121 (PGM VII); LDAB 5166; VH 1077	CE3late	pap.	roll (opis.)	spells, different/ later hand from rest of pap.

Text	Identification	Date	Material	Form	Comment
214. **Magical text	*BKT* 8.17 (= P.Berl. 11778); VH 275; Rahlfs 974	CE3early	pap.	reused sheet	prayer/invocation with Job quotation
215. *Sibylline Oracles* (5.484-504)	P.Oslo 2.14; VH 581; LDAB 4797	CE2	pap.	sheet? roll?	doc. text on v. (Jewish?)
216. Prayer	P.Oxy. 407; VH 952; LDAB 5531	CE3-4	pap.	sheet	amulet (?), short account on v. Unabbreviated *nom.sac.* words
217. Prayer (ana-phora?)	P.Würzb. 3; VH 1036; LDAB 5475	CE3late	pap.	sheet?	damaged lines on both sides
218. Jewish/ Christian Dia-logue	P.Oxy. 2070; VH 1154; LDAB 5404	CE3end	pap.	roll	later cursive text on v., ιη
219. Homily or letter (eschatololgical subject)	P.Mich. 18.764; LDAB 0562	CE2-3	pap.	roll	diacritics & punc.
220. Homily or letter	P.Mich. 18.763; LDAB 5071	CE2-3	pap.	roll (opis.)	r. = doc. text
221. Homily?	*BKT* 9.22; LDAB 4973	CE2-3	pap.	codex	cites Exod. & Deut.
222. Homily?	P.Lit.Lond. 228; LDAB 5306; VH 1145	CE3	pap.	roll (opis.)	doc. on r. (dated CE237)
223. Unidenti-fied text	P.Med.inv. 71.84; LDAB 3117	CE3late/ end	pap.	roll? (frg.)	cites Isa. 58:6-9
224. Medical text?	P.Mich. 18.766; LDAB 5546	CE3-4	pap.	roll (opis.)	
225. Theol. text	P.Strasb.inv. 1017; VH 1178; LDAB 5570	CE3-4	pap.	roll (opis.)	doc. text on r.; text divisions
226. School ex-ercise?	P.Laur. 4.140; LDAB 3136	CE3-4	pap.	sheet (or roll)?	Ps. 1:1-2 with sylla-ble marks
227. Name list (Gk.-Heb.)	P.Oxy. 2745; VH 1158; LDAB 3503	CE3-4	pap.	opis.	doc. on r.

Christian Apocrypha

Text	Identification	Date	Material	Form	Comments
228. *Gospel of Thomas* (logia 26-33,77a)	P.Oxy. 1; LDAB 4028; VH 0594	CE3early	pap.	codex	reformed doc. hand; page number (ια); ιθ et al.; leaf-edge repaired
229. *Gospel of Thomas* (logoi 24,36-39)	P.Oxy. 655; LDAB 4029; VH 595	CE3early	pap.	roll	"well-written specimen"; ca. 16cm. roll height
230. *Gospel of Thomas* (Prologue, logoi 1-7)	P.Oxy. 654; LDAB 4030; VH 593	CE3mid/ late	pap.	opis., land survey on r.	cursive hand, pars.; coronis marks; corr.; ιης
231. *Protevangelium of James* (1-25)	P.Bod. V; LDAB 2565; VH 599	CE3-4	pap.	codex (14.2× 15.5cm.)	same copyist as VH 681; composite, + P.Bod. VII, X-XIII, XX
232. Corinthian/ Paul's letters (3 *Cor* 1:1-16; 3:1-40)	P.Bod. X; LDAB 2565; VH 611	CE3-4	pap.	codex	composite, + P.Bod. VII, XI-XIII, XX
233. *Apocryphon of Moses*	P.GM 13 (P.Ludg.Bat. 2W); VH 1071; LDAB 5670	CE3-4	pap.	codex	"Gnostic"? (VH)
234. *Gospel of Mary* (end)	P.Ryl. 463; LDAB 5329; VH 1065	CE3early	pap.	codex (8.9×9.9cm.)	only ανος, pag., title
235. *Gospel of Mary*	P.Oxy. 3525; LDAB 5406;	CE3	pap.	roll	excerpt? "practised cursive," "amateur copy"; ανος, but κυριε?, σωτηρ
236. Unknown Gospel (Peter?)	P.Oxy. 2949; LDAB 5111; VH 592	CE2-3	pap.	roll? (or sheet? v. blank)	See also P.Oxy. 4009
237. Unknown Gospel (Peter?)	P.Oxy. 4009; LDAB 4872	CE2	pap.	codex	miniature or 2 cols.? See also P.Oxy. 2949
238. Unknown Gospel (Egerton)	P.Lond.Christ. 1+P.Köln 6.255; LDAB 4736; VH 586	CE2-3	pap.	codex	ιη, et al
239. Unknown (Fayum) Gospel	LDAB 5462; VH 589; P.Vindob.G. 2325	CE3	pap.	roll (v. blank)	

Text	Identification	Date	Material	Form	Comments
240. *Acts of Paul*	P.Berl.inv. 13893+P.Mich. 3788+1317; LDAB 5543; VH 607+608	CE3-4	pap.	codex	cf. VH 605 & 608; = VH 263
241. *Acts of Paul*	Hamburg pap. bil. 1; VH 605; LDAB 3138	CE3	pap.	codex (20×26cm.)	composite Gk. & Sahidic ms. (cf. VH 263)
242. *Acts of Paul & Thecla*	P.Fackelmann 3; LDAB 5234	CE3	pap.	codex	
243. **Apocalypse of Peter?*	P.Vindob.G. 39756+Bodl. MS Gr.th.f4(P.); LDAB 5583; VH 619	CE3-4	parch.	miniature codex	Bodl. MS Gr.th.f4 dated CE5 in VH
244. ***"Naasene Psalm"?*	P.Fay. 2; VH 1066; LDAB 5049	CE2-3	pap.	roll	pagan account of underworld visit? (Roberts)
245. **Hermetic Treatise*	P.Vindob.G. 29456r+29828r; VH 1068; LDAB 8118	CE3early	pap.	roll	pre/non-Christian?
246. *Apocryphon of Jannes & Jambres*	P.Vindob.G. 29456v+29828v; VH 1069; LDAB 5467	CE3	pap.	opis. (v. of VH 1068)	

Photographic Plates of Selected Manuscripts

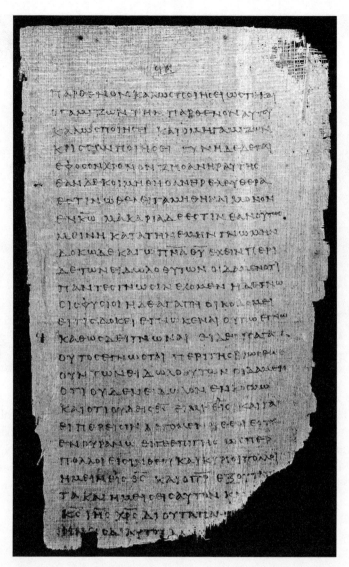

Plate 1: P. Chester Beatty II, 𝔓46 (folio 47 verso 1 Cor. 7:37–8:7)
Page number (= 92) at top. Top, left and right margins, stitching holes for
binding in left margin. Sense-unit spaces: lines 3, 4, 8, 15. *Nomina sacra:* ΚΩ
(line 8), ΠΝΑ, ΘΥ (line 10), ΘΣ (lines 19, 23), ΠΡ (line 23), ΚΣ, ΙΗΣ, ΧΡΣ
(line 25).   Image used by permission of the Chester Beatty Library, Dublin.

Plate 2: P. Chester Beatty I, 𝔓45 (folio 13 recto Luke 12:18-37)
Left-hand portion of folded papyrus sheet (right-hand portion = folio 14
recto). Left and right margins, with stitching holes on right margin.
Nomina sacra: ΘΣ (lines 11, 18), ΘΥ (line 22), ΠΡ (lines 21, 23), ΚΝ (line
30). Punctuation: high/middle stops (e.g., lines 6, 8, 9, 12). Image used by
permission of the Chester Beatty Library, Dublin.

Plate 3: P. Chester Beatty VI (folio 12 verso Num. 7:31-49)
Page number (ΚΓ = 23). Two columns, 35 lines, in skilled hand. Top, left
and right margins (portions). Note many instances of numbers written as
alphabetical letters with an overstroke (e.g., col. 1, lines 1, 6, 8, 11, 13, 14, 15).
Sense-unit space, col. 2, line 29.   Image used by permission of the Chester Beatty Library, Dublin.

I.fr. XIV, 26 - XV

Plate 4: P. Bodmer XIV, 𝔓75 (Luke 14:26b–15:3)

Portions of all margins. Single column, 40 lines, competent and clear hand. *Tau-rho* (staurogram) end of line 4 in abbreviated form of σταυρον with overstroke (close-up in plate 5). *Nomina sacra:* ΑΝΟΣ (line 14). Cf. abbreviation by suspension at end of lines 19 (εστι[ν]) and 38 (συ[ν]). Punctuation: high stops in lines 4, 8, 12, 16, 18, 22, 24, 28, 30, 32, 33, 39, and low stops in lines 15, 23, 27, 29. Diaeresis over initial *iota*, line 10. Sense-unit space, line 28. Ekthesis, lines 29, 33.   Photo used by permission of the Fondation Martin Bodmer, Geneva.

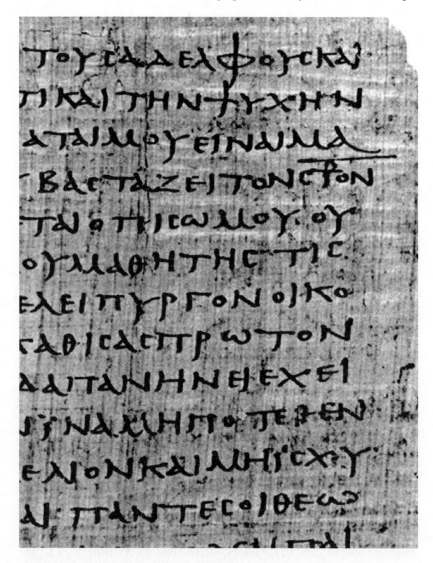

Plate 5: Close-up of P. Bodmer XIV, 𝔓75 (Luke 14:27)
Close-up of parts of lines 1-13, showing *tau-rho* (staurogram) in abbreviated form of σταυρον, line 4.   Photo used by permission of the Fondation Martin Bodmer, Geneva.

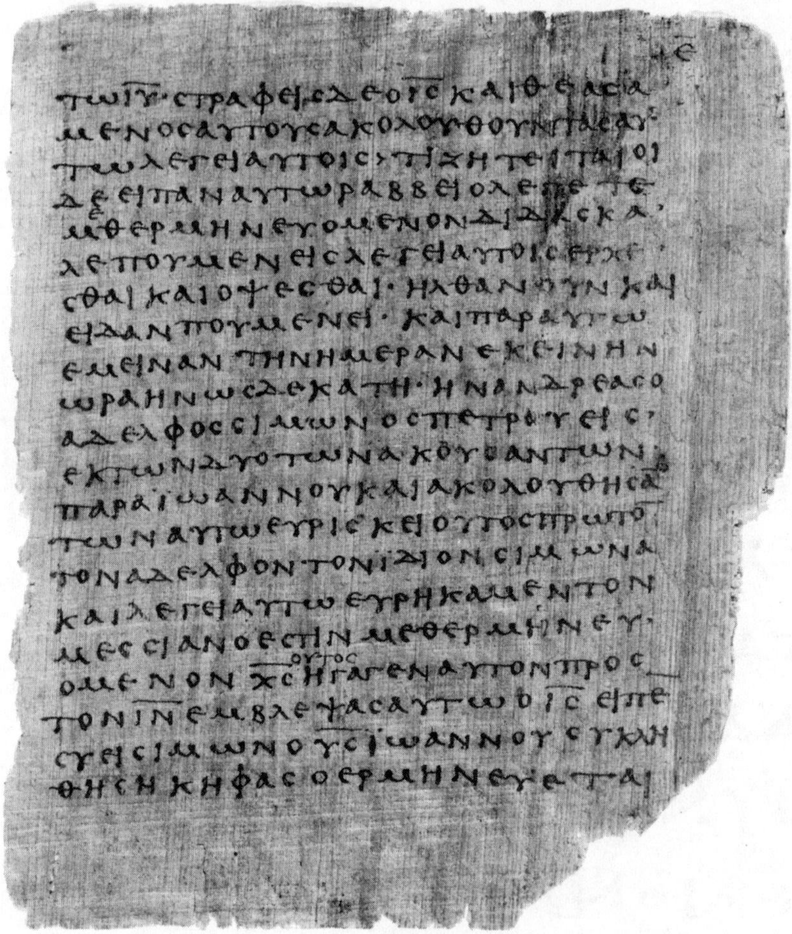

Plate 6: P. Bodmer II, 𝔓66 (John 1:37-42)
Single column, 21 lines, in competent hand. Page number top right (E = 5).
Nomina sacra: IY (line 1), IΣ (lines 1, 19), IN (line 19), XΣ (line 18), YΣ (line
20). Cf. abbreviation by suspension of final letter(s) at end of lines 13, 14,
19), with stroke over last letter and extending into margin. Punctuation:
high stops, lines 1, 7, 8, 10, 12. Diaeresis over initial *iota* (in ιδιον), line 15.
Corrections by insertion above line in lines 5 and 18.   Photo used by permission of the Fondation Martin Bodmer, Geneva.

Plate 7: P. Oxyrhynchus 1; Bodleian MS. Gr. th. e 7 (P) (Corresponds to sayings 26-29, 30 + 77, *Gospel of Thomas*)
Codex leaf (verso), twenty-one lines (last line fragmented) in informal but competent hand. Top and both side margins extant. Page number upper right-hand corner (IA = 11). *Nomina sacra:* IΣ (line 5, and probably in line 11), ΘΥ (line 8), ΠΡΑ (line 11), ΑΝΩΝ (line 19). End-of-line filler mark (lines 3, 9, 17, 18). Photo used by permission of the Bodleian Library, Oxford.

Plate 8: P. Oxyrhynchus 654; British Museum Pap. 1531 (corresponds to prologue and sayings 1-7 of *Gospel of Thomas*)

Part of a reused roll (opisthograph), this text written in a competent hand on the outer side with vertical fibers, remnants of a land survey on the inner side. *Nomina sacra:* ΙΗΣ (line 2, 27, 36). Note horizontal strokes at left margin to separate sayings (lines 6, 10, 22, 28, 32), and forked marks before λεγει Ις (lines 5, 9, 36), and after the phrase in line 27. Diaeresis over initial *upsilon* (line 21). Corrections inserted in line 19 (υμεις) and line 25 (οτι).

Photo used by permission of the British Library, London.

Plate 9: P. Oxyrhynchus 655; Harvard Semitic Museum Pap. 4367 (corresponds to sayings 24, 36-39 of *Gospel of Thomas*)
The largest of eight fragments of a roll, parts of two columns visible in this one, written in an informal book hand. No punctuation or division between sayings, and no extant instances of words usually written as *nomina sacra*.   Photo used by permission of the Houghton Library, Harvard University.

INDEX OF AUTHORS

Bagnall, Roger, 13
Black, C. Clifton, 30-31
Blanchard, Alain, 100
Brown, Schuyler, 97, 107

Charlesworth, Scott, 75n.108
Comfort, Philip, 12n.26

Dagenais, John, 10n.21
de Savignac, Jean, 143-45, 146

Epp, Eldon J., 9, 26-27, 74-80, 157

Foster, Paul, 33n.82

Gamble, Harry, 1, 11-12, 70, 73-74, 80, 187, 192
Gonis, Nick, 32n.78
Grenfell, Bernard P., 25, 82

Haines-Eitzen, Kim, 12
Head, Peter, 36, 156n.4
Hill, Charles E., 30, 32
Horsley, G. H. R., 32n.78, 68-69
Howard, George, 111
Hunt, Arthur S., 25, 82
Hurtado, Larry W., 5n.11, 61, 112, 121, 150, 153, 187n.85

Jensen, Robin, 151-52
Judge, Edwin A., 12

Kenyon, Frederic G., 168, 175n.68
Kraft, Robert A., 18n.9, 61-63, 107-10, 121
Kraus, Thomas J., 12n.26

Llewelyn, Stephen R., 30, 41

McCormick, Michael, 74, 75n.105, 76-77
Metzger, Bruce M., 192
Millard, Alan, 12, 119n.78
Milne, H. J. M., 185

Nicklas, Tobias, 12n.26

O'Callaghan, José, 119n.75, 129-30
Osiek, Carolyn, 33

Paap, A. H. R. E., 106-7, 113, 129-30, 132
Pickering, Stuart R., 12

Roberts, C. H., 12, 39, 47n.15, 52-53, 59, 63, 64, 65, 70-74, 124, 126, 132, 150, 178-80, 182, 183

Sanders, Henry A., 180
Skeat, T. C., 36, 53, 63-67, 70-74, 169, 185
Snyder, Graydon, 153

Sulzberger, Max, 142-43, 145-46

Tov, Emanuel, 66, 102-3, 109, 183-84, 185
Traube, Ludwig, 95, 106-7, 120, 133
Treu, Kurt, 61-63, 107-10, 121
Trobisch, David, 122
Tuckett, C. M., 109-10, 116n.68, 122-28,
 130, 132

Turner, Eric G., 52n.30, 66, 77, 155-65,
 168, 171-73, 174, 192

van Haelst, Joseph, 4n.10

Zuntz, Günther, 39

OLD TESTAMENT

Berlin Staats.Bib.Cod.
gr. fol. 66 I,II   56n.48, 163n.25, 167
Bodl.MS.Gr.bibl.g.5   50
8HevXIIgr   18n.9, 103, 184
P.Alex.inv. 203   20n.18, 59, 108
P.Ant. 1.8   159
P.Ant. 1.9   158
P.Baden 4.56   167
P.Barc.inv. 2   19n.16, 55
P.Barc.inv. 3   19n.14, 159
P.Bod. VII   98n.12
P.Bod. VII-IX   35n.85
P.Bod. VIII   98n.12
P.Bod. XXIV   163n.25
P.Chest.Beatty IV   147n.37
P.Chest.Beatty V   162, 174
P.Chest.Beatty VI   126n.94, 127, 130,
            158, 162, 163n.27, 167-68, 184,
                                  231 (pl.)
P.Chest.Beatty VII   130, 162
P.Chest.Beatty VIII   54n.40, 163n.25
P.Chest.Beatty IX   163n.25
P.Chest.Beatty IX-X   20n.19, 66, 163n.27,
                                    172-73

P.Chest.Beatty X   184
P.Fouad 266a   18n.9, 19n.12, 184
P.Fouad 266b   18n.9, 19n.12, 184
P.Fouad 266c   18n.9, 19n.12, 184
P.Harris 2.166   19n.13, 59
P.Harris 31   19n.16, 59
P.Leip.inv. 170   54n.40
P.Lit.Lond. 202   159
P.Lit.Lond. 204   160
P.Lit.Lond. 207   19n.16
P.Lit.Lond. 211   20n.20, 59
P.Lond.Christ. 3   19n.14
P.Med. 1.13   19n.17
P.Mich. 3.135   19n.17
P.Monts. II Inv. 10   19n.16
P.Oxy. 656   19n.12, 62n.65, 63, 124,
                                    163n.25
P.Oxy. 1007   19n.12, 103n.27, 108-9
P.Oxy. 1075   19n.13, 59
P.Oxy. 1166   19n.12, 59, 108
P.Oxy. 1594   160, 161n.19
P.Oxy. 3522   18n.9, 103
P.Oxy. 4443   18n.9, 19n.15, 55, 184
P.Ryl. 458   18n.9, 182-83
P.RylPSI 8.921v.   19n.16, 54
P.Vindob.G. 39777   19n.16, 103n.27

P.Yale 1 — 147n.37, 162
Schøyen Codex 187 — 54n.40

QUMRAN

4Q119 — 18n.9
4Q120 — 18n.9, 103
4Q121 — 18n.9
4Q122 — 18n.9
4Q126 — 18n.9
4Q127 — 18n.9
4Q167 — 103
4Q173 — 103
4Q174 — 75n.109
4Q175 — 75n.109
7Q1 — 18n.9
7Q2 — 18n.9
11Q22 — 102

NEW TESTAMENT

$\mathfrak{P}$1 (P.Oxy. 2) — 163n.25
$\mathfrak{P}$4 — 20n.24, 20n.26, 36, 72, 88, 129, 159, 167-68, 170
$\mathfrak{P}$5 (P.Oxy. 208) — 163n.25
$\mathfrak{P}$9 (P.Oxy. 402) — 21n.32
$\mathfrak{P}$12 (P.Amherst 1.3) — 21n.29, 27n.64
$\mathfrak{P}$13 (P.Oxy. 657, *PSI* 12.1292) — 21n.29, 57n.49
$\mathfrak{P}$15 (P.Oxy. 1008) — 38, 163n.25
$\mathfrak{P}$16 (P.Oxy. 1009) — 38
$\mathfrak{P}$18 (P.Oxy. 1079) — 21n.34, 31-32, 54n.42, 57n.49
$\mathfrak{P}$22 (P.Oxy. 1228) — 57n.49, 58n.51, 127n.96
$\mathfrak{P}$23 (P.Oxy. 1229) — 21n.30
$\mathfrak{P}$28 (P.Oxy. 1596) — 162
$\mathfrak{P}$29 (P.Oxy. 1597) — 37n.90
$\mathfrak{P}$30 (P.Oxy. 1598) — 38

$\mathfrak{P}$32 (P.Ryl. 1.5) — 162
$\mathfrak{P}$37 — 163n.25
$\mathfrak{P}$38 — 37n.90
$\mathfrak{P}$39 (P. Oxy. 1780) — 20n.27, 163n.25
$\mathfrak{P}$40 (P.Heidelberg 45) — 21n.28
$\mathfrak{P}$45 (P.Chest.Beatty I) — 20nn.24-26, 30, 33, 36, 36n.89, 37-38, 113, 118n.74, 72, 85, 87-88, 124, 130, 141-44, 151, 162, 174-76, 177, 181-82, 188, 230 (pl.)
$\mathfrak{P}$46 (P.Chest.Beatty II) — 31, 36n.87, 38-39, 85, 88, 118n.74, 124, 127, 129-30, 162, 173, 181, 188, 229 (pl.)
$\mathfrak{P}$47 (P.Chest.Beatty III) — 112n.54, 127n.96, 162, 174, 188
$\mathfrak{P}$48 — 37n.90
$\mathfrak{P}$49 — 38
$\mathfrak{P}$50 — 37n.90
$\mathfrak{P}$52 — 124, 159n.13, 162, 170, 174, 179, 182
$\mathfrak{P}$53 — 20n.24, 37n.90
$\mathfrak{P}$64 — 20n.24, 20n.26, 36, 72, 88, 159, 167-68, 170, 179
$\mathfrak{P}$65 — 38
$\mathfrak{P}$66 (P.Bod. II) — 72, 127n.96, 130, 140-44, 151, 159, 169, 180, 182, 188, 234 (pl.)
$\mathfrak{P}$67 — 20n.24, 20n.26, 36, 72, 88, 159, 167-68, 170
$\mathfrak{P}$72 (P.Bod. VIII) — 124, 175n.71, 188
$\mathfrak{P}$75 (P.Bod. XIV-XV) — 20n.26, 36, 72, 88, 141-44, 151, 162, 169, 173, 180, 182, 188, 232 (pl.), 233 (pl.)
$\mathfrak{P}$77 (P.Oxy. 2683 + P.Oxy. 4405) — 72, 159, 182, 188
$\mathfrak{P}$78 (P.Oxy. 2684) — 160
$\mathfrak{P}$80 — 20n.27
$\mathfrak{P}$90 (P.Oxy. 3523) — 72, 159
$\mathfrak{P}$91 — 37n.90
$\mathfrak{P}$92 — 38

𝔓95   20n.27
𝔓98 (P.IFAO 2.31)   21n.34, 31, 32, 54,
                                     57n.49, 159n.12
𝔓100 (P.Oxy. 4449)   21n.30, 163n.26, 182
𝔓101   163n.26
𝔓102 (P.Oxy. 2943)   163n.26, 182
𝔓103 (P.Oxy. 4403)   72, 159, 182, 188
𝔓104 (P.Oxy. 4404)   72, 163n.26, 182
𝔓106 (P.Oxy. 4445)   163n.26, 182
𝔓107 (P.Oxy. 4446)   182
𝔓108 (P.Oxy. 4447)   162
𝔓109 (P.Oxy. 4448)   163n.26
𝔓113 (P.Oxy. 4497)   163n.26, 167, 182
𝔓114 (P.Oxy. 4498)   163n.26
𝔓115 (P.Oxy. 4499)   163n.26, 182
0162 (P.Oxy. 847)   20n.27
0171 (P.Berl. 11863)   20n.24, 20n.26
0232 (P.Ant. 1.12)   21n.33, 39, 160,
                                        161n.19

OTHER CHRISTIAN TEXTS

BKT 6.2.1   57
BKT 6.6.1   57
BKT 9.22   56
P.Dura 10   58
P.Fouad 203   18n.9, 24n.57
P.Gen. 3.125   54
P.Harris 1.55   54
P.Haun. 1.8   57
P.Iand. 1.4   32n.78, 56
P.Iand. 5.70   57
P.Lond.Christ 2   167
P.Med.inv. 71.84   57
P.Mich. 18.763   54
P.Mich. 18.764   55, 57
P.Mich. 130, 54   124
P.Mich. 6427   32n.78
P.Oslo 2.14   55, 57

P.Oxy. 3.407   98n.11
P.Oxy. 5   23n.48, 32n.78
P.Oxy. 404   23n.47
P.Oxy. 405   55
P.Oxy. 407   24n.55, 123, 125
P.Oxy. 412   57
P.Oxy. 840   161
P.Oxy. 1173   57
P.Oxy. 1226   163n.25
P.Oxy. 1356   57
P.Oxy 1782   161
P.Oxy. 1783   23n.47, 161
P.Oxy. 1786   24n.56
P.Oxy. 1828   23n.47
P.Oxy. 2070   24n.54, 57
P.Oxy. 2158   57
P.Oxy. 3527   167
P.Oxy. 3528   56
P.Oxy. 4442   184
P.Oxy. 4706   32n.78
P.Ryl. 3.469   57
P.Ryl. 460   76
PSI 11.1200   55, 57
PSI 11.1207   57
Schyen Codex 193   167

CHRISTIAN APOCRYPHA

Bodl. MS Gr.th.f4   23n.44
P.Ant. 1.13   161
P.Bod. V   159
P.Egerton 2   22n.39, 97, 118n.74, 129, 182
P.Fay. 2   22n.36
P.Grenfell 1.8   161
P.Köln 6.255   57
P.Lond.Christ. 1   57, 113
P.Ludg.Bat. II W   23n.46
P.Oxy. 1   56, 81n.124, 82, 98, 127,
                                     235 (pl.)

P.Oxy. 654   81-82, 98, 236 (pl.)

P.Oxy. 655   58, 81n.124, 83, 237 (pl.)

P.Oxy. 849   98, 161n.19

P.Oxy. 850   98

P.Oxy. 2949   22n.40, 33-34, 55

P.Oxy. 3525   124, 125

P.Oxy 4009   22n.40, 33-34, 55n.44, 57

P.Ryl.463   58, 127n.96

P.Vindob.G. 2325   22n.41, 58

P.Vindob.G. 39756   23n.44

EXTRABIBLICAL TEXTS

AF11357   50

B.A.M. Papyrus Sammlung P. 14283   50

BIFAO 61   50

P.Hamb. 2.134   50

P.Lit.Lond. 127   52n.32

P.Mur. 164a   137

P.Oxy. 30   50

P.Oxy. 108   112n.52

P.Oxy. 470   50n.25

P.Oxy. 3321   53n.38

P.Oxy. 4174   50n.25

P.Oxy. 4196a   50n.25

P.Oxy. 4220 frag. 3   50n.25

P.Oxy. 4220 frag. 4   50n.25

P.Oxy. 4231a   50n.25

P.Ross.Georg. 1.19   50